PRAISE FOR

Where Shall Wisdom Be Found?

"Passionate and prolific literary critic Bloom grows more munificent in sharing his erudition and appreciation, discoveries, and opinions with each book. [His] immersion in and gratitude for these diverse and inexhaustible works will inspire readers to be on the lookout for wisdom in every work that speaks to them." —*Booklist*

"Bloom . . . has launched another masterly work." —*Library Journal*

"Emulating one of his favorite critics, Dr. Samuel Johnson, Bloom returns once more to sift through the Western canon, this time to discern and describe those writers whose brand of wisdom he holds in highest esteem. Beginning with Job and Ecclesiastes, and ranging from Plato, Homer, Cervantes, Shakespeare, Montaigne, Francis Bacon, Johnson and Goethe to Emerson, Nietzsche, Freud and Proust, Bloom writes gracefully about each as he evaluates by comparision and teases out indicators of their subtle interrelationships. He justifies his tastes with close readings of *King Lear* and *Macbeth* that find a Shakespearean variety of nihilism, a form of wisdom Bloom identifies as central to the poetic tradition. In his intricate discussion of each great writer, Bloom offers the rich perceptions of a scholar drawing on the whole of a long and thoughtful career." —*Publishers Weekly*

PRAISE FOR HAROLD BLOOM AND

Shakespeare: The Invention of the Human

A National Book Award Finalist
A National Book Critics Circle Award Finalist
A *New York Times* Notable Book of the Year
An ALA Booklist Editors' Choice
A *Publishers Weekly* Best Book of the Year

"A fiercely argued exegesis of Shakespeare's plays in the tradition of Samuel Johnson, Hazlitt, and A. C. Bradley, a study that is as passionate as it is erudite." —Michiko Kakutani, *The New York Times*

"Bloom in love—lavishly quoting and contagiously savoring huge chunks of poetry, detailing the luxuriance of Shakespeare's imagination and the prodigiousness of his intelligence—is a pleasure to read."
—*The Boston Globe*

"Bloom has given us the crowning achievement of his career. . . . If any piece of literary criticism can have a practical effect—on our stage and imaginations—this is the one." —Salon.com

"A huge cloak-bag of ideas . . . It is a feast." —*The Wall Street Journal*

"An enraptured, incantatory epic . . . dazzling . . . You could hardly ask for a more capricious and beneficent work than *Shakespeare: The Invention of the Human*." —*The New Yorker*

"The legend of Bloom's genius . . . spans four decades."
—*The New York Times Magazine*

"No critic—not even Bloom's masters A. C. Bradley or Harold Goddard—writes as well for actors and directors, or understands as clearly the *performability* of the plays." —*Publishers Weekly* (starred review)

"Should this be the one book you read if you're going to read one book about Shakespeare? Yes." —*The New York Observer*

ALSO BY HAROLD BLOOM

Jesus and Yahweh: The Names Divine (2005)

The Best Poems of the English Language (2004)

Hamlet: Poem Unlimited (2003)

Genius: A Mosaic of One Hundred Exemplary Creative Minds (2002)

Stories and Poems for
Extremely Intelligent Children of All Ages (2001)

How to Read and Why (2000)

Shakespeare: The Invention of the Human (1998)

Omens of Millennium (1996)

The Western Canon (1994)

The American Religion (1992)

The Book of J (1990)

Ruin the Sacred Truths (1989)

Poetics of Influence (1988)

The Strong Light of the Canonical (1987)

Agon: Towards a Theory of Revisionism (1982)

The Breaking of the Vessels (1982)

The Flight to Lucifer: A Gnostic Fantasy (1979)

Wallace Stevens: The Poems of Our Climate (1977)

Figures of Capable Imagination (1976)

Poetry and Repression (1976)

Kabbalah and Criticism (1975)

A Map of Misreading (1975)

The Anxiety of Influence (1973)

The Ringers in the Tower: Studies in Romantic Tradition (1971)

Yeats (1970)

Commentary on David V. Erdman's Edition of
The Poetry and Prose of William Blake (1965)

Blake's Apocalypse (1963)

The Visionary Company (1961)

Shelley's Mythmaking (1959)

WHERE SHALL

WISDOM BE

FOUND?

HAROLD BLOOM

RIVERHEAD BOOKS

NEW YORK

THE BERKLEY PUBLISHING GROUP
Published by the Penguin Group
Penguin Group (USA) Inc.
375 Hudson Street, New York, New York 10014, USA
Penguin Group (Canada), 90 Eglinton Avenue East, Suite 700, Toronto, Ontario M4P 2Y3, Canada
(a division of Pearson Penguin Canada Inc.)
Penguin Books Ltd., 80 Strand, London WC2R 0RL, England
Penguin Group Ireland, 25 St. Stephen's Green, Dublin 2, Ireland
(a division of Penguin Books Ltd.)
Penguin Group (Australia), 250 Camberwell Road, Camberwell, Victoria 3124, Australia
(a division of Pearson Australia Group Pty. Ltd.)
Penguin Books India Pvt. Ltd., 11 Community Centre, Panchsheel Park, New Delhi—110 017, India
Penguin Group (NZ), cnr Airborne and Rosedale Roads, Albany, Auckland 1310, New Zealand
(a division of Pearson New Zealand Ltd.)
Penguin Books (South Africa) (Pty.) Ltd., 24 Sturdee Avenue, Rosebank, Johannesburg 2196,
South Africa

Penguin Books Ltd., Registered Offices: 80 Strand, London WC2R 0RL, England

First Riverhead hardcover edition: October 2004
First Riverhead trade paperback edition: October 2005
Riverhead trade paperback ISBN: 1-59448-138-5

The Library of Congress has catalogued the Riverhead hardcover edition as follows:

Bloom, Harold.
Where shall wisdom be found? / Harold Bloom.
p.   cm.
Includes bibliographical references.
ISBN 1-57322-284-4
1. Wisdom in literature
2. Wisdom literature—Criticism, interpretation, etc.
I. Title
PN56.W54B58   2004   2004043777
809'.93384—dc22

PRINTED IN THE UNITED STATES OF AMERICA

10   9   8   7   6   5   4   3   2

FOR RICHARD RORTY

Acknowledgments

I am grateful to my editor, Celina Spiegel. I thank also my wife, Jeanne, and Brad Woodworth, Brett Foster, Jesse Zuba, Deborah Copland, Elizabeth Meriwether, and Stuart Watson, as well as my copy editor, Toni Rachiele, and my agents, Glen Hartley and Lynn Chu, and their associate, Katy Sprinkel.

HAROLD BLOOM

Timothy Dwight College, Yale University

March 15, 2004

how I said can I be glad and sad: but a man goes
    from one foot to the other:
wisdom wisdom:
        to be glad and sad at once is also unity
and death:
    wisdom wisdom: a peachblossom blooms on a particular
tree on a particular day:
        unity cannot do anything in particular:

                        A. R. AMMONS, "GUIDE"

The greatest ideas are the greatest events.

                        NIETZSCHE

CONTENTS

WISDOM

All of the world's cultures—Asian, African, Middle Eastern, European/Western Hemisphere—have fostered wisdom writing. For more than a half-century I have studied and taught the literature that emerged from monotheism and its later secularizations. *Where Shall Wisdom Be Found?* rises out of personal need, reflecting a quest for sagacity that might solace and clarify the traumas of aging, of recovery from grave illness, and of grief for the loss of beloved friends.

I have only three criteria for what I go on reading and teaching: aesthetic splendor, intellectual power, wisdom. Societal pressures and journalistic fashions may obscure these standards for a time, but mere Period Pieces never endure. The mind always returns to its needs for beauty, truth, and insight. Mortality hovers, and all of us learn the triumph of time. "We have an interval, and then our place knows us no more."

Christians who believe, Muslims who submit, Jews who trust—all in or to God's will—have their own criteria for wisdom, yet each needs to realize those norms individually if the words of God are to enlighten or comfort. Secularists take on a different kind of responsibility, and their turn to wisdom literature sometimes is considerably more wistful or anguished, depending on temperament. Whether pious or not, we all of us learn to crave wisdom, wherever it can be found.

In the early twenty-first century of the Common Era, the United States and Western Europe are parted by nearly as many factors as those that keep them uneasily allied. Pragmatically the New World or Evening Land lives just as secular an existence as most of Europe, but Americans tend to separate their outer and inner lives. Many of them have conversations with Jesus, and their testimony can be persuasive, on its own terms. Religion, for them, is not the opiate but the poetry of the people, which is why they reject what they know of Marx, Darwin, and Freud. And yet they too can thirst for human wisdom to supplement their encounters with the divine.

Wisdom writing, for me, has its own implicit standards of aesthetic and cognitive strength. This book attempts to present norms that engross literate women and men, common readers, as Virginia Woolf followed Samuel Johnson in calling them. Debasements of wisdom traditions flood the marketplace: pop divas flaunt red strings that purport to be Kabbalistic, thus invoking the hidden lore of the Zohar, the masterwork of Jewish esotericism. Kierkegaard's wisdom, desperately urgent despite its ironic mask-

ings, halts at the frontiers of the esoteric, at what the great Kabbalistic scholar Moshe Idel terms "the Perfection that absorbs."
Idel gently plays against his heroic precursor in Kabbalah scholarship, the majestic Gershom Scholem, who had spoken of "the
strong light of the canonical, of a Perfection that destroys." Wisdom, whether esoteric or not, seems to me a Perfection that can
either absorb or destroy us, depending on what we bring to it.

2

What is the use of wisdom, if it can be reached only in solitude,
reflecting on our reading? We most of us know that wisdom
immediately goes out the door when we are in crisis. Becoming
Job is for most of us a mitigated experience: but his house falls in,
his children are slain, he is covered with sore boils, and his superbly
laconic wife advises him, "Dost thou still retain thine integrity?
curse God, and die" (2:9). That is all we ever hear her say, and it is
difficult to withstand. The Book of Job is a structure of gathering
self-awareness, in which the protagonist comes to recognize himself in relation to a Yahweh who will be absent when he will be
absent. And this wisest of works in the Hebrew Bible grants us no
comfort in accepting such wisdom.

In Psalm 22, King David begins by lamenting, "My God, my
God, why hast thou forsaken me?" the outcry of his descendant,
Jesus of Nazareth, upon the cross. Psalm 23 is sung by Sir John Fal-
staff on his deathbed in *Henry V,* as we learn from Mistress Quickly,

who garbles together "He maketh me to lie down in green pastures" and "Thou preparest a table before me in the presence of mine enemies." Instead she gives us "and a table of green fields." W. H. Auden thought that Falstaff was for Shakespeare something like an image of Christ. That seems to me a garbling also, but is greatly preferable to the dismissal of Falstaff as a besotted old glutton, a lord of misrule. Auden's poignance is a kind of wisdom, while scholars who denigrate Falstaff are the undead, at best.

I have not found that wisdom literature is a comfort: Job could not console Herman Melville and his Captain Ahab, but provoked them to furious response when God rhetorically questions Job, "Canst thou draw out Leviathan with a hook?" Myself, I react even more angrily to God's "Will he make a covenant with thee?" though I appreciate that the poet of the Book of Job so superbly evokes the initial Yahweh of the J writer, primal author of the palimpsest we now read as Genesis, Exodus, Numbers. Capricious and even sarcastic, this uncanny Yahweh is to be feared, a fear that is the beginning of wisdom.

Job and Ecclesiastes, Homer and Plato, Cervantes and Shakespeare teach a harsh wisdom, suspended between irony and tragedy. The irony of one era or culture is not likely to be that of another, yet irony always tends to say one thing while meaning something else. Tragedy, even if you view it as joyful, as W. B. Yeats did, was not acceptable to Plato, who repudiated what seems to most of us the tragic vision of the *Iliad*. Change and mortality are not wisdom for Plato, who would have been even unhappier with Cervantes and Shakespeare than he was with Homer.

3
—

Wisdom literature teaches us to accept natural limits. The secular wisdom of Cervantes and of Shakespeare (both of them compelled to conceal personal skepticism) can verge upon a kind of transcendence in *Don Quixote* and in *Hamlet*, but the Knight of the Sad Countenance falls into the sane disenchantment of a Christian grave, and the Prince achieves apotheosis only in the restful silence of annihilation.

Since childhood, I have been comforted by Talmudic wisdom, which is concentrated in the *Pirke Aboth*, "Sayings of the Fathers." In old age, I keep returning to *Aboth,* which is a later addition to the massive Mishnah, the "Oral Torah," a huge volume that teaches us to adhere to rabbinic admonitions. *Pirke Aboth* is all epigrams, aphorisms, original proverbs, and softens the fierce Mishnah, which is marked by moral and legal debate. There are two splendid translations and commentaries of *Pirke Aboth* in English, by the English Unitarian R. Travers Herford (1925) and by the great scholar Judah Goldin (1957). I remember Goldin telling me, when he kindly gave me the little book, that he admired Herford's work, but wished to have a more Talmudic version of *Aboth*. Both volumes are splendid, and I will sometimes use them here interchangeably.

> *Hillel used to say: If I am not for myself who is for me? And when I am for myself what am I? and if not now, when?*

[HERFORD, page 34]

Hillel used to say: If not I for myself, who then? And being for myself, what am I? And if not now, when?

[GOLDIN, page 69]

There is perfect, balanced wisdom. I affirm myself, but if I am for myself only, it is inadequate, and unless standing up both for myself and for others happens right now, whenever can it happen? Hillel also remarked, "Say not when I am at leisure I will study—perhaps you will not ever be at leisure." Who can forget Hillel's "In a place where there are no men, strive to be a man"? Humorous even when acidulous, Hillel achieves total memorability:

He used to say:—More flesh, more worms; more wealth, more care; more women, more witchcraft; more maidservants, more lewdness; more menservants, more thieving; more Torah, more life; more assiduity, more wisdom; more counsel, more understanding; more charity, more peace. He who has acquired a good name acquired it for himself. He who has acquired words of Torah has acquired for himself the life of the world to come.

I render for myself my favorite aphorism in the Wisdom of the Fathers, Rabbi Tarphon's subtly weighed admonition "You are not required to complete the work, but neither are you free to desist from it." However many classes had to be taught and however much writing had to be done, when I was ill, depressed, or weary, I rallied, with Tarphon's cognitive music in my inner ear. But I bring these introductory musings to a close with the greatest figure among the founders of Judaism as we know it today, Rabbi Akiba,

martyred by the Romans for inspiring Bar Kochba's insurrection against them in the second century of the Common Era.

> *He used to say: All is given in pledge, and the net is spread over all the living; the shop is open and the shopman gives credit, and the account-book is open and the hand writes, and every one who would borrow let him come and borrow; and the collectors go round continually every day and exact payment from a man whether with or without his knowledge. And they have whereon to rely, and the judgment is a judgment of truth, and all is made ready for the banquet.*

[HERFORD, page 89]

> *He used to say: everything is given against a pledge and a net is cast over all the living: the shop is open, the shopkeeper extends credit, the ledger lies open, the hand writes, and whoever wishes to borrow may come and borrow; and the collectors make the rounds continually, every day, and exact payment of man with his consent or without it. They have what to base their claims on. And the judgment is a judgment of truth. And everything is prepared for the feast.*

[GOLDIN, page 144]

This sharpens the Covenant, as little else can. If wisdom is trust in the Covenant, then I cannot see how wisdom can go further.

THE

POWER OF

WISDOM

CHAPTER 1

THE HEBREWS:

JOB AND ECCLESIASTES

No scholar doubts that the wisdom literature of ancient Israel was influenced by Egyptian and Sumerian forerunners. Both modes of wisdom—prudential and skeptical—were bequeathed to the Hebrews, the former in the Proverbs, and the darker quest for God's justice in Job and Ecclesiastes. The canons of Eastern Orthodoxy and Roman Catholicism include these as well as the Wisdom of ben Sirach (second century B.C.E.) and the Wisdom of Solomon (first century B.C.E.), both of which Shakespeare read in the Apocrypha of the Protestant Geneva Bible, and most of us read in the King James Apocrypha. I will place major emphasis on Job and Ecclesiastes, both literary masterpieces, with Job in a sphere apart.

Sages are universally present in almost all the world's spiritual traditions, East and West. Sometimes the wisdom of a tradition is assigned to a single, representative individual. We know that the Five Books of Moses were not composed by Moses, and the Hebrews pre-

sumably knew this also. King David was a poet, but hardly could have written the entire Book of Psalms. The founder of Hebrew wisdom supposedly was David's son, King Solomon, who did not write the Song of Songs, or the Proverbs, or Ecclesiastes, let alone the Wisdom of Solomon. Still, Solomon dominated a sophisticated culture, and his court poets and sages were evidently proud to ascribe their words to his authority and patronage. More than David, Solomon had a capacious spirit, and his court seems to have produced both the book of J, or the Yahwist text, the most powerful work in ancient Hebrew, and the magnificent history we call II Samuel.

The Book of Proverbs, though some of its aphorisms belong to the Solomonic era, almost certainly comes after the age of the Redactor, the term that has come to stand for the editor of genius who compiled the Genesis-to-Kings structure of the Hebrew Bible, as we know it. Proverbs is a pasted-together book, disregarding history and its calamities. Roughly the first twenty-two chapters have some reference to the Solomonic court; after that we are offered a miscellany. The earlier group are the wiser and more famous. No formal term is apt for them except "aphorism," and yet they have little in common with the French and German traditions that fuse in the aphorisms of Goethe and Nietzsche, a tradition that for me culminates in the superb anti-Freudian eloquence of the Viennese Jewish satirist Karl Kraus: "Psychoanalysis is itself that disease of which it purports to be the cure."

Prudential wisdom, which achieves its apotheosis in Samuel Johnson and in Goethe, is not easily assimilated to the more fascinating skepticism (to call it that) of Job and of Ecclesiastes. The Book of

Job traditionally is described as theodicy, akin to John Milton's *Paradise Lost*, the supposed purpose of each the justification of God's ways to men and women. Job is the greatest aesthetic triumph of the Hebrew Bible, but I am baffled by its reputation as theodicy. "Patient Job" is actually about as patient as King Lear, and neither the ancient work nor *King Lear* gives us a justified God or the gods. More vitally, both poems are demonstrations that we have no language appropriate for our confrontations with the Divine.

Ken Frieden, in a very useful essay (reprinted in my *Modern Critical Interpretations: The Book of Job,* 1988), centered on names: Job's, the Adversary's, God's. Job's name seems related to the Arabic *awah,* the returner to God, but rabbinic interpretation saw the name as antithetical to itself, meaning both "just" and the "enemy" (of God). Yahweh, in the Prologue and Epilogue, is named directly, but in the poem proper is called *El, Elosh, Elohim,* and *Shaddai* by Job and his companions. That leaves *Ha-Satan,* the Adversary or Accuser but not Satan in the Miltonic sense.

The most powerful commentators on Job's book, for me, remain John Calvin, in his sermons, and Kierkegaard, but I defer them until the end of this discussion, as they are difficult Protestant statements. Job is one of the world's great poems, though complex and ambivalent. A common reader, working through the King James version, encounters a five-part work, to adapt the useful analogies of Marvin H. Pope's translation and commentary in the Anchor Bible (*Job,* third edition, 1985). There is a two-chapter Prologue, a Debate (Chapters 3–31), the remarkable harangues of Elihu (32–37), the Voice of Yahweh out of the Whirlwind (38–41), and finally a dubious Epilogue (42).

The notorious Prologue centers on a remarkable exchange between Yahweh and the Satan, here not an outcast but an authorized Accuser of Sin:

> Now there was a day when the sons of God came to present themselves before the LORD, and Satan came also among them.
>
> And the LORD said unto Satan, Whence comest thou? Then Satan answered the LORD, and said, From going to and fro in the earth, and from walking up and down in it.
>
> And the LORD said unto Satan, Hast thou considered my servant Job, that there is none like him in the earth, a perfect and an upright man, one that feareth God, and escheweth evil?
>
> Then Satan answered the LORD, and said, Doth Job fear God for nought?
>
> Hast not thou made a hedge about him, and about his house, and about all that he hath on every side? thou hast blessed the work of his hands, and his substance is increased in the land.
>
> But put forth thine hand now, and touch all that he hath, and he will curse thee to thy face.
>
> And the LORD said unto Satan, Behold, all that he hath is in thy power; only upon himself put not forth thine hand. So Satan went forth from the presence of the LORD.
>
> [JOB 1:6–12, *King James Version, as throughout this book*]

Palpably, both Yahweh and the Satan are unsympathetic personages, in the extreme. We are not far from *Moby-Dick*, or from Kafka. Except for prosperity, Job has no faults, though his Comforters will search out their nonsense the best they can. As a

troublemaker, the Accuser is merely laboring in his vocation, but Yahweh's motivation appears to be either His usual bad temper, or merely a CEO's skepticism concerning his most faithful employee. Justifying Yahweh here would take all the scandalous talents of Tony Kushner's Roy Cohn in *Perestroika*. But the poet of the Book of Job (whoever he was—we cannot even know that he was an Israelite) probably did not write the Prologue. He begins in the Debate of Chapters 3–31, and I suspect continues through Yahweh's celebration of Leviathan as his own Moby-Dick. The inept Epilogue is an absurdity written by any pious fool whatsoever.

I have some doubts as to the nation and creed of the wisdom writer who composed Job, just as I hold to my prior surmise that the J writer of the Hebrew Bible might well have been a Hittite woman. It does not much matter: Solomon's court must have been crowded with international wisdom writers. Whoever the poet was, he strikes me as no more pious than Herman Melville, who did not exactly trust in the Covenant, any more than Captain Ahab did. Melville called *Moby-Dick* "a wicked book"; Job is more complex, but I read its wisdom as being more wicked than not. Job, not being an Ahab, would not have hunted Leviathan with a harpoon.

Behemoth and Leviathan plainly represent the sanctified tyranny of nature over men. But that is to rate them too tamely. Yahweh is proud of them, and his pride taunts Job and the reader, superbly in Chapter 41, above all:

Canst thou draw out Leviathan with a hook? or his tongue with a cord which thou lettest down?

Canst thou put a hook into his nose? or bore his jaw through with a thorn?

Will he make many supplications unto thee? will he speak soft words unto thee?

Will he make a covenant with thee? wilt thou take him for a servant for ever?

Wilt thou play with him as with a bird? or wilt thou bind him for thy maidens?

Shall the companions make a banquet of him? shall they part him among the merchants?

Canst thou fill his skin with barbed irons? or his head with fish spears?

Lay thine hand upon him, remember the battle, do no more.

Behold, the hope of him is in vain: shall not one be cast down even at the sight of him?

None is so fierce that dare stir him up: who then is able to stand before me?

Who hath prevented me, that I should repay him? whatsoever is under the whole heaven is mine.

I will not conceal his parts, nor his power, nor his comely proportion.

Who can discover the face of his garment? or who can come to him with his double bridle?

Who can open the doors of his face? his teeth are terrible round about.

His scales are his pride, shut up together as with a close seal.

One is so near to another, that no air can come between them.

They are joined one to another, they stick together, that they cannot be sundered.

By his sneezings a light doth shine, and his eyes are like the eyelids of the morning.

Out of his mouth go burning lamps, and sparks of fire leap out.

Out of his nostrils goeth smoke, as out of a seething pot or caldron.

His breath kindleth coals, and a flame goeth out of his mouth.

In his neck remaineth strength, and sorrow is turned into joy before him.

The flakes of his flesh are joined together: they are firm in themselves; they cannot be moved.

His heart is as firm as a stone; yea, as hard as a piece of the nether millstone.

When he raiseth up himself, the mighty are afraid: by reason of breakings they purify themselves.

The sword of him that layeth at him cannot hold: the spear, the dart, nor the habergeon.

He esteemeth iron as straw, and brass as rotten wood.

The arrow cannot make him flee: sling stones are turned with him into stubble.

Darts are counted as stubble: he laugheth at the shaking of a spear.

Sharp stones are under him: he spreadeth sharp pointed things upon the mire.

He maketh the deep to boil like a pot: he maketh the sea like a pot of ointment.

He maketh a path to shine after him; one would think the
deep to be hoary.
    Upon earth there is not his like, who is made without fear.
    He beholdeth all high things: he is a king over all the children
of pride.

This is brutal, highly accessible wisdom, and may represent a Hebrew transmutation of an Arab poem. And yet the revision touches upon sublimity, of a highly negative kind: "Will he make a covenant with thee?" Even as a child, I blinked at this divine sarcasm. As a bombardment of exuberances, it is unanswerable, and substitutes power for justification. Perhaps only Saint Augustine can render theodicy palatable. The poet of Job gives us a Yahweh who could not care less, and who substitutes power for reason. Is this because Job is a Gentile? I think not. Leviathan makes no covenant with anyone, and the Book of Job is skeptical as to whether its God is still interested in covenants.

Maimonides denied Job's wisdom, his boundless patience in the face of calamity. Yet who can be wise in a poem where God knows only the wisdom of force? Job's Comforters take joy in God's wisdom, but pragmatically they are more satanic than the accuser. Their apologist is John Calvin, who strengthens their case with a kind of mad eloquence:

For Job could not better prove his patience than by resolving to be
entirely naked, inasmuch as the good pleasure of God was such.
Surely, men resist in vain; they may grit their teeth, but they

must return entirely naked to the grave. Even the pagans have
said that death alone shows the littleness of men. Why? For we
have a gulf of covetousness, that we would wish to gobble up all
the earth; if a man has many riches, vines, meadows, and pos-
sessions, it is not enough; God would have to create new worlds,
if He wished to satisfy us.

[JOHN CALVIN, SECOND SERMON ON JOB]

Is that the meaning of the Book of Job, that God would
have to create new worlds, if He wished to satisfy us? Calvin is
more Yahwistic than Yahweh, and gets the God he wants and
deserves.

Meanwhile God will be condemned among us. This is how men
exasperate themselves. And in this what do they do? It is as if
they accuse God of being a tyrant.

Are we then to be even more Jobean? Kierkegaard, subtler than
Calvin, thought that was our desire:

And yet there is no hiding place in the wide world where troubles
may not find you, and there has never lived a man who was able
to say more than you can say, that you do not know when sorrow
will visit your house. So be sincere with yourself, fix your eyes
upon Job; even though he terrifies you, it is not this he wishes, if
you yourself do not wish it.

[SØREN KIERKEGAARD, EDIFYING DISCOURSES]

Kierkegaard insists that it is the Creator, and not the creation, that overcomes Job. Leviathan and Behemoth are *beyond* Job, even as the Creator is. The Book of Job offers wisdom, but it is not anything we can comprehend. Hence the superb poem of Chapter 28:12–28, which gives us no choice except yielding to its eloquence:

But where shall wisdom be found? and where is the place of understanding?

Man knoweth not the price thereof; neither is it found in the land of the living.

The depth saith, It is not in me: and the sea saith, It is not with me.

It cannot be gotten for gold, neither shall silver be weighed for the price thereof.

It cannot be valued with the gold of Ophir, with the precious onyx, or the sapphire.

The gold and the crystal cannot equal it: and the exchange of it shall not be for jewels of fine gold.

No mention shall be made of coral, or of pearls: for the price of wisdom is above rubies.

The topaz of Ethiopia shall not equal it, neither shall it be valued with pure gold.

Whence then cometh wisdom? and where is the place of understanding?

Seeing it is hid from the eyes of all living, and kept close from the fowls of the air.

Destruction and death say, We have heard the fame thereof with our ears.

God understandeth the way thereof, and he knoweth the place thereof.

For he looketh to the ends of the earth, and seeth under the whole heaven;

To make the weight for the winds; and he weigheth the waters by measure.

When he made a decree for the rain, and a way for the lightning of the thunder;

Then did he see it, and declare it; he prepared it, yea, and searched it out.

And unto man he said, Behold, the fear of the Lord, that is wisdom; and to depart from evil is understanding.

Is this appropriate for Job? Joseph Blenkinsopp suggests that this injunction to religious observance belongs to Job's Comforter, Zophar, and that the text is scrambled. I think not, and fear that poetry is defeated here by wisdom. Perhaps Plato, or rather his Socrates, would approve, but do we, when we read Job? God does not defend his justice: He devastates us rhetorically, as Moby-Dick destroys Ahab, the *Pequod,* and all the crew except Ishmael, who escapes alone to tell us. No one can dispute the literary power of the Book of Job, but what is wisdom literature if it abnegates wisdom?

Paul Ricoeur, in his *The Symbolism of Evil* (1967), interpreted this as tragic reaffirmation, but the Book of Job is not Sophocles, and wisdom literature is not tragedy. I would not call *Hamlet* a tragedy, since the prince dies into an apotheosis of will or free wisdom, more gain than loss. No more than the Book of Job is *Hamlet* a justification of God's ways to men and women.

Reductively, Behemoth appears to be a hippo and Leviathan a crocodile, but William Blake and Herman Melville between them transcend the text, and both beasts together fuse into Thomas Hobbes's vision of state tyranny and Melville's indestructible albino whale. Truly the beasts *are* the poem, and are the emblems of the incommensurateness of Yahweh's wisdom and humankind's.

The translator Stephen Mitchell, in his interesting version of Job (1986), poignantly remarks that Job truly loves God. Spinoza admonished us that it was necessary to love God without ever expecting Him to love us in return, a very un-American sentiment, since the Gallup poll every second year tells us that eighty-nine percent of Americans believe that God loves them on a personal and individual basis. The American God, like the American Jesus, is surprisingly nonbiblical, but then Americans are not very Jobean.

Where shall wisdom be found? Is the fear of God wisdom? That is God's poetry, not Job's. Can you love fear? It does not work in human erotic partnership, and it turns democracy into plutocracy, where our nation seems to be heading. The difficult pleasures of the Book of Job are the crown of Hebrew poetry, and Job himself, in yielding to the Whirlwind, doubtless achieves peace. I myself, searching for wisdom in the Hebrew Bible, prefer Ecclesiastes or the Preacher, Solomon, as Koheleth, as teacher and dark orator.

ECCLESIASTES

The Book of Job may have been written as early as the seventh century B.C.E. Ecclesiastes is post-Exilic, and it is likely that it was com-

posed, most probably by a single sage, no later than 200 B.C.E. The
Jewish Alexandrian translation of the Bible, the Septuagint, rendered the Hebrew *koheleth* by the word *ekklesiastes,* meaning congregation. *Koheleth* evidently meant a speaker or preacher to an
assembly or congregation. The unlikely identification with King
Solomon is based on I Kings 8:1, where Solomon preaches to the
notables of Jerusalem.

As Ecclesiastes is my personal favorite among all the works of
the Bible, I will comment upon it rather fully. My ideal literary
critic, Samuel Johnson, was profoundly affected by it. Besides, a
book on wisdom and literature must brood upon Koheleth, for it
comes first to mind whenever wisdom literature is mentioned.

There is a tradition that the Solomonic Song of Songs was
included in the canonical Hebrew Bible primarily because the great
Rabbi Akiba insisted on it. I think it even more a wonder that
Koheleth made its way into the canonical text, since its main concern is mortality, and it sees fate and fortune, which are not mentioned elsewhere in the Bible, since they are pagan concepts, as being
decisive in determining the dating of death. In certain passages,
Koheleth can seem a Hellenistic Stoic, but normative Judaism
remains the staple of his work. Some of these normative strands
may be later interpolations—but I doubt that, on the purely internal literary experience of having reread the work so many times.
There is a definite and idiosyncratic personality revealed throughout, as there is in Jeremiah or the first Isaiah.

Like many other readers, I find that my own medical ordeals, life-
threatening just a year ago, have given a finer edge to rereading
Koheleth. The Preacher's sense of life as a waning but extraordinary

gift has also been intensified by recent experiences, personal and public, and our appreciation of his full range of consciousness is now much enhanced. Though he has religious interests, they are heterodox. God is never called Yahweh in Ecclesiastes, and seems rather remote. And yet he cites passages from Genesis and Deuteronomy, which he shrewdly modifies into what is more his own.

From the opening of his book onward, Koheleth manifests what will be his enormous eloquence throughout the twelve brief chapters:

> *The words of the Preacher, the son of David, king in Jerusalem.*
>
> *Vanity of vanities, saith the Preacher, vanity of vanities; all is vanity.*
>
> *What profit hath a man of all his labour which he taketh under the sun?*
>
> *One generation passeth away, and another generation cometh: but the earth abideth for ever.*
>
> *The sun also ariseth, and the sun goeth down, and hasteth to his place where he arose.*
>
> *The wind goeth to the south, and turneth about unto the north; it whirleth about continually, and the wind returneth again according to his circuits.*
>
> *All the rivers run into the sea; yet the sea is not full; unto the place from whence the rivers come, thither they return again.*
>
> *All things are full of labour; man cannot utter it: the eye is not satisfied with seeing, nor the ear filled with hearing.*
>
> *The thing that hath been, it is that which shall be; and that*

which is done is that which shall be done: and there is no new thing under the sun.

Is there any thing whereof it may be said, See, this is new? it hath been already of old time, which was before us.

There is no remembrance of former things; neither shall there be any remembrance of things that are to come with those that shall come after.

I the Preacher was king over Israel in Jerusalem.

And I gave my heart to seek and search out by wisdom concerning all things that are done under heaven: this sore travail hath God given to the sons of man to be exercised therewith.

I have seen all the works that are done under the sun; and, behold, all is vanity and vexation of spirit.

That which is crooked cannot be made straight: and that which is wanting cannot be numbered.

I communed with mine own heart, saying, Lo, I am come to great estate, and have gotten more wisdom than all they that have been before me in Jerusalem: yea, my heart had great experience of wisdom and knowledge.

And I gave my heart to know wisdom, and to know madness and folly: I perceived that this also is vexation of spirit.

For in much wisdom is much grief: and he that increaseth knowledge increaseth sorrow.

[ECCLESIASTES 1]

The persona of Solomon, clearly a fiction, serves admirably to bind the verses together. Dr. Johnson, in his one great poem, "The

Vanity of Human Wishes," captures the core meaning of "vanity of vanities," primarily a reference to our desires, whether erotic or pertaining to ambition. Verse 5 was captured forever by Hemingway for the title of his best novel. But so much here is part of our lives: "there is no new thing under the sun" and "That which is crooked cannot be made straight."

The second chapter, less memorably, vexes itself with who shall inherit one's particular labors and achievements, but greatness returns in the first eight verses of Chapter 3:

> To every thing there is a season, and a time to every purpose under the heaven:
>
> A time to be born, a time to die; a time to plant, and a time to pluck up that which is planted;
>
> A time to kill, and a time to heal; a time to break down, and a time to build up;
>
> A time to weep, and a time to laugh; a time to mourn, and a time to dance;
>
> A time to cast away stones, and a time to gather stones together; a time to embrace, and a time to refrain from embracing;
>
> A time to get, and a time to lose; a time to keep, and a time to cast away;
>
> A time to rend, and a time to sew; a time to keep silence, and a time to speak;
>
> A time to love, and a time to hate; a time of war, and a time of peace.

Few can come into their seventies without a chill at these repetitive rhythms. Koheleth, whose genius shows us that beneath every deep a lower deep opens, achieves a more reverberating pathos in the opening verses of Chapter 4:

> So I returned, and considered all the oppressions that are done under the sun: and behold the tears of such as were oppressed, and they had no comforter; and on the side of their oppressors there was power; but they had no comforter.
>
> Wherefore I praised the dead which are already dead, more than the living which are yet alive.
>
> Yea, better is he than both they, which hath not yet been, who hath not seen the evil work that is done under the sun.
>
> Again, I considered all travail, and every right work, that for this a man is envied of his neighbor. This is also vanity and vexation of spirit.

As his eloquence attains a higher pitch, Koheleth redefines wisdom literature for us:

> Whatsoever thy hand findeth to do, do it with thy might; for there is no work, nor device, nor knowledge, nor wisdom, in the grave, whither thou goest.
>
> I returned, and saw under the sun, that the race is not to the swift, nor the battle to the strong, neither yet bread to the wise, nor yet riches to men of understanding, nor yet favor to men of skill; but time and chance happeneth to them all.

Here the two verses are antithetical to each other, since even your mightiest labor will not win the race or the battle, or return bread for your wisdom. One is moved to ask, Is this universal or specifically Hebraic wisdom? Vanity or vain desire belongs to all traditions, indeed to human nature itself, and only Koheleth, in the Bible, truly competes with the universality of Shakespeare. Nothing else in the Bible *finds* me with the force that begins the final chapter:

> Remember now thy Creator in the days of thy youth, while the evil days come not, nor the years draw nigh, when thou shalt say, I have no pleasure in them;
>
> While the sun, or the light, or the moon, or the stars, be not darkened, nor the clouds return after the rain:
>
> In the day when the keepers of the house shall tremble, and the strong men shall bow themselves, and the grinders cease because they are few, and those that look out of the windows be darkened,
>
> And the doors shall be shut in the streets, when the sound of the grinding is low, and he shall rise up at the voice of the bird, and all the daughters of musick shall be brought low;
>
> Also when they shall be afraid of that which is high, and fears shall be in the way, and the almond tree shall flourish, and the grasshopper shall be a burden, and desire shall fail: because man goeth to his long home, and the mourners go about the streets:
>
> Or ever the silver cord be loosed, or the golden bowl be broken,

or the pitcher be broken at the fountain, or the wheel broken at the cistern.

Then shall the dust return to the earth as it was: and the spirit shall return unto God who gave it.

Vanity of vanities, saith the Preacher; all is vanity.

These eight verses deserve repetition until you possess them by memory, as you should much of Shakespeare. If wisdom in Job costs too much for its confirmation, so in Koheleth all wisdom becomes personal, fragments of a confession. The Preacher accepts the Hebrew God, yet scarcely knows Him. In the second century B.C.E., a disciple of Koheleth appeared in Jesus ben Sirach, whose book we know in the Apocrypha as Ecclesiasticus. Like Koheleth, Jesus ben Sirach was not a Pharisee, and so did not believe in the resurrection of the body. Here he is at his strongest, overcoming a certain long-windedness that generally compares unfavorably with Koheleth's fierce economy:

Let us now praise famous men, and our fathers that begat us.

The Lord hath wrought great glory by them through his great power from the beginning.

Such as did bear rule in their kingdoms, men renowned for their power, giving counsel by their understanding, and declaring prophecies:

Leaders of the people by their counsels, and by their knowledge of learning meet for the people, wise and eloquent in their instructions:

Such as found out musical tunes, and recited verses in writing:

Rich men furnished with ability, living peaceably in their habitations:

All these were honoured in their generations, and were the glory of their times.

There be of them, that have left a name behind them, that their praises might be reported.

And some there be, which have no memorial; who are perished, as though they had never been; and are become as though they had never been born; and their children after them.

But these were merciful men, whose righteousness hath not been forgotten.

With their good seed shall continually remain a good inheritance, and their children are within the covenant.

James Agee, with his fine ear, appropriated the start of this for his poignant volume that fuses superb prose with the photographs of Walker Evans at his best. For once, Jesus ben Sirach beautifully extended the tradition of wisdom writing. The last stand of that Hebraic tradition comes in the Apocrypha's Wisdom of Solomon, a crucial influence on *King Lear*, as I will show in Chapter 2. I turn, though, elsewhere in the Wisdom of Solomon, 2:1–9, which I surmise had a more general influence on Shakespeare:

For the ungodly said, reasoning with themselves, but not aright, Our life is short and tedious, and in the death of a man there is no remedy: neither was there any man known to have returned from the grave.

For we are born at all adventure: and we shall be hereafter as though we had never been: for the breath in our nostrils is as smoke, and a little spark in the moving of our heart:

Which being extinguished, our body shall be turned into ashes, and our spirit shall vanish as the soft air,

And our name shall be forgotten in time, and no man shall have our works in remembrance, and our life shall pass away as the trace of a cloud, and shall be dispersed as a mist, that is driven away with the beams of the sun, and overcome with the heat thereof.

For our time is a very shadow that passeth away; and after our end there is no returning: for it is fast sealed, so that no man cometh again.

Come on therefore, let us enjoy the good things that are present: and let us speedily use the creatures like as in youth.

Let us fill ourselves with costly wine and ointments: and let no flower of the spring pass by us:

Let us crown ourselves with rosebuds, before they be withered:

Let none of us go without his part of our voluptuousness: let us leave tokens of our joyfulness in every place: for this is our portion, and our lot is this.

This is the wisdom of annihilation, of Hamlet and Lear, and perhaps of Shakespeare himself. His great tragedies culminate wisdom literature, though I hope to show its aphoristic survival in Montaigne and Francis Bacon, Samuel Johnson and Goethe, Emerson and Nietzsche, Freud and Proust, before I end with the wisdom of the Catholic Church at its strongest, in Saint Augustine.

CHAPTER 2

THE GREEKS:

PLATO'S CONTEST

WITH HOMER

The wise Emerson called Hamlet a Platonist, by which the Sage of Concord meant that Hamlet, like Plato, is so subtle an ironist that we cannot know when the prince and the philosopher speak what they mean, or quite mean what is said. Had Homer come up to the border of Plato's Republic, I doubt that Plato would have turned him back. That contravenes what Plato says about poets, but should we trust the polemic? I am not competent to judge Plato as a philosopher, but his dialogues, at their best, are unique dramatic poems, unmatchable in literary history.

Homer has been dated as middle to late eighth century before the Common Era, and was challenged for poetic excellence by Hesiod in the early seventh. The even stronger agon, Plato's, began with the advent of Socrates (469–399 B.C.E.) and was culminated by his "son," seer of the *Republic* and the *Symposium*. Plato (429–347 B.C.E.) was defeated by Homer, to judge by strictly liter-

ary criteria, but then he engaged in mental fight with him not so much against him as poet but against Homer's role as teacher of the Greeks. Homer had become the textbook on all subjects for them. There, also, Plato lost, but the nearly two and a half millennia since have taken Plato as teacher of philosophy, and Homer as founder of poetry.

Together, Homer and Plato are so strong that their only rival before Dante, Cervantes, and Shakespeare is the Yahwist, who composed the earliest and most crucial stratum of Torah (in Genesis, Exodus, Numbers, with many later insertions by the Redactor, in the Babylonian exile) sometime between 980 and 900 B.C.E., before Homer lived and died. The ultimate agon has to be that between the Yahwist's Moses, enigmatic hero of the Torah, and Socrates, captured forever by Plato, despite the genius of Aristophanes in his great farce *The Clouds* (424 B.C.E.), and the devoted candor of the pragmatic Xenophon, heroic chronicler of *Anabasis, or The Persian Expedition*, in which Xenophon leads an army of Greek freebooters, and marches them back to safety after their patron, Cyrus the Younger, is killed in battle by the forces of his enemy brother, the Persian king. Xenophon's Socrates is so different from Plato's that I used to give credence to the late Gregory Vlastos (one of my undergraduate teachers at Cornell) in his genial dismissal of the Spartan (in spirit) general as a prophecy of Lytton Strachey's *Eminent Victorians*. Now I am a touch uncertain, after rereading Robin Waterfield's version, Xenophon's *Conversations of Socrates* (Penguin, 1990). It may be that Plato's Socrates is a superb fiction, and not the historical Socrates, but then the Yahwist's Moses is a sublimely ironic fiction, quite unlike the hero of Deuteronomy and of the priestly author's

layer of the Exodus–Numbers palimpsest constructed by the Ezra-like Redactor.

Xenophon's Socrates does not ironically assert his own ignorance, but teaches goodness because he knows himself as the Good. This Socrates is not a genius of deliberate comedy, but fit teacher for a military man. Shall we postulate—though I am uneasy in gainsaying Vlastos, the most thorough of all scholars of Socrates—that the sage of Athens taught what each student was capable of understanding? Was Xenophon aware of his teacher's unsurpassed control of irony? Or did Plato project his own magnificence at irony so as to create a heroic precursor? Nietzsche, who, like Kierkegaard, manifested lifelong ambivalence toward Socrates, remarked that if one hadn't a good father, it was necessary to invent one.

2
—

Susan B. Levin, in a revisionist study of Plato's relation to the Greek literary tradition, has us accompany her on *The Ancient Quarrel Between Philosophy and Poetry Revisited* (Oxford, 2001). Though she accurately notes Plato's stance that philosophers don't need poetry (which prophesies David Hume and Ludwig Wittgenstein on Shakespeare), she also catches a certain urgency in Plato's determination to triumph over Homer. This disagrees with Iris Murdoch's contention that, for Plato, poetry is mere sophistry. What Plato, and his Socrates, know about the uses of etymology,

particularly for the meaning of names, is finally Homeric. Plato insisted that only Socrates was his teacher, and yet involuntarily, like all the Greeks, Homer also served as Plato's teacher.

The best recent guide I know to the literary culture of ancient Greece is Andrew Ford's *The Origin of Criticism* (Princeton, 2002), which gives a wry account of the background to Plato's enigmatic exile of the poets:

> A capsule history of Greek criticism before Plato is given to us by Plato himself when he apologizes for dismissing poets from his ideal city by referring to an "ancient quarrel between poetry and philosophy" (Republic 607B). Plato may not be altogether serious: he documents the poets' side of the quarrel with snatches of lyric and comic verse that have nothing to do with philosophy but that do speak of pompous and arrogant types who may win a reputation among the undiscerning. And whether he is joking or not, we should be wary of Platonic constructions of literary history that make it culminate in his own philosophical positions. Yet most histories of Greek criticism have taken him at his word and traced this war to the later sixth century, when Xenophanes and his younger contemporary Heraclitus criticized the songs of Homer and Hesiod. A turning point—the beginning of the end of traditional reverence for poets—is recognized when Xenophanes said, "Homer and Hesiod have attributed to the gods every kind of behavior that among men is the object of reproach: stealing, adultery, and cheating each other." Although Hesiod and Solon, and no doubt popular wisdom, already knew that singers

(aoidoi) *often lie, with Xenophanes the rational Greek critical spirit is supposed to awaken.*

Ford usefully indicates that Plato creatively misreads Xenophanes, who was a wisdom writer, and not a philosopher, and indeed was himself a poet. In the sixth century B.C.E., wisdom and poetry scarcely could be distinguished as categories, and Xenophanes, who wandered about until a great age, attacking Homer and commending himself, earned his living as a performing rhapsode. It seems almost comic that the aristocratic Plato should have put the disreputable Xenophanes to use as another dart to toss at Homer, but we very probably don't always apprehend Plato's comedy. He would have known that Xenophanes, like the more solemn Pythagoras and Empedocles, was a kind of shaman, and so the "ancient quarrel" with Homer and Hesiod was not on behalf of anything rational.

Another of Andrew Ford's contributions is to strengthen the realization that Homeric singers (*aoidoi*) did not begin to be called "poets" or "makers" (*poietai*) until the fifth century B.C.E., and then the term rarely was used or liked by the poets themselves. Of the high tragedians, only Euripides accepts the word, and his ironies are as prevalent as Plato's. And yet Plato's resentment of Homer was profound, however complexly expressed. The *Iliad* and the *Odyssey* do not have the same relation to the *Oresteia* of Aeschylus and the *Oedipus* cycle of Sophocles that they have to the *Symposium* and the *Republic,* works intended to at least rival Homer. Plato was too vastly intelligent to believe he could actually do that, any more than Hume and Wittgenstein could think Shakespeare might

be set aside. At our dreadful moment in education, the *Iliad* and the *Odyssey* are not as universally taught as in my youth, but they remain far more widely studied than are the *Symposium* and the *Republic*. Homer, as Dr. Johnson said, was (except for Shakespeare) the first among all poets.

Plato, better than any now alive, perceived the aesthetic supremacy of Homer, but regarded Socrates as the truer guide to wisdom both moral and religious. Whether the epic tragedy of Achilles and the epic comedy of Odysseus possess less truth than the discourses of Plato's Socrates is a highly disputable contention, yet I am *alogos*, averse to philosophy, since first I fell in love with the poetry of William Blake and Hart Crane. I do not read Hume and Wittgenstein except as a searcher for arresting aphorisms, and I turn incessantly back to Shakespeare in quest for truth, power, beauty, and for persons, above all else. I say this so as to admit that the *Republic* makes me unhappy. Just as I reread Jonathan Swift's superbly acidulous *A Tale of a Tub* twice a year, to subdue myself, so I regularly reread the *Republic*, also to receive a wisdom that chastens my fury against all ideology. What Andrew Ford calls "the sound of ideology" rises up from the *Republic*, ultimate ancestor of all the current commissars of Resentment who throng our academies, and who zealously continue the destruction of literary study. "The aesthetics of song," Ford writes, is in the *Republic* "always discussed in terms of a social psychology and in relation to political goals." I have returned to teaching after a year spent recovering from ill health, and I have resumed my practice of advising any potential student to vote with her or his feet (grand American idiom!) if they expect to discuss cultural politics in my

classroom. It is a long way down and out from Plato to our contemporary lemmings, but the *Republic* inaugurates their Puritanism.

As a hermetic aesthete, I am not exactly the auditor the *Republic* desires, but negation has its uses in the art of reading. Plato's gods do not include Yahweh, who in the Book of Amos and the Epistle of James cries out against the exploiters of the poor, who now dominate the plutocracy and oligarchy that has replaced democracy in America. Platonic "justice" would shrug this off, but then so would Homeric wisdom. Our civilization is still split between a Hellenic cognition and aesthetic and a Hebraic morality and religion. One might say that the hand of Western (indeed of much Eastern also) civilization has five ill-assorted fingers: Moses, Socrates, Jesus, Shakespeare, Freud. Plato's culture is entirely Socratic, by design, yet also Homeric, unwillingly. Between the *Republic* and ourselves come Moses, Jesus, Shakespeare, Freud, and though we cannot abandon Athens, still less could we avoid our tongues' cleaving to the roofs of our mouths if we do not prefer Jerusalem to Athens.

The *Republic*, I find, makes intense but unpleasant reading, principally because Plato accurately argues that most citizens never grow up, and therefore need to be fed benign fictions rather than the Homeric epics, where the gods are selfish, nasty spectators, all too happy to see us suffering in their theater of cruelty. I detect neither Socratic nor Platonic irony in this cultural materialism. If criticism is the art of judging poetry, "judging" remains a powerful metaphor in that definition. Plato is a bad judge in regard to Homer, whatever qualifications scholars might bring to my discomfort.

3

And yet Plato was a great reader, a sublime writer, and the most gifted of all of the auditors of Socrates. It is not possible that Plato did not know how outrageous was his "banishment" of the poet proper, "creator" (as we would say) of Achilles and Odysseus. Part of the puzzle is that as Hebraic monotheists (in heritage anyway, be it Judaism, Christianity, Islam) we cannot conceive of setting philosophy against the poetry of Job, the Psalms, the Song of Solomon, the war song of Deborah and Barak (Judges 5). There was no Hebraic philosophy or theology before Philo of Alexandria and the Platonized Jews who came after him. The most extraordinary of Hebrew wisdom writings, as we have seen in Chapter 1, are the poems embedded in Proverbs, Job, Isaiah. Plato deeply influenced the second-century-C.E. rabbis, since their notion that Torah study could be redemption has no warrant in the Hebrew Bible, yet is strangely Platonic in spirit.

Leo Strauss mused on a reconciliation between Athens and Jerusalem, which I believe is not possible. I was touched when recently I unearthed, after many years, the late Allan Bloom's translation/commentary of the *Republic,* which he gave me in Ithaca, New York, in June 1969, with the affectionate inscription "for the continuation of our Athens–Jerusalem collaboration." True disciple of Strauss, Allan defended Plato against Homer:

From this viewpoint, one can also understand what Socrates meant by treating the poet as an imitator of artifacts. In one

*sense man is a natural being, but in another he is a product of
nomos, convention. Men and men's ways differ from place to
place as trees and their ways do not. The law transforms men to
such an extent that many can doubt whether there is such a thing
as human nature at all. Even if there is a natural man, or, more
classically expressed, a man who lives according to nature, civil
society and its laws must aid in his coming to be. Civil men, the
dwellers in the cave, are in the decisive sense the artifacts of the
legislator: their opinions are made by him. Human making has a
great deal to do with our perception of even the things which
seem most unambiguously natural. Men see the beautiful sunset,
the noble river, the terrifying storm or the sacred cow. To know
these things we must separate what belongs to them naturally
from what opinion adds to them. Poetry tends to blend the natural and conventional elements in things; and it charms men in
such a way that they no longer see the seams of the union of
these two elements.* [pages 433–34]

At *Republic* 398A, Plato insists no one can compose both tragedy
and comedy, but at the close of the *Symposium*, Socrates says that
the same dramatist ought to be good at both comedy and tragedy.
Athens had no such playwright, but Shakespearean women and
men are both comic and tragic: Hamlet, Falstaff, Cleopatra, even
Iago. I recall that, after reading the paragraph above, I asked Allan,
"But what if the poet was Shakespeare and not Homer?" Is
the truth revealed by Shakespeare only a partial truth? Even the
Straussian Allan was not willing to argue for Plato's wisdom over
Shakespeare's, though he fell back upon context, since Shake-

speare began two thousand years after Plato. As a lifelong antihistoricist, I shrugged off this contention. Plato's *Republic* is eternal, or it is nothing, and it is almost ludicrous that the poet of *Hamlet* and of *King Lear* might be allowed to return by Socrates if only he could learn to argue, to justify himself before a tribunal of philosophers.

The scholars of Socrates and Plato who impress me most include G. M. A. Grube, Paul Friedländer, Gregory Vlastos, and Alexander Nehamas, but they too make me wonder why Plato's Socrates wants to exile Homer and Hesiod. Grube (1935) gives us a Socrates who sounds to me like Dr. Johnson on Shakespeare, insisting upon "a study of goodness." *King Lear* appalled Johnson, who could not accept the murder of Cordelia, and who endorsed Nahum Tate's parody in which Cordelia survives to marry Edgar and be happy ever after.

Friedländer, a little warier, ironically set Plato against Plato, in a Hegelian dispute between right and right, moralism against Homer's aesthetic magnificence. That seems to me another dead end. Rather dazzlingly, Vlastos indicts Socrates for a failure in love, which startles me into the analogy of Hamlet's lack of love for everyone, himself included. Nehamas defends the Platonic Socrates by insisting that what is being attacked is not Homer's art but its use as Athenian entertainment, which is regarded by Nehamas as akin to our cinema, TV, and computer debasements that dumb down even Shakespeare, Jane Austen, and Dickens. With all respect, philosophers become somewhat desperate in attempting to

defend a ban or curtailment of the *Iliad*, and surely they know it. Iris Murdoch, philosopher and novelist, to me seems best in unvexing this unfortunate quarrel. The fault, she says, is in Plato's firm sense of hierarchy: "Wisdom is *there*, but belongs to gods and very few mortals." Which has more wisdom: the *Republic* or the *Iliad*? I think we cannot prefer Plato to Homer, any more than we can choose Francis Bacon over Shakespeare.

4

I remember, after my amiable disagreement with Allan Bloom, going back to the house my wife and I were renting in Ithaca, and settling down for the evening to reread Richmond Lattimore's *Iliad* and Allan's *Republic* side by side. Sometimes, I would interpolate scenes from *King Lear,* further to intensify the agon. Any philosopher I know would say I was far from the point, since Socrates condemns poetry for untruth and for erotic desire, and is disputing Homer's wisdom and his effect on the supposed public good. Plato therefore would dismiss the agonistic notion that he was struggling against Homer for the foremost place in what we now would call literary achievement.

As antithesis to my quest for wisdom fused with aesthetic supremacy, I will consider the title essay of the philosopher Stanley Rosen's *The Quarrel Between Philosophy and Poetry* (London, 1988). Rosen follows Plato in distinguishing between Socrates' erotics and Homer's depiction of desire, to Plato a path to tyranny. I find this too ironic even for Plato, since his Socrates professes igno-

rance of everything *except* erotics. The literary critic in me is also unhappy with Rosen's attempt to be equitable, which faults Plato over Homer:

> *Philosophy has the advantage over poetry of being able to explain what it understands by wisdom. But poetry has the advantage over philosophy in that part of wisdom, and indeed, the regulative part, is poetic.* [page 13]

Is Shakespeare implicitly unable to explain what Hamlet understands by wisdom? The arrogance here is Plato's, not Rosen's, since Homer dramatizes the wisdom of Odysseus and the doomeager unwisdom of Achilles. How are we to believe that Homer, unlike Socrates, does not lay hold of the Truth? Socrates knows the difference between images and reality, while Homer supposedly does not. And yet Homer knows that the poetry of the past, however wise, is not necessarily true. Must we become Platonists in order to believe Plato, or is he again ironic when he answers us that Socrates knows the truth? Only dualism, the distinction between ideal Forms and ordinary realities, is truth for Plato's Socrates. Odysseus is pragmatically a monist, while Achilles is childlike. Who decides what is true?

Homer, according to Plato's Socrates, has educated Greece, but the only socially valuable part of that education consists of "hymns to gods or celebration of good men." Is that all that Achilles and Odysseus have contributed to our instruction? Absurd as that

question sounds, how much more outrageous it would be if we asked, Do Hamlet and Lear teach us how to praise the gods and how to celebrate good men? So far as I can tell, Hamlet has no gods, while Lear abandons his. Who are the good men in *Hamlet* and in *Lear*? In *Hamlet,* there is only the straight man, Horatio, while *Lear* gives us Edgar and Gloucester, both duped by Edmund, and the faithful Kent, accurate from the start. Plato might have approved of Kent, hardly central to the drama.

A great mythmaker, Plato shrewdly disarms lovers of Homer by concluding Book X, where Homer is exiled, and so the whole of the *Republic,* with the astonishingly wise and powerful myth of Er, an ultimate vision of moral and theophanic judgment. Er dies in battle, but is resurrected on the twelfth day, and reports to us on the judgment of the just and the unjust in the afterlife. This certainly is not Homer's Hades, to which Odysseus descends, though only as a visitor. Implicitly, Socrates intimates that Achilles and Odysseus are meaningless compared with his Er. I take it that the intimation is unfair, because Socrates is purifying Homer into a moral poet, but with no belief in the survival of individual consciousness. Meaning is wholly a question of justice and injustice: there is no vision of what was to become the Christian Platonism of Saint Paul and Saint Augustine.

Manifestly, the attack on Homer will not satisfy any reader who rightly values the *Iliad* as one of the crowns of imaginative literature, and yet the issue of wisdom here is religious, though certainly not in any Hebraic sense. Plato's Socrates wants the gods to be devoid of personality: free of lust, fury, envy, and everything else that interests us in Homer's Zeus, much of the time. Like the

Christian Platonists who were to follow him, the divine Plato is obsessed with salvation, hardly a Homeric notion. Unlike the biblical Hebrews, who had no theology, Plato most certainly did, though it is difficult to summarize. Something in me does not altogether ascribe Plato's resentment of Homer to the philosopher's spirituality, but doubtless it intensified Plato's agon with the teacher of all Hellas. That Plato's god keeps cosmological distance from the disciple of Socrates has something to do with the origins of Gnosticism, a post-Platonic heresy that strongly misreads both Plato and the Bible. An exiled God is still God, and Homer's all-too-human gods sincerely offended Plato.

Homer may have seemed to Plato a trifler with magic, almost a shaman. That isn't the *Iliad* as we read it now, or as most Greeks read it then. What did Plato make of Homer's Achilles, who destroys men as part of a private war against death itself, even as a child might mangle an already wounded kitten?

Iris Murdoch, in her brilliant *The Fire and the Sun*, reads the banishment of Homer as the poet Plato's protest against the poet-in-himself, uneasy brother of the Socratic philosopher-theologian. Perhaps Homer rendered Plato even more troubled, for even the most luminous exchanges in the dialogues cannot challenge the heroic pathos of the *Iliad*, which, with the Yahwist, Dante, Cervantes, and Shakespeare, continues to set the standard for high literature. Who can underestimate Plato's ambitions? He wanted to be the poet-philosopher-theologian-educator first of Greece and then of all humankind. Homer would not budge, and is there still. When the gods join the battle between Greeks and Trojans, the aesthetic effect eclipses Plato at his most imaginative, while

spiritually it may have disgusted him. As Richmond Lattimore observes, Homer's Olympians are primarily immortal men and women, no better than the rest of us, and only rarely are they paradigms of wisdom.

Plato's Socrates would not get high marks as a literary critic of Homer, who decidedly was not a philosopher. But then I would fail Hume and Wittgenstein as critics of Shakespeare, and I suspect that neither could admit to himself the disconcerting truth that Shakespeare, most capacious of intellects, could outflank any philosopher. Hegel, who loved Shakespeare, praised the poet-dramatist for creating a host of people who were "free artists of themselves." Plato, a free artist of himself, was not Shakespeare, or Homer. That, I venture, remains the true, ongoing quarrel between poetry and philosophy.

Plato carries what, to me, is a darker burden, for the more anguished quarrel is between poetry and theology, inaugurated by Plato's Socrates in the *Republic,* and still prevalent, except that the ideologies of Resentment have largely displaced theology. Thus, I have heard Emerson and Whitman denounced as "racists," and some years back, after teaching *King Lear,* I received an anonymous note informing me that every class I had ever conducted was "an act of violence against the women of Yale." Doubtless it is unfair to call such lemmings "Platonists," since probably they have never read the *Republic* or the *Laws,* but the legacy is clear enough.

The supreme poets—Homer, Dante, Petrarch, Chaucer, Shake-

speare, Milton, Goethe, Walt Whitman, Yeats—would none of them be acceptable to the Platonic Socrates. When we read Homer, Dante, Shakespeare, can we really believe that the supreme music is philosophy? That Plato, in aesthetic eminence, stands near to Homer and Dante reasonably could be argued, but he dwindles in proximity to Shakespeare, as all must do. Why did Plato—or at least his Socrates—challenge Homer as a wisdom writer? Is poetry, of the highest order, a corruption of the intellect? Did Homer, Dante, Shakespeare not know what they were doing? Eric Havelock, in his still lively *Preface to Plato* (1963), permanently startles me by bluntly stating the Platonic polemic at its most outrageous:

> *To assume that Plato would subscribe to the pretensions of the Hebrew prophets, or alternatively of the Romantic poets, is to stand Platonism on its head.* [page 34]

There go Isaiah, Ezekiel, William Blake, Shelley, Hart Crane: let Plato then stand upon his head, so far as at least this one literary critic is concerned. To save Plato from himself is to do him violence, he being so majestical. The dilemma is that wisdom and literature cannot be brought together either with or without Plato and his Socrates: the *Symposium* is very nearly as essential a work as the *Iliad, The Divine Comedy, Hamlet,* and *King Lear* and *Macbeth.* I am not foolish enough to join in saving Plato from himself, and yet I badly need to be saved from Plato.

Francis M. Cornford, introducing his translation of the *Timaeus* in his *Plato's Cosmology* (1937), remarks:

The Republic *had dwelt on the structural analogy between the state and the human soul.*

That may be the center of the catastrophic farewell to Homer. Plato dismisses him as Prince Hal/Henry V exiles Falstaff, whose soul is not exactly statist. Socrates, in Plato, formulates ideas of order: the *Iliad*, like Shakespeare, knows that a violent disorder is a great order.

If the Hebrew prophets and William Blake entertained any "pretensions," it was because they heard the voice of God even as Socrates listened to his daimon. Plato's strength, as all his legatees know, cannot be separated from his very individual "religion" (to call it that), and the pursuit of his wisdom must bring us there.

5
—

Gregory Vlastos, commenting on the *Republic,* precisely characterizes Plato's idiosyncratic mysticism:

This is the mystical element at the core of Plato's metaphysics. I call it "mystical" because no fully rational explanation can be given of the implosion set off in the philosopher's soul by the vision of Form which makes a new man out of him. The varieties of mysticism are legion. It can be wholly this-worldly, as in Zen. In Plato it is radically otherworldly—as much so as in Augustine or Paul. Through Plato we get a glimpse of what Christian otherworldliness would have been like if it had not

been informed by agapē and its ethics had not been humanized by the man-centeredness of its Jewish God. A moment ago, speaking for humanistic ethics, I said that when I ask, "What is excellence for?" I can only reply, "For humanity." Plato would protest that my question is senseless: excellence, he would say, eternally complete in the world of Form, is not for anything or anyone: it simply is, and its imperative to us is only the imperious love its being evokes in any soul capable of knowing it. He would turn my question around: "What is humanity for?" he would ask. And his reply would not be so unlike the one in the Westminster Confession. Substitute "Form" for "God" and it would be the same: The chief end of man is to glorify Form and enjoy it for ever. If you are a Platonic philosopher, you have found the meaning of your life, your true vocation, in faithful service to the Forms of Justice, Beauty, Goodness, and the rest. You are possessed by a transcendent love beside which earthly passions pale. You have discovered bliss which turns the prizes of this world into trash.

[*SOCRATES, PLATO, AND THEIR TRADITION*, pages 96–97]

The Forms cannot be described except in Plato's vision: they are his icons. If God is transcendent Form, then the problem of Job is solved, at the high cost of dehumanizing God. Commenting on the *Timaeus*, Vlastos frees both God and the soul from any responsibility for evil:

When you find a physical cause for irrational choice, you must exculpate God of the disorderly motion that has caused it. And

you cannot stop short of the primitive chaos. This ultimate cause
of evil must exist, uncaused by God, and (short of reopening the
problem all over again) uncaused by soul. [page 260]

Job would have found no comfort (or indeed sense) in this absolutely un-Hebraic kind of discourse: "Behold now Behemoth which I made with you" takes away any Platonic murmuring about "disorderly motions." The Neoplatonists—and, in a rebel mode, the Gnostics—seem to have understood Plato's God as we, mostly, cannot. Alexander Nehamas, a rare exception, comments on the *Symposium* in a way that suggests that it is there, not in the *Timaeus,* that we ought to seek Plato on divine things:

And so erōs, *which we first approached as the desire to possess*
sexually the body of another person, turns out to be a desire for
immortality, for wisdom, and for the contemplation of an object
that is not in any way bodily or physical. [page 311]

Socrates, both the lover and the beloved (of Alcibiades, among others), is a daimon or spirit, interpreted by Nehamas as neither a god nor a mortal. These days, in the United States, the followers of the erotic Plato are joined in dubious battle with American Religionists, led by the twice-born George W. Bush. The issue of gay marriage will not go away, nor should it. The Hebrew Bible and the Platonic dialogues refuse reconciliation, because Yahweh and Plato's God cannot share dominion.

And yet our cognition—science and technology, as well as philosophy—is Greek, as is our aesthetic, though not altogether.

Religion and morality, despite the long tradition of Christian Platonism, will remain Hebraic-Christian-Islamic, though perhaps increasingly Platonized.

The Hebrews strove to trust in the Covenant; Plato theologized, really inaugurating the mode. The crucial Platonic work is Book 10 of the *Laws,* the philosopher's final work, in old age, and the only dialogue where Socrates does not appear at all. There is a superb study by Friedrich Solmsen, *Plato's Theology* (1942). Solmsen was one of my teachers of Greek, when I was a Cornell undergraduate, and after fifty-five years I remember him with reverence and gratitude. Of *Laws* 10, Solmsen remarked that in it Plato abandons all efforts to found religion upon individual human life. Belief must be cosmic, and imposed by the state. That is already distasteful (to understate it), but matters develop into something far worse.

The aged Plato founded a new religion, which in one sense never gained a single adherent (Plato included) but in another was to alter all Western monotheisms: Judaism, Christianity, Islam, and in yet another produced every Western esotericism: Neoplatonism, Gnosticism, Sufism, Kabbalah, and the variants thereof. I cannot think of anything in spiritual history comparable to Plato's power of contamination. *Laws* 10 is a sublime disaster, and yet that hardly matters, even where it is least humane:

Now since impiety has three causes, which we've already described, and each is divided into two kinds, there will be six categories of religious offenders worth distinguishing; and the punishment imposed on each should vary in kind and degree.

Consider first a complete atheist: he may have a naturally just character and be the sort of person who hates scoundrels, and because of his loathing of injustice is not tempted to commit it; he may flee the unjust and feel fondness for the just. Alternatively, besides believing that all things are 'empty of' gods, he may be a prey to an uncontrollable urge to experience pleasure and avoid pain, and he may have a retentive memory and be capable of shrewd insights. Both these people suffer from a common failing, atheism, but in terms of the harm they do to others the former is much less dangerous than the latter. The former will talk with a complete lack of inhibition about gods and sacrifices and oaths, and by poking fun at other people will probably, if he continues unpunished, make converts to his own views. The latter holds the same opinions but has what are called 'natural gifts': full of cunning and guile, he's the sort of fellow who'll make a diviner or a demagogue or a general, or a plotter in secret rites; and he's the man who invents the tricks of the so-called 'sophists'. So there can be many different types of atheist, but for the purpose of legislation they need to be divided into two groups. The dissembling atheist deserves to die for his sins not just once or twice but many times, whereas the other kind needs simply admonition combined with incarceration. The idea that gods take no notice of the world similarly produces two more categories, and the belief that they can be squared another two. So much for our distinctions.

That is beyond my capacity for response. Is this the author of the *Symposium*, who took Socrates, master of erotics, as his father? What seems to have transformed Plato from a supreme composer

of cognitive music, prose poet of the earlier and middle dialogues, into an Orwellian nightmare was his own genius for cosmological speculation. That may be only a literary critic's misapplied interpretation, and yet clearly Plato developed and did not just unfold, as perhaps Socrates did. The judicial murder of Socrates (which the sage accepted, uncannily akin to Jesus' murder by crucifixion) may have malformed Plato, though only after some decades. If there is irony in the *Laws,* I cannot locate it. And yet Socrates' god within, his daimon, is not the God of the elder Plato. Perhaps it is a mistake to regard Plato as the disciple of Socrates, early or late. I begin to doubt the argument of Vlastos, that Plato's is the historical Socrates. Unless we are philosophers, and I decidedly am not, then we do not descend from Socrates. But lovers of imaginative literature, however heterodox their religious temperaments, necessarily are involuntarily Platonists. All of our still current Alexandrian culture—pagan, Jewish, Muslim, Christian—was and remains Platonist, and you cannot harvest Hellenism without incessantly rereading Plato. Emerson cheerfully remarked that Hamlet is Plato's heir (doubtless by way of Montaigne, who preferred Socrates), and Hamlet, like Plato, I regard as fascinating bad news.

Solmsen, admirably dispassionate, ended his *Plato's Theology* with a superb paragraph that presents both our debt to Plato's spirituality and our departures from it:

> *If we are right in suggesting that Plato thinks of God as the*
> *mediator between the intelligible and the physical worlds, we are*

bound to admit that Aristotle's concept of God as the apex of Being won out over his master's view; but it is fitting to repeat that some elements of Plato's own thought were combined with and modified the Aristotelian concept of the Prime Mover. The World-Soul, conceived as it was by Plato as mediating between the eternal and the perishable, could for this very reason be placed no higher than on the third plane by the Neoplatonists, whereas the Christians very naturally refused to recognize a cosmic Soul, and were more attracted by the concept of a Universe of souls than by that of a Universe governed by a Soul. On the other hand, the idea of a mediator between the Godhead and this world is of vital importance for Christianity, and its theological formulation owes much to Plato's concept of the Demiurge. Still more important is the fact that the spiritual world of Christian thinkers enjoys the kind of reality that Plato had ascribed to his Ideas. Not only the Ideas themselves, which survive in mediaeval philosophy as the thoughts of God, but the intelligible world as a whole constitutes the most essential debt of Christianity to the Platonic account of true Being. To think of God as the apex of this realm has become so customary that even modern interpreters of Plato tend to treat his God as identical with his highest Idea, and to overlook or misunderstand the peculiar situation out of which Plato's theology developed. Plato conceived of the Deity as mediating between two worlds and as imparting to the visible world; but his concept was obscured in the history of Platonism. We can in fact trace this process through some stages. Although the tension between Being and Becoming

has since reappeared in the history of philosophy, there has been
no revival of the Platonic position, since through the combined
influence of Aristotelianism, Neoplatonism, and Christianity the
concept of God had in the meantime been fixed as the consum-
mation of Being.

Unpacking Solmsen has its rewards. Plato's final vision of God sees Him as mediating between nature and the world of ideas, a stationing not taken up by Aristotle, or Neoplatonism, or Christianity. A long foreground informs Plato's ultimate formulation. There are no neutral gods in Homer, where Athena supports the Greeks against the Trojans. Though she personifies Athens, she wins no approval from Plato. The patroness of Achilles is not what Plato means by a spiritual path to the achievement of wisdom. In the *Republic*, Homer is indicted, together with Hesiod and other poets, for composing false stories about the gods warring and plotting against one another, thus destroying Olympian religion.

G. M. A. Grube, in his *Plato's Thought* (1935), emphasizes that, after the *Republic*, a distance opens up between the Ideas, or transcendental Forms, and the gods. "Ideas" is a bad translation for the Socratic *eidos*, which means what Wallace Stevens called "the look of things," the appearance that the supposed materialist Freud, like the supposed transcendentalist Plato, judged to constitute absolute reality. Forms, to all Platonists (Stevens and Freud included), are the world in which we live and must die (a grim acceptance

mitigated by Neoplatonists, mystics, and Christian Platonists). Grube usefully warns us (page 168) that the Forms do not emanate from God, as they do in the Jewish Kabbalah, which is an extraordinary fusion of Neoplatonism and an anti-Platonic Gnosticism (the latter favored by Gershom Scholem, titan of Kabbalah scholarship). This still leaves us to confront the central issue between Plato's irony and Homer's: How can Plato's God and Homer's outrageous gods coexist?

According to Solmsen, Plato began by expurgating everything colorful and all-too-human in the Homeric gods. That destroys the *Iliad* and the *Odyssey,* or would, except that Homer—like Dante, Shakespeare, Cervantes, Chaucer—is indestructible, which was a lifelong frustration for the moralizing and finally totalitarian Plato, who in the *Laws* sets the prototype for Franco, Stalin, Mao. Since expurgating Homer did not work, Plato resorted to cosmological movement as a grand machine, a theory of change to sweep away Homeric dominance of Greek education. A weird astrology ensued that remains of interest only to scholars, while students go on reading Homer (or would, if we still had universities, rather than mediaversities of multiculturalism).

Plato, endlessly persistent in his resentment of Homer, resorted to his own mythmaking, one of the most extraordinary of his bewildering endowments of creative gifts. His *Timaeus* forsakes expurgation and identifies the entire Cosmos with God. That makes us only items, however important (as Solmsen notes), in a scheme that moves to a purpose that dwarfs us. I do not think that Achilles and Odysseus are absorbed comfortably into that scheme. Neither are Abraham, Moses, David, Jesus, and Muhammad.

6

Whatever the ancient quarrel between poetry and philosophy meant to the pre-Socratics, it became the center of the contest between Plato's Socrates and Homer. Socratic irony professes ignorance, while Homeric pride palpably manifests encyclopedic knowledge. Eric Havelock, whose *Preface to Plato* (1963) cheerfully takes Plato's side against Homer, delighted in telling me, when I was a young enthusiast for Blake and Shelley, that poetry corrupted the intellect. I was charmed by Havelock, yet hardly could be persuaded. Even Freud, neither a Christian nor a Platonist, nevertheless shared Plato's distrust of the power of poetry.

Let us set aside the *Timaeus* and the *Laws*. Will the common reader, now as always, absorb more wisdom from the *Republic* and the *Symposium* than from the *Iliad* and the *Odyssey*? Do Hume and Wittgenstein make us wiser than *Hamlet* and *King Lear*? In search of wisdom, ought I to reread (most reluctantly) Foucault on power and sadomasochism, or Proust's *In Search of Lost Time*? The questions are absurd: competing with Homer, Shakespeare, and Proust is hopeless unless you are Aeschylus, Cervantes, and Joyce. Plato is unique among philosophers because, as Emerson said, "he has clapped copyright upon the world." Yet Homer *is* the world, and could not be copyrighted.

In his "Socratic Reflections," Nehamas (*The Art of Living*, 1998) warns us that "Socrates' ironic gaze is turned not only toward his

interlocutors but toward his interpreters as well," among whom Plato is foremost. Homer's ironies, like Chaucer's and Shakespeare's, are so enormous that our vision is not large enough to see them; Plato's stories are marvelous but brief. The fury of Achilles and the cunning of Odysseus sustain tremendous epics—Hemingway, in his cups, would boast that he was in training to go a dozen rounds with Tolstoy; El Sordo's last stand in *For Whom the Bell Tolls* is superb, but try to read it side by side with the Chechen hero's final battle in *Hadji Murad,* the strongest narrative I have ever read. Plato, courageous almost beyond belief, secure in his own literary powers, nevertheless appears to discard his own defensive irony when he rejects Homer in the *Republic.* Scholars of philosophy are not very wary in regard to Plato's blunder, because (at their best) philosophy is for them a way of life. But Plato sought to replace Homer as the culture of Greece, which was as likely as demoting Shakespeare for the English-speaking world, Goethe for the Germans, Tolstoy for the Russians, Montaigne and Descartes for the French. I would add Walt Whitman for the New World, except that we have not yet learned how to read him, except for a handful: Thoreau, Hart Crane, Borges, Pessoa, Neruda.

7
—

What Is Ancient Philosophy? is the title of a seminal book by Pierre Hadot (translated from the French by Michael Chase, 2002). At the start (page 4), Hadot remarks that one of his fundamental themes is "the distance which separates philosophy from wisdom." Later

(page 47), Hadot's Plato is compared to Eros and Socrates, both homeless:

> *Philosophy's tonality is also tragic, because the bizarre being, the "philosopher," is tortured and torn by the desire to attain this wisdom which escapes him, yet which he loves. Like Kierkegaard, the Christian who wanted to be a Christian but knew that only Christ is a Christian, the philosopher knows that he cannot reach his model and will never be entirely that which he desires. Plato thus establishes an insurmountable distance between philosophy and wisdom. Philosophy is defined by what it lacks— that is, by a transcendent norm which escapes it, yet which it nevertheless possesses within itself in some way, as in the famous, and very Platonic, words of Pascal: "You would not seek me if you had not already found me."*

Poignant as this clearly is, I would set against Hadot the assertion that High Literature (Shakespeare, Homer, Dante, Cervantes, Milton, Tolstoy, Proust) is not a preparatory exercise for wisdom. Doubtless, philosophy is needed, but what I desire, the wisdom I never can possess, is available to me, and to most readers, only in Shakespeare and those few who are almost his peers, who share some portion of his incredible richness. Plato could not have called what takes place in *Hamlet* and in *King Lear* only a copy of a copy, rather than the Form of reality itself. Samuel Johnson and Goethe, Emerson and Nietzsche, knew better, and so did Freud, though he evaded confronting that deep knowledge.

Plato's Socrates is his Supreme Fiction. As I remarked earlier, I

no longer believe Gregory Vlastos: Xenophon's *is* the historical Socrates. Homer's fictions almost transcend the work of making: Achilles and Odysseus seem more like foundational beings than poets' imaginings. With Shakespeare, the idea of fiction becomes somewhat irrelevant (except for the mass of those who teach Shakespeare). If Falstaff and Hamlet, Iago and Cleopatra, Lear and Macbeth are only roles for performances, then what are we? Wisdom is there to be found, in Job and Koheleth, in the Gospel of Mark and the Gospel of Thomas, in Cervantes and in Shakespeare. If your quest is for a wisdom within the bounds of reason, rather than of wonder, then go back to Plato and his progeny, down through David Hume to Wittgenstein. Plato, I think, would have approved the reservations concerning Shakespeare expressed by Hume and by Wittgenstein. But even a long life is too short to receive everything Shakespeare is capable of giving you.

8
—

This chapter is subtitled "Plato's Contest with Homer," and I have said little of Homer except as Plato's target. Yet I feel obliged to say more about Plato's figure of Socrates before I pass on to Plato's disfiguration of Homer, and then to say something of Homer himself.

Is there a difference between Socratic eros and Socratic irony, or are they both structures of need, of an emptiness craving fulfillment? Freud, who now seems to me more and more an unknowing Platonist, thought that we fell in love in order not to get ill, not

from lack but from an over-sense-of-self. I do not underestimate Freud's own irony, which competes with Proust's, Joyce's, Kafka's, and Beckett's, and appears to be parodied by Thomas Mann's. Socratic eros, as Iris Murdoch observed, is "cunning" and "homeless," which would be an apt description of the Freudian transference, that shamanistic exchange of the patient's love and the analyst's supposed benignity. I go on believing that the most destructive remark ever made about psychoanalysis was the unanswerable aphorism of the Viennese satirist Karl Kraus: "It is itself that illness of which it purports to be the cure." Can we not transpose this to the Socratic polemic against Homer: "It is itself that resentment which it proposes to legislate out of existence"? Achilles is a killing machine because he desires a god's immortality, but his human father intimates the hero's death. Plato, never a warrior, took Socrates as his heroic father, and gave Socrates immortality *as a literary character,* yet the Homeric irony in this is that Plato achieved a poetic immortality as a dialogical dramatist and mythmaker.

Plato's precursor, as the Hellenistic literary critic Longinus ironically implied, was Homer, and not Socrates, who declined to compose anything whatsoever. Could the *Republic* and the *Symposium* have been written without Homer as precursor, antagonist, provocation?

Xenophon's Socrates has most of the Homeric virtues: he is the best of the Greeks, whether in war or in argument, and is a match for Achilles in honor and for Odysseus in precise propriety when encountering difficult occasions. A Platonist generally

replies that Xenophon was a professional military man, who preferred Sparta to Athens. That hardly seems relevant: his rugged Socrates has no quarrel with Homer. What then was the critical relationship, if any, between Socrates and Plato? Like Wallace Stevens, Plato avoids the capital I. Kierkegaard's "indirect communication" seems based on Plato's, perhaps as a swerve away from Hegel. The persona of Socrates, invented by Plato, in part was Plato's defense against Homer, the poet eternally present in Greece. Nietzsche's Schopenhauer played the same role, another ironic mask for Nietzsche-as-educator.

When Odysseus disguised himself as a beggar, he influenced the actual Socrates, the eros whom Diotima, wise woman of the *Symposium,* called poor, filthy, barefoot. Socrates is not exactly a Platonic Form, visually speaking, though Plato found in him the Form-of-Forms. Both a mortal and a daimon, Socrates is half a god, like Achilles, and also a resourceful deceiver, as cunning as Odysseus. He is the third major Homeric hero, as Plato clearly understood. Homer, Plato insisted, was a liar, whereas the lies of Socrates were "noble," and necessary if Athens was to be reeducated.

Plato's shrewdness is that of strong poets throughout the ages: creatively misinterpret the dominant poetic forerunner, in order to clear imaginative space for yourself. Here, too, Plato set the pattern. Philosophy is a literary art, akin to but superior to Homer's, and also the art of dialectics, of conversation sharpened and refined. Plato, though out of his class in facing off against Homer, is at least a plausible challenger, yet no other philosopher has been so major a literary artist. The Socrates of Plato incarnates the art of eros, and Homer is not primarily a poet of eros but of strife between

men and gods. Only the *Symposium* is not destroyed by being read in the company of the *Iliad*.

Wisdom is the aim of Plato, and of his Socrates. What is Homer's relation to wisdom? Wallace Stevens, miscalled (by some) a Platonist, affirmed that poetry was superior to philosophy. Shelley, even more absurdly named by many scholars as a Platonist, wrote the finest discourse on poetry's greater wisdom in 1821 in *A Defence of Poetry*, not published, however, until 1840, eighteen years after the poet drowned. Homer receives accurate tribute:

> The poems of Homer and his contemporaries were the delight of infant Greece; they were the elements of that social system which is the column upon which all succeeding civilization has reposed. Homer embodied the ideal perfection of his age in human character; nor can we doubt that those who read his verses were awakened to an ambition of becoming like to Achilles, Hector, and Ulysses: the truth and beauty of friendship, patriotism, and persevering devotion to an object, were unveiled to their depths in these immortal creations: the sentiments of the auditors must have been refined and enlarged by a sympathy with such great and lovely impersonations, until from admiring they imitated, and from imitation they identified themselves with the objects of their admiration. Nor let it be objected, that these characters are remote from moral perfection, and that they are by no means to be considered as edifying patterns for general imitation. Every epoch, under names more or less specious, has deified its peculiar

errors; Revenge is the naked idol of the worship of a semi-barbarous age; and Self-deceit is the veiled image of the unknown evil, before which luxury and satiety lie prostrate. But a poet considers the vices of his contemporaries as the temporary dress in which his creations must be arrayed, and which cover without concealing the eternal proportions of their beauty. An epic or dramatic personage is understood to wear them around his soul, as he may the ancient armour or modern uniform around his body; whilst it is easy to conceive a dress more graceful than either. The beauty of the internal nature cannot be so far concealed by its accidental vesture, but that the spirit of its form shall communicate itself to the very disguise, and indicate the shape it hides from the manner in which it is worn. A majestic form and graceful motions will express themselves through the most barbarous and tasteless costume. Few poets of the highest class have chosen to exhibit the beauty of their conceptions in its naked truth and splendour; and it is doubtful whether the alloy of costume, habit, &c., be not necessary to temper this planetary music for mortal ears.

Plato would have been very unhappy with this, and unhappier still when Shelley turned to the disciple of Socrates, just before the praise of Homer:

An observation of the regular mode of the recurrence of harmony in the language of poetical minds, together with its relation to music, produced metre, or a certain system of traditional

forms of harmony and language. Yet it is by no means essential that a poet should accommodate his language to this traditional form, so that the harmony, which is its spirit, be observed. The practice is indeed convenient and popular, and to be preferred, especially in such composition as includes much action: but every great poet must inevitably innovate upon the example of his pre-decessors in the exact structure of his peculiar versification. The distinction between poets and prose writers is a vulgar error. The distinction between philosophers and poets has been anticipated. Plato was essentially a poet—the truth and splendour of his imagery, and the melody of his language, are the most intense that it is possible to conceive. He rejected the measure of the epic, dramatic, and lyrical forms, because he sought to kindle a harmony in thoughts divested of shape and action, and he forbore to invent any regular plan of rhythm which would include, under determinate forms, the various pauses of his style.

This is sly and fierce of Shelley; Plato is exalted for imagery and melody, for mastery of cadence, but not for wisdom, while Homer gives us truth as well as beauty. Achilles, Hector, and Odysseus prompt heroic emulation, and again we recall the military heroism of Xenophon's Socrates. Despite continued personal fondness for the late Eric Havelock, I grow ever more skeptical of his famous *Preface to Plato* of 1963. That Homer was memorized and so became the major source of later Greek popular thinking is indisputable, but the author of the *Iliad* was rather more than an encyclopedist. Plato's Socrates says he knows nothing except eros,

but Homer asserts total knowledge and proves his apparent extrav-
agances. He does teach how to live, and what to do, *if you happen
not to be a philosopher.*

After half a century of teaching poetry, I have come to believe
that I must urge my better students to possess great poems by
memory. Choose a poem that *finds* you, as Coleridge says, and
read it deeply and often, out loud to yourself and to others. Inter-
nalizing the poems of Shakespeare, Milton, Whitman will teach
you to think more comprehensively than Plato can. We cannot all
become philosophers, but we can follow the poets in their ancient
quarrel with philosophy, which may be a way of life but whose
study is death. I do not think that poetry offers a way of life (except
for a handful like Shelley and Hart Crane); it is too large, too
Homeric for that. At the gates of death, I have recited poems to
myself, but not searched for an interlocutor to engage in dialectic.

Homer's is poetic argument, and not the mode of Plato's
Socrates, who seeks perfection of the work, the life, the state. And
Homer's lies are beyond time and so against time, unlike the "noble"
lies Plato assigns to his Socrates. Perhaps Plato (or his Socrates) was
the first and last philosopher, even as Jesus was the first and last Christian. We do not have to choose between Plato and Homer, though
Plato wants us to choose. If finally we must choose, read Homer.

9

The *"Homeric problem,"* which exercised the scholars of the generation before my own, has little relevance for the common reader of

the early twenty-first century. I begin to believe that whether Homer was one poet, or two, or a whole phalanx of singers of tales, is pragmatically no more useful than our deranged obsessions which insist that Shakespeare was written by anyone except Shakespeare: the Earl of Oxford, Francis Bacon, Christopher Marlowe, Queen Elizabeth, Lucy Negro (London's leading East Indian sex worker), or the impostor named William Shakespeare who impersonated William Shakespeare. I delight in the London society that, each month, unsolicitedly sends me its circulars demonstrating that all of Lewis Carroll was composed by Queen Victoria. Recently, I mourned when reading the obituary of the founder of the American Flat Earth Society.

We have the Iliad and the *Odyssey,* and those who cannot read ancient Greek can be served admirably by a garland of translators, including Richmond Lattimore, Robert Fitzgerald, and Robert Fagles. Further back are George Chapman, Alexander Pope (rather overpraised by Samuel Johnson himself), and even Lawrence of Arabia. Though much is lost in translation, much abides. Ironically, Plato is more hurt by translation than Homer is, because his pervasive ironies and private jokes all too often vanish.

Any major poem is a wisdom writing, since even a great unwisdom is wisdom. Plato's Socrates, in the *Republic,* rather weakly chooses to censure Homer for demeaning the gods, who after all are already below the threshold of debasement. The Olympians at best are an audience looking at human beings as so many victims playing roles upon a great stage of fools. W. K. C. Guthrie, in his

The Greeks and Their Gods (1950), emphasizes the authority of Homer for the Greeks, so that "a great deal in later Greek religion is only a development of Homeric ideas." One of Guthrie's sentences haunts me, since it makes clear the strong differences between Homeric and Hebraic religion, and also between Homer and Plato: "What made the gods approach our level was an element of human nature in them, not a hint of the divine in us" (page 120).

What divides gods and men in Homer, Guthrie says, are questions of rank, prestige, power, but never of mere morality. What we call "personal religion" did not exist for most ancient Greeks. But when the Macedonian kings Philip and Alexander the Great, his son, ended the city-states, they essentially concluded Homeric religion also. Plato, in Guthrie's view, desired to revive the city-state, but in conjunction with a purification of the Homeric gods. Only philosophers, possessing something like divine wisdom, were to rule the Platonic Republic. To attain a kind of divine wisdom, you had to cultivate theology, of which Homer was largely innocent. Sometimes, reading the *Iliad,* you can get the impression that the gods are a storytelling convenience. And yet the poem rarely lets you forget that men must die, while gods live on forever, perfectly cheerful as they contemplate our sufferings.

Homer's Zeus, the god in Plato, and Yahweh have almost nothing in common. Zeus is the god of the wind and the weather. He lives in the sky, where he gathers clouds and rains down thunderbolts. Though Zeus had a father, Kronos, the auditors of Homer knew only Zeus as father and tyrant. Plato, or at least his Socrates, was compelled to regard Homer's Zeus as a travesty, an immorality masking as a deity.

10

Are our wars *Hebrew* or *Greek*, prophetic or Platonic? Here, curiously, the irony is Hebraic. Contrast the earliest of biblical battle odes, the war song of Deborah and Barak, with a parallel moment in book 9 of the *Iliad*.

> *Hektor in his ecstasy of power*
> *is mad for battle, confident in Zeus,*
> *deferring to neither men nor gods. Pure frenzy*
> *fills him, and he prays for the bright dawn*
> *when he will shear our stern-post beaks away*
> *and fire all our ships, while in the shipways*
> *amid that holocaust he carries death*
> *among our men, driven out by smoke. All this*
> *I gravely fear; I fear the gods will make*
> *good his threatenings, and our fate will be*
> *to die here, far from the pastureland of Argos.*
> *Rouse yourself, if even at this hour*
> *you'll pitch in for the Akhaians and deliver them*
> *from Trojan havoc. In the years to come*
> *this day will be remembered pain for you*
> *if you do not.*
>
> [*Translated by* ROBERT FITZGERALD]

For the divisions of Reuben there were great thoughts of heart.
  Why abodest thou among the sheepfolds, to hear the bleatings

of the flocks? For the divisions of Reuben there were great
searchings of heart.

   Gilead abode beyond Jordan: and why did Dan remain in ships?
Asher continued on the sea shore, and abode in his breaches.

   Zebulon and Naphtali were a people that jeoparded their lives
unto the death in the high places of the field.

[JUDGES 5:15–18]

The prophetess Deborah ironically chastises the tribes of Reuben, Dan, and Asher, and then gloriously celebrates the heroism of the tribes Zebulon and Naphtali.

Simone Weil, who loved both the *Iliad* and the Gospels, rather oddly associated them, as though Jesus had been a Greek and not a Jew:

The Gospels are the last marvelous expression of the Greek genius, as the Iliad is the first. . . . With the Hebrews, misfortune was a sure indication of sin and hence a legitimate object of contempt; to them a vanquished enemy was abhorrent to God himself and condemned to expiate all sorts of crimes—this is a view that makes cruelty permissible and indeed indispensable. And no text of the Old Testament strikes a note comparable to the note heard in the Greek epic, unless it be certain parts of the book of Job. Throughout twenty centuries of Christianity, the Romans and the Hebrews have been admired, read, imitated, both in deed and word; their masterpieces have yielded an appropriate quotation every time anybody had a crime he wanted to justify.

Though vicious in regard to the Hebrew Bible, this is also merely banal, being another in that weary procession of instances of Jewish self-hatred, and even of Christian anti-Semitism. What is interesting in it, however, is Weil's strong misreading of the *Iliad* as "the poem of force," as when she says, "Its bitterness is the only justifiable bitterness, for it springs from the subjections of the human spirit to force, that is, in the last analysis, to matter." Of what "human spirit" did Weil speak? That sense of the spirit is of course Hebraic, and not at all Greek, and is totally alien to the text of the *Iliad*. Cast in Homer's terms, her sentence should have ascribed justifiable bitterness, the bitterness of Achilles and Hector, to "the subjections of the human force to the gods' force and to fate's force." For that is how Homer sees men; they are not spirits imprisoned in matter but forces or drives that live, perceive, and feel. I adopt here Bruno Snell's famous account of "Homer's view of man," in which Achilles, Hector, and all the other heroes, even Odysseus, "consider themselves a battleground of arbitrary forces and uncanny powers." Abraham, Jacob, Joseph, and Moses clearly do not view themselves as a site where arbitrary forces clash in battle, and neither of course does David nor his possible descendant, Jesus. The *Iliad* is as certainly the poem of force as Genesis, Exodus, Numbers is the poem of the will of Yahweh, who has his arbitrary and uncanny aspects but whose force is justice and whose power is also canny.

The poet of the Iliad seems to me to have only one ancient rival, the prime and original author of much of Genesis, Exodus, Numbers,

known as the Yahwist or J writer to scholars. Homer and J have absolutely nothing in common except their uncanny sublimity, and they are sublime in very different modes. In a profound sense, *they* are agonists, though neither ever heard of the other, or listened to the other's texts. They compete for the consciousness of Western nations, and their belated strife may be the largest single factor that makes for a divided sensibility in the literature and life of the West. For what marks the West is its troubled sense that its cognition goes one way and its spiritual life goes in quite another. We have no ways of thinking that are not Greek, and yet our morality and religion—outer and inner—find their ultimate source in the Hebrew Bible.

The burden of the word of the Lord, as delivered by Zechariah (9:12–13), has been prophetic of the cultural civil war that, for us, can never end:

> *Turn you to the stronghold, ye prisoners of hope: even today do*
> *I declare that I will render double unto thee;*
> *   When I have bent Judah for me, filled the bow of Ephraim,*
> *and raised up thy sons, O Zion, against thy sons, O Greece, and*
> *made thee as the sword of a mighty man.*

Like the Hebrew Bible, Homer is both scripture and book of general knowledge, and these are necessarily still the prime educational texts, with only Shakespeare making a third, a third who evidences most deeply the split between Greek cognition and Hebraic spirituality. To read the *Iliad* in particular without distorting it is

now perhaps impossible, and for reasons that transcend the differences between Homer's language and implicit socioeconomic structure, and our own. The true difference, whether we are Gentile or Jew, believer or skeptic, Hegelian or Freudian, is between Yahweh, and the tangled company of Zeus and the Olympians, fate and the daemonic world. Christian, Moslem, Jew, or their mixed descendants, we are children of Abraham and not of Achilles. Homer is perhaps most powerful when he represents the strife of men and gods. The Yahwist or J is as powerful when she shows us Jacob wrestling a nameless one among the Elohim to a standstill, but the instance is unique, and Jacob struggles not to overcome the nameless one but to delay him. And Jacob is no Heracles; he wrestles out of character, as it were, so as to give us a giant metaphor for Israel's persistence in its endless quest for a time without boundaries.

The *Iliad*, except for the Yahwist, Dante, and Shakespeare, is the most extraordinary writing yet to come out of the West, but how much of it is spiritually acceptable to us, or would be, if we pondered it closely? Achilles and Hector are hardly the same figure, since we cannot visualize Achilles living a day-to-day life in a city, but they are equally glorifiers of battle. Defensive warfare is no more an ideal (for many of us) than is aggression, but in the *Iliad* both are very near to the highest good, which is victory. What other ultimate value is imaginable in a world where the ordinary reality is battle? It is true that the narrator, and his personages, are haunted by similes of peace, but as James M. Redfield observes, the rhetorical purpose of these similes "is not to describe the

world of peace but to make vivid the world of war." Indeed, in the *Iliad*, the world of peace is essentially a war between humans and nature, in which farmers rip out the grain and fruit as so many spoils of battle. This helps explain why the *Iliad* need not bother to praise war, since reality is a constant contest anyway, in which nothing of value can be attained without despoiling or ruining someone or something else.

To compete for the foremost place was the Homeric ideal, which is not exactly the biblical ideal of honoring your father and your mother. I find it difficult to read the *Iliad* as "the tragedy of Hector," as Redfield and others do. Hector is stripped of tragic dignity, indeed very nearly of all dignity, before he dies. The epic is the tragedy of Achilles, ironically enough, because he retains the foremost place, yet cannot overcome the bitterness of his sense of his own mortality. To be only half a god appears to be Homer's implicit definition of what makes a hero tragic. But this is not tragedy in the biblical sense, where the dilemma of Abraham arguing with Yahweh on the road to Sodom, or of Jacob wrestling with the angel of death, is the need to act as if one were everything in oneself while knowing also that, compared with Yahweh, one is nothing in oneself. Achilles cannot act as if he were everything in himself, nor can he believe that, compared even with Zeus, he is nothing in himself. Abraham and Jacob, therefore, and not Achilles, are the cultural ancestors of Hamlet and the other Shakespearean heroes.

What after all is it to be the "best of the Achaeans," Achilles, as contrasted to the comparable figure, David (who in Yahweh's eyes is clearly the best among the children of Abraham)? It is certainly

not to be the most complete man among them. That, as James Joyce rightly concluded, is certainly Odysseus. The best of the Achaeans is the one who can kill Hector, which is to say that Achilles, in an American heroic context, would have been the fastest gun in the West. Perhaps David would have been that also, and certainly David mourns Jonathan as Achilles mourns Patroklos, which reminds us that David and Achilles both are poets. But Achilles, sulking in his tent, is palpably a child, with a wavering vision of himself—inevitable, since his vitality, his perception, and his affective life are all divided from one another, as Bruno Snell demonstrated. David, even as a child, is a mature and autonomous ego, with his sense of life, his vision of other selves, and his emotional nature all integrated into a new kind of man, the hero whom Yahweh had decided not only to love but also to make immortal *through his descendants,* who would never lose Yahweh's favor. Jesus, *contra* Simone Weil, can only be the descendant of David, and not of Achilles. Or to put it most simply, Achilles is the son of a goddess, but David is a Son of God.

The single "modern" author who compels comparison with the poet of the *Iliad* and the writer of the J text is Tolstoy, whether in *War and Peace* or in the short novel that is the masterpiece of his old age, *Hadji Murad*. Rachel Bespaloff, in her essay on the *Iliad* (rightly commended by the superb Homeric translator Robert Fitzgerald as conveying how distant, how refined, the art of Homer was), seems to have fallen into the error of believing that the Bible and Homer, since both resemble Tolstoy, must also resemble each

other. Homer and Tolstoy share the extraordinary balance between the individual in action and groups in action that alone permits the epic accurately to represent battle. The Yahwist and Tolstoy share an uncanny mode of irony that turns on the incongruities of incommensurable entities, Yahweh or universal history, and man, meeting in violent confrontation or juxtaposition. But the Yahwist has little interest in groups; she turns away in some disdain when the blessing, on Sinai, is transferred from an elite to the mass of the people. And the clash of gods and men, or of fate and the hero, remains in Homer a conflict between forces not wholly incommensurable, though the hero must die, whether in or beyond the poem.

The crucial difference between the Yahwist and Homer, aside from their representations of the self, necessarily is the indescribable difference between Yahweh and Zeus. Both are personalities, but such an assertion becomes an absurdity directly they are juxtaposed. Erich Auerbach, comparing the poet of the *Odyssey* and the Elohist, the Yahwist's revisionist, traced the mimetic difference between the *Odyssey*'s emphasis on "foregrounding" and the Bible's reliance on the authority of an implied "backgrounding." There is something to that distinction, but it tends to fade out when we move from the *Odyssey* to the *Iliad* and from the Elohist to the Yahwist. The *Iliad* may not demand interpretation as much as the Yahwist does, but it hardly can be apprehended without any reader's considerable labor of aesthetic contextualization. Its man, unlike the Yahwist's, has little in common with the "psychological man" of Freud.

Joseph, who may have been the model for the Yahwist's por-

trait of King David, provides a fascinating post-Oedipal contrast to his father, Jacob, but Achilles seems never to have approached any relation whatever to his father, Peleus, who is simply a type of ignoble old age wasting toward the wrong kind of death. Surely the most striking contrast between the *Iliad* and the J text of the Bible is that between the mourning of Priam and the grief of Jacob when he believes Joseph to be dead. Old men in Homer are good mostly for grieving, but in the Yahwist they represent the wisdom and the virtue of the fathers. Yahweh is the God of Abraham, the God of Isaac, the God of Jacob, even as He will be the God of Moses, the God of David, the God of Jesus. But Zeus is nobody's god, as it were, and Achilles might as well not have had a father at all.

Priam's dignity is partly redeemed when his mourning for Hector is joined to that of Achilles for Patroklos, but the aged Jacob is dignity itself, as his grandfather Abraham was before him. Nietzsche's characterization is just. A people whose ideal is the agon for the foremost place must fall behind in honoring their parents, while a people who exalt fatherhood and motherhood will transfer the agon to the temporal realm, to struggle there not for being the best at one time, but rather for inheriting the blessing, which promises more life into a time without boundaries.

Yahweh is the source of the blessing, and Yahweh, though frequently enigmatic in J, is never an indifferent onlooker. No Hebrew writer could conceive of a Yahweh who is essentially an audience, whether indifferent or engrossed. Homer's gods are human—all too human—particularly in their abominable capacity to observe suffering almost as a kind of sport. The Yahweh of Amos and the

prophets after him could not be further from Homer's Olympian Zeus.

It can be argued that the spectatorship of the gods gives Homer an immense aesthetic advantage over the writers of the Hebrew Bible. The sense of a divine audience constantly in attendance both provides a fascinating interplay with Homer's human auditors and guarantees that Achilles and Hector will perform in front of a sublimity greater even than their own. To have the gods as one's audience enhances and honors the heroes who are Homer's prime actors. Yahweh frequently hides Himself, and will not be there when you cry out for Him, or He may call out your name unexpectedly, to which you can only respond, "Here I am." Zeus is capricious and is finally limited by fate. Yahweh surprises you, and has no limitation. He will not lend you dignity by serving as your audience, and yet He is anything but indifferent to you. He fashioned you out of the moistened red clay, and then blew his own breath into your nostrils, so as to make you a living being. You grieve Him or you please Him, but fundamentally He is your longing for the father, as Freud insisted. Zeus is not your longing for anyone, and he will not save you even if you are Heracles, his own son.

In Homer, you fight to be the best, to take away the women of the enemy, and to survive as long as possible, short of aging into ignoble decrepitude. That is not why you fight in the Hebrew Bible. There you fight the wars of Yahweh, which so appalled that harsh saint, Simone Weil. I want to close this chapter by comparing two

great battle odes, the war song of Deborah and Barak, in Judges 5, and the astonishing passage in book 18 of the *Iliad* when Achilles reenters the scene of battle, in order to recover his arms, his armor, and the body of Patroklos.

> *At this,*
> *Iris left him, running downwind. Akhilleus,*
> *whom Zeus loved, now rose. Around his shoulders*
> *Athena hung her shield, like a thunderhead*
> *with trailing fringe. Goddess of goddesses,*
> *she bound his head with golden cloud, and made*
> *his very body blaze with fiery light.*
> *Imagine how the pyre of a burning town*
> *will tower to heaven and be seen for miles*
> *from the island under attack, while all day long*
> *outside their town, in brutal combat, pikemen*
> *suffer the wargod's winnowing; at sundown*
> *flare on flare is lit, the signal fires*
> *shoot up for other islanders to see,*
> *that some relieving force in ships may come:*
> *just so the baleful radiance from Akhilleus*
> *lit the sky. Moving from parapet*
> *to moat, without a nod for the Akhaians,*
> *keeping clear, in deference to his mother,*
> *he halted and gave tongue. Not far from him*
> *Athena shrieked. The great sound shocked the Trojans*
> *into tumult, as a trumpet blown*

by a savage foe shocks an encircled town,
so harsh and clarion was Akhilleus' cry.
The hearts of men quailed, hearing that brazen voice.
Teams, foreknowing danger, turned their cars
and charioteers blanched, seeing unearthly fire,
kindled by the grey-eyed goddess Athena,
brilliant over Akhilleus. Three great cries
he gave above the moat. Three times they shuddered,
whirling backward, Trojans and allies,
and twelve good men took mortal hurt
from cars and weapons in the rank behind.
Now the Akhaians leapt at the chance
to bear Patroklos' body out of range.
They placed it on his bed,
and old companions there with brimming eyes
surrounded him. Into their midst Akhilleus
came then, and he wept hot tears to see
his faithful friend, torn by the sharp spearhead,
lying cold upon his cot. Alas,
the man he sent to war with team and chariot
he could not welcome back alive.

[*Translated by* ROBERT FITZGERALD]

Exalted and burning with Athena's divine fire, the unarmed Achilles is more terrible even than the armed hero would be. It is his angry shouts that panic the Trojans, yet the answering shout of the goddess adds to their panic, since they realize that they face

preternatural powers. When Yahweh roars, in the prophets Isaiah and Joel, the effect is very different, though He too cries out "like a man of war." The difference is in Homer's magnificent antiphony between man and goddess, Achilles and Athena. Isaiah would not have had the king and Yahweh exchanging battle shouts in mutual support, because of the shocking incommensurateness that does not apply to Achilles and Athena.

I began this section by juxtaposing two epigraphs, Odysseus shrewdly warning Achilles that "this day," on which Hector may burn the Achaean ships, "will be remembered pain for you," if Achilles does not return to the battle, and a superb passage from Deborah's war song in Judges 5. Hector's "ecstasy of power" would produce "remembered pain" for Achilles, as power must come at the expense of someone else's pain, and ecstasy results from the victory of inflicting memorable suffering. Memory depends upon pain, which was Nietzsche's fiercely Homeric analysis of all significant memory. But that is not the memory exalted in the Hebrew Bible. Deborah, with a bitter irony, laughs triumphantly at the tribes of Israel that did not assemble for the battle against Sisera, and most of all at Reuben, with its scruples, doubts, hesitations: "great searchings of heart." She scorns those who kept to business as usual, Dan, who remained in ships, and Asher, who continued on the seashore. Then suddenly, with piercing intensity and moral force, she utters a great paean of praise and triumph, for the tribes that risked everything on behalf of their covenant with Yahweh, for those who transcended "great thoughts" and "great searchings of heart":

Zebulon and Naphtali were a people that jeoparded their lives unto the death in the high places of the field.

The high places are both descriptive and honorific; they are where the terms of the covenant were kept. Zebulon and Naphtali fight not to be the foremost among the tribes of Israel, and not to possess Sisera's women, but to fulfill the terms of the covenant, to demonstrate *emunah,* which is trust in Yahweh. Everyone in Homer knows better than to trust in Zeus. The aesthetic supremacy of the *Iliad* again must be granted. Homer is the best of the poets, and always will keep the foremost place. What he lacks, even aesthetically, is a quality of trust in the transcendent memory of a covenant fulfilled, a lack of the sublime hope that moves the Hebrew poet Deborah:

They fought from heaven; the stars in their courses fought against Sisera.
The river of Kishon swept them away, that ancient river, the river Kishon. O my soul, thou hast trodden down strength.

CHAPTER 3

CERVANTES AND

SHAKESPEARE

MIGUEL DE CERVANTES

Cervantes and Shakespeare share the supremacy among all Western writers from the Renaissance to this moment. Fictive selves of the last four centuries are Cervantean or Shakespearean, or more frequently blend the two. In this book, I wish to consider them as the masters of wisdom in our modern literature, equals of Ecclesiastes and the Book of Job, of Homer and Plato. The fundamental difference between Cervantes and Shakespeare is exemplified by the comparison between Don Quixote and Hamlet.

The knight and the prince alike are questers whose goals are uncertain, whatever they say to the contrary. What is the true object of Don Quixote's quest? I find that unanswerable. What are Hamlet's authentic motives? We are not permitted to know. Since Cervantes's magnificent Knight's quest has cosmological scope

and reverberation, no object seems beyond reach. Hamlet's frustration is that he is allowed only Elsinore and revenge tragedy. Shakespeare composed a poem unlimited, in which only the protagonist is beyond all limits.

Cervantes and Shakespeare, who died almost simultaneously, are the central Western authors, at least since Dante, and no writer since has matched them, not Tolstoy nor Goethe, Dickens, Proust, Joyce. Context cannot hold Cervantes and Shakespeare: the Spanish Golden Age and the Elizabethan-Jacobean era are secondary when we attempt a full appreciation of what we are given.

W. H. Auden found in Don Quixote a portrait of the Christian saint, as opposed to Hamlet, who "lacks faith in God and in himself." Though Auden *sounds* perversely ironic, he was quite serious, and I think wrongheaded. Against Auden I set Miguel de Unamuno, my favorite critic of *Don Quixote*. For Unamuno, Alonso Quixano is the Christian saint, while Don Quixote is the originator of the actual Spanish religion, Quixotism.

Herman Melville blended Don Quixote and Hamlet in Captain Ahab (with a touch of Milton's Satan added for seasoning). Ahab desires to avenge himself upon the White Whale, while Satan would destroy God, if only he could. Hamlet is death's ambassador to us, according to G. Wilson Knight. Don Quixote says that his quest is to destroy injustice. The final injustice is death, the ultimate bondage. To set captives free is the Knight's pragmatic way of battling against death.

2

You cannot locate Shakespeare in his own works, not even in the Sonnets. It is this near-invisibility that encourages the zealots who believe that almost anyone wrote Shakespeare except Shakespeare himself. So far as I know, the Hispanic world does not harbor covens who labor to prove that Lope de Vega or Calderón de la Barca composed *Don Quixote.* Cervantes inhabits his great book so pervasively that we need to see that it has three unique personalities: the Knight, Sancho, and Cervantes himself.

And yet how sly and subtle is the presence of Cervantes! At its most hilarious, *Don Quixote* is immensely somber. Shakespeare again is the illuminating analogue: Hamlet at his most melancholic will not cease his punning or his gallows humor, and Falstaff's boundless wit is tormented by intimations of rejection. Just as Shakespeare wrote in no genre, *Don Quixote* is tragedy as well as comedy. Though it stands forever as the birth of the novel out of the prose romance, and is still the best of all novels, I find its sadness augments each time I reread it, and does make it "the Spanish Bible," as Unamuno termed this greatest of all narratives. Novels are written by George Eliot and Henry James, by Balzac and Flaubert, or by the Tolstoy of *Anna Karenina.* Although *Don Quixote* may not be a scripture, it so contains us that, as with Shakespeare, we cannot get out of it, in order to achieve perspectivism. We are inside the vast book, privileged to hear the superb conversations between the Knight and his squire, Sancho Panza. Sometimes we are fused

with Cervantes, but more often we are invisible wanderers who accompany the sublime pair in their adventures and debacles.

If there is a third Western author with universal appeal from the Renaissance on, it could only be Dickens. Yet Dickens purposely does not give us "man's final lore," which Melville found in Shakespeare, and presumably in Cervantes also. *King Lear*'s first performance took place as Part I of *Don Quixote* was published. *Contra* Auden, Cervantes, like Shakespeare, gives us a secular transcendence. Don Quixote does regard himself as God's knight, but he continuously follows his own capricious will, which is gloriously idiosyncratic. King Lear appeals to the skyey heavens for aid, but on the personal grounds that they and he are old. Battered by realities that are even more violent than he is, Don Quixote resists yielding to the authority of church and state. When he ceases to assert his autonomy, there is nothing left except to be Alonso Quixano the Good again, and no action remaining except to die.

I return to my initial question: the sorrowful Knight's object. He is at war with Freud's reality principle, which accepts the necessity of dying. But he is neither a fool nor a madman, and his vision always is at least double: he sees what we see, yet he sees something else also, a possible glory that he desires to appropriate, or at least share. Unamuno names this transcendence as literary fame, the immortality of Cervantes and Shakespeare. Certainly that is part of the Knight's quest; much of Part II turns upon his and Sancho's delightful apprehension that their adventures in Part I are recognized everywhere. Perhaps Unamuno underestimated the complexities involved in so grand a disruption in the aesthetics of

representation. *Hamlet* again is the best analogue: from the entrance of the players in Act II through the close of the performance of *The Mousetrap* in Act III, all the rules of normative representation are tossed away, and everything is theatricality. Part II of *Don Quixote* is similarly and bewilderingly advanced, since the Knight, Sancho, and everyone they encounter are acutely conscious that fiction has disrupted the order of reality.

3

We need to hold in mind as we read *Don Quixote* that we cannot condescend to the Knight and Sancho, since together they know more than we do, just as we never can catch up to the amazing speed of Hamlet's cognitions. Do we know exactly who we are? The more urgently we quest for our authentic selves, the more they tend to recede. The Knight and Sancho, as the great work closes, know exactly who they are, not so much by their adventures as through their marvelous conversations, be they quarrels or exchanges of insights.

Poetry, particularly Shakespeare's, teaches us how to talk to ourselves, but not to others. Shakespeare's great figures are gorgeous solipsists: Shylock, Falstaff, Hamlet, Iago, Lear, Cleopatra, with Rosalind the brilliant exception. Don Quixote and Sancho really listen to each other, and change through this receptivity. Neither of them *overhears* himself, which is the Shakespearean mode. Cervantes or Shakespeare: they are rival teachers of how we change, and why. Friendship in Shakespeare is ironic at best, treacherous

more commonly. The friendship between Sancho Panza and his Knight surpasses any other in literary representation.

We do not have *Cardenio,* the play Shakespeare wrote, with John Fletcher, after reading Thomas Shelton's contemporaneous translation of *Don Quixote.* Therefore we cannot know what Shakespeare thought of Cervantes, though we can surmise his delight. Cervantes, an unsuccessful dramatist, presumably never heard of Shakespeare, but I doubt that he would have valued Falstaff and Hamlet, both of whom choose the self's freedom over obligations of any kind. Sancho, as Kafka remarked, is a free man, but Don Quixote is metaphysically and psychologically bound by his dedication to knight-errantry. We can celebrate the Knight's endless valor, but not his literalization of the romance of chivalry.

4

But does Don Quixote altogether believe in the reality of his own vision? Evidently, he does not, particularly when he (and Sancho) are surrendered by Cervantes to the sadomasochistic practical jokes, indeed the vicious and humiliating cruelties, that afflict the Knight and squire in Part II. Nabokov is very illuminating on this in his *Lectures on Don Quixote,* published posthumously in 1983:

> *Both parts of* Don Quixote *form a veritable encyclopedia of cruelty. From that viewpoint it is one of the most bitter and barbarous books ever penned. And its cruelty is artistic.*

To find a Shakespearean equivalent to this aspect of *Don Quixote,* you would have to fuse *Titus Andronicus* and *The Merry Wives of Windsor* into one work, a grim prospect, because they are, to me, Shakespeare's weakest plays. Falstaff's dreadful humiliation by the merry wives is unacceptable enough (even if it formed the basis for Verdi's sublime *Falstaff*). Why does Cervantes subject Don Quixote to the physical abuse of Part I, and the psychic tortures of Part II? Nabokov's answer is aesthetic: the cruelty is vitalized by Cervantes's characteristic artistry. That seems to me something of an evasion. *Twelfth Night* is comedy unsurpassable, and on the stage we are consumed by hilarity at Malvolio's terrible humiliations. When we reread the play, we become uneasy, because Malvolio's socioerotic fantasies echo in virtually all of us. Why are we not made at least a little dubious by the torments, bodily and social, suffered by Don Quixote and Sancho Panza?

Cervantes himself, as a constant if disguised presence in the text, is the answer. He was the most battered of eminent writers. At the great naval battle of Lepanto, he was wounded, and so at twenty-four permanently lost the use of his left hand. In 1575, he was captured by Barbary pirates, and spent five years as a slave in Algiers. Ransomed in 1580, he served Spain as a spy in Portugal and Oran, and then returned to Madrid, where he attempted a career as a dramatist, almost invariably failing after writing at least twenty plays. Somewhat desperately, he became a tax collector, only to be indicted and imprisoned for supposed malfeasance in 1597. A fresh imprisonment came in 1605; there is a tradition that he began to compose *Don Quixote* in jail. Part I, written at

incredible speed, was published in 1605. Part II, spurred by a false continuation of *Don Quixote* by one Avellaneda, was published in 1615.

Fleeced of all royalties from Part I by the publisher, Cervantes would have died in poverty except for the belated patronage of a discerning nobleman in the last three years of his life. Though Shakespeare died at just fifty-two (why, we do not know), he was an immensely successful dramatist, and became quite prosperous by shareholding in the actors' company that played at the Globe Theatre. Circumspect, and only too aware of the government-inspired murder of Christopher Marlowe, and the torture of Thomas Kyd, and the branding of Ben Jonson, Shakespeare kept himself nearly anonymous, in spite of being the reigning dramatist of London. Violence, slavery, imprisonment were the staples of Cervantes's life. Shakespeare, wary to the end, had an existence almost without a memorable incident, so far as we can tell.

The physical and mental torments suffered by Don Quixote and Sancho Panza had been central to Cervantes's endless struggle to stay alive and free. And yet Nabokov's observations are accurate: cruelty is extreme throughout *Don Quixote*. The aesthetic wonder is that this enormity fades when we stand back from the huge book and ponder its shape and endless range of meaning. No critic's account of Cervantes's masterpiece agrees with, or even resembles, any other critic's impressions. *Don Quixote* is a mirror held up not to nature but to the reader. How can this bashed and mocked knight-errant be, as he is, a universal paradigm?

5
—

Hamlet does not need or want our admiration and affection, but Don Quixote does, and receives it, as Hamlet generally does also. Sancho, like Falstaff, is replete with self-delight, though Sancho does not rouse moralizing critics to wrath and disapproval, as the sublime Falstaff does. Much more has been written about the Hamlet/Don Quixote contrast than about Sancho/Falstaff, two vitalists in aesthetic contention as masters of reality. But no critic has called Don Quixote a murderer or Sancho an immoralist. Hamlet is responsible for eight deaths, his own included, and Falstaff is a highwayman, a warrior averse to battle, and a fleecer of everyone he encounters. Yet Hamlet and Falstaff are victimizers, not victims, even if Hamlet dies properly fearing a wounded name, and Falstaff is destroyed by Hal/Henry V's rejection. It does not matter. The fascination of Hamlet's intellect and of Falstaff's wit is what endures. Don Quixote and Sancho are victims, but both are extraordinarily resilient, until the Knight's final defeat and dying into the identity of Quixano the Good, whom Sancho vainly implores to take to the road again. The fascination of Don Quixote's endurance and of Sancho's loyal wisdom always remains.

Cervantes plays upon the human need to withstand suffering, which is one reason that the Knight awes us. However good a Catholic he may (or may not) have been, Cervantes is interested in heroism, and not in sainthood. Shakespeare, I think, was not interested in either, since none of his heroes can endure close scrutiny: Hamlet, Othello, Antony, Coriolanus. Only Edgar, the recalcitrant

survivor who inherits the nation, most unwillingly, in *King Lear*, abides our skepticism, and at least one prominent Shakespeare critic weirdly has called Edgar "weak and murderous." The heroism of Don Quixote is by no means constant: he is perfectly capable of flight, abandoning poor Sancho to be beaten up by an entire village. Cervantes, a hero at Lepanto, wants Don Quixote to be a new kind of hero, neither ironic nor mindless, but one who wills to be himself, as José Ortega y Gasset accurately phrased it.

Hamlet subverts the will, while Falstaff satirizes it. Don Quixote and Sancho Panza both exalt the will, though the Knight transcendentalizes it, and Sancho, the first postpragmatic, wants to keep it within limits. It is the transcendent element in Don Quixote that ultimately persuades us of his greatness, partly because it is set against the deliberately coarse, frequently sordid context of the panoramic book. And again it is important to note that this transcendence is secular and literary, and not Catholic. The Quixotic quest is erotic, yet even the eros is literary. Crazed by reading (as so many of us still are), the Knight is in quest of a new self, one that can overgo the erotic madness of Orlando (Roland) in Ariosto's *Orlando Furioso* or of the mythic Amadis of Gaul. Unlike Orlando's or Amadis's, Don Quixote's madness is deliberate, self-inflicted, a traditional poetic strategy. Still, there is a clear sublimation of the sexual drive in the Knight's desperate courage. Lucidity keeps breaking in, reminding him that Dulcinea is his own Supreme Fiction, transcending an honest lust for the peasant girl Aldonza Lorenzo. A fiction, believed in even though you know it is a fiction, can only be validated by sheer will.

Erich Auerbach argued for the book's "continuous gaiety," which

is not at all my own experience as a reader. But *Don Quixote,* like the best of Shakespeare, will sustain any theory you bring to it, as well or as badly as any other. The woeful Knight is more than an enigma: he seeks an undying name, literary immortality, and finds it, but only through being all but dismantled in Part I, and all but teased into real madness in Part II: Cervantes performs the miracle, nobly Dante-like, of presiding over his creation like a Providence, but also subjecting himself to the subtle changes brought about both in the Knight and Sancho Panza by their wonderful conversations, in which a shared love manifests itself by equality and grumpy disputes. They are brothers, rather than father and son. To describe the precise way that Cervantes regards them, whether with ironic love, or loving irony, is an impossible critical task.

6

Harry Levin shrewdly phrased what he called "Cervantes' formula":

> *This is nothing more nor less than a recognition of the difference between verses and reverses, between words and deeds,* palabras and hechos—*in short, between literary artifice and that real thing which is life itself. But literary artifice is the only means that a writer has at his disposal. How else can he convey his impression of life? Precisely by discrediting those means, by repudiating that air of bookishness in which any book is inevitably wrapped. When Pascal observed that the true eloquence makes fun of eloquence, he succinctly formulated the principle that*

could look to Cervantes as its recent and striking exemplar. It
remained for La Rochefoucauld to restate the other side of the
paradox: some people would never have loved if they had not
heard of love.

It is true that I cannot think of any other work in which the
relations between words and deeds are as ambiguous as in *Don
Quixote*, except (once again) for *Hamlet*. Cervantes's formula is also
Shakespeare's, though in Cervantes we feel the burden of the
experiential, whereas Shakespeare is uncanny, since nearly all of
his experience was theatrical. Still, the ironizing of eloquence characterizes the speeches of both Hamlet and Don Quixote. One
might at first think that Hamlet is more word-conscious than is the
Knight, but Part II of Cervantes's dark book manifests a growth in
the Woeful Face's awareness of his own rhetoricity.

I want to illustrate Don Quixote's development by setting him
against the wonderful trickster Ginés de Pasamonte, whose first
appearance is as a galley-bound prisoner in Part I, Chapter 22, and
who pops up again in Part II, Chapters 25–27, as Master Pedro, the
divinator and puppeteer. Ginés is a sublime scamp and picaroon
confidence man, but also a picaresque romance writer on the
model of *Lazarillo de Tormes* (1533), the anonymous masterpiece of
its mode (see W. S. Merwin's beautiful translation, from 1962).
When Ginés reappears as Master Pedro in Part I, he has become a
satire upon Cervantes's hugely successful rival Lope de Vega, the
"monster of literature," who turned out a hit play nearly every
week, whereas Cervantes had failed hopelessly as a dramatist.

Every reader has her or his favorite episodes in *Don Quixote*;

mine are the two misadventures the Knight inaugurates in regard to Ginés/Master Pedro. In the first, Don Quixote gallantly frees Ginés and his fellow prisoners, only to be beaten nearly to death (with poor Sancho) by the ungrateful convicts. In the second, the Knight is so taken in by Master Pedro's illusionism that he charges at the puppet show, and cuts the puppets to pieces, in what can be regarded as Cervantes's critique of Lope de Vega. Here first is Ginés, in the admirable new translation by Edith Grossman:

> "He's telling the truth," said the superintendent. "He wrote his own history himself, that's all I can say, and he pawned the book in prison for two hundred reales."
>
> "And I intend to redeem it," said Ginés, "even if the amount had been two hundred ducats."
>
> "Is it that good?" said Don Quixote.
>
> "It is so good," responded Ginés, "that it's too bad for Lazarillo de Tormes and all the other books of that genre that have been written or will be written. What I can tell your grace is that it deals with truths, and they are truths so appealing and elegant that no lies can equal them."
>
> "And what is the title of the book?" asked Don Quixote.
>
> "The Life of Ginés de Pasamonte," he replied.
>
> "And is it finished?" asked Don Quixote.
>
> "How can it be finished," he responded, "if my life isn't finished yet? What I've written goes from my birth to the moment when they sentenced me to the galleys this most recent time."
>
> "Then you have been there before?" said Don Quixote.
>
> "To serve God and the king, I've already spent four years on

the galleys, and I know the taste of hardtack and the overseer's whip," responded Ginés. "And I'm not too sorry to go there, because I'll have time to finish my book, for I still have lots of things to say, and on the galleys of Spain there's more than enough peace and quiet, though I don't need much for what I have to write, because I know it by heart."

Ginés, admirable miscreant, is a demonic parody of Cervantes himself, who had served five years in Algerian slavery, and whose total *Don Quixote* became nearly unfinishable. The death of Cervantes came only a year after the publication of the Second Part of the great saga. Doubtless, Cervantes regarded Lope de Vega as his own demonic shadow, which is made clearer in the magnificent assault upon Master Pedro's puppet show. The picaroon Ginés follows the general law of Part Two, which is that everyone of consequence either has read Part One or is aware that he was a character in it. Master Pedro evades identity with Ginés, but at the high cost of witnessing another furious assault by the Knight of the Woeful Face. But this comes just after Master Pedro is strongly identified with Lope de Vega:

The interpreter said nothing in reply, but went on, saying:
"There was no lack of curious eyes, the kind that tend to see everything, to see Melisendra descend from the balcony and mount the horse, and they informed King Marsilio, who immediately gave orders to sound the call to arms: and see how soon this is done, and how the city is flooded with the sound of the bells that ring from all the towers of the mosques."

"No, that is wrong!" said Don Quixote. "Master Pedro is incorrect in the matter of the bells, for the Moors do not use bells but drums and a kind of flute that resembles our flageolet, and there is no doubt that ringing in Sansueña is a great piece of nonsense." This was heard by Master Pedro, who stopped the ringing and said:

"Your grace should not concern yourself with trifles, Señor Don Quixote, or try to carry things so far that you never reach the end of them. Aren't a thousand plays performed almost every day that are full of a thousand errors and pieces of nonsense, and yet are successful productions that are greeted not only with applause, but with admiration? Go on, boy, and let them say what they will, for as long as I fill my purse, there can be more errors than atoms in the sun."

"That is true," replied Don Quixote.

When Don Quixote assaults the puppet show, Cervantes assaults the popular taste that had preferred the theater of Lope de Vega to his own:

And Don Quixote, seeing and hearing so many Moors and so much clamor, thought it would be a good idea to assist those who were fleeing, and rising to his feet, in a loud voice he said:

"I shall not consent, in my lifetime and in my presence, to any such offense against an enamored knight so famous and bold as Don Gaiferos. Halt, you lowborn rabble; do not follow and do not pursue him unless you wish to do battle with me!"

And speaking and taking action, he unsheathed his sword,

leaped next to the stage, and with swift and never before seen fury began to rain down blows on the crowd of Moorish puppets, knocking down some, beheading others, ruining this one, destroying that one, and among many other blows he delivered so powerful a downstroke that if Master Pedro had not stooped, crouched down, and hunched over, he would have cut off his head more easily than if it had been so much marzipan. Master Pedro cried out, saying:

"Your grace must stop, Señor Don Quixote, and realize that the ones you are overthrowing, destroying, and killing are not real Moors but only pasteboard figures. Sinner that I am, you are destroying and ruining everything I own!"

But this did not keep Don Quixote from raining down slashes, two-handed blows, thrusts, and backstrokes. In short, in less time than it takes to tell about it, he knocked the puppet theater to the floor, all its scenery and figures cut and broken to pieces: King Marsilio was badly wounded, and Emperor Charlemagne's head and crown were split in two. The audience of spectators was in a tumult, the monkey ran out the window and onto the roof, the cousin was fearful, the page was frightened, and even Sancho Panza was terrified, because, as he swore when the storm was over, he had never seen his master in so wild a fury. When the general destruction of the puppet theater was complete, Don Quixote calmed down somewhat and said:

"At this moment I should like to have here in front of me all those who do not believe, and do not wish to believe, how much good knights errant do in the world: if I had not been here, just think what would have happened to the worthy Don Gaiferos

and the beauteous Melisendra; most certainly, by this time those dogs would have overtaken them and committed some outrage against them. In brief, long live knight errantry, over and above everything in the world today!"

This gorgeous, mad intervention is also a parable of the triumph of Cervantes over the picaresque, and of the triumph of the novel over the romance. The downward stroke that nearly decapitates Ginés/Master Pedro is a metaphor for the aesthetic power of *Don Quixote*. So subtle is Cervantes that he needs to be read at as many levels as Dante. Perhaps the Quixotic can be accurately defined as the literary mode of an absolute reality, not as impossible dream but rather as a persuasive awakening into mortality.

7
—

The aesthetic truth of Don Quixote is that, again like Dante and Shakespeare, it make us confront greatness directly. If we have difficulty fully understanding Don Quixote's quest, its motives and desired ends, that is because we confront a reflecting mirror that awes us even while we yield to delight. Cervantes is always out ahead of us, and we never quite can catch up. Fielding and Sterne, Goethe and Thomas Mann, Flaubert and Stendhal, Melville and Mark Twain, Dostoevsky: these are among Cervantes's admirers and pupils. *Don Quixote* is the only book that Dr. Johnson desired to be even longer than it already was.

And yet Cervantes, although a universal pleasure, is in some

respects even more difficult than are Dante and Shakespeare upon their heights. Are we to believe everything that Don Quixote says to us? Does *he* believe it? He (or Cervantes) is the inventor of a mode now common enough, in which figures, within a novel, read prior fictions concerning their own earlier adventures, and have to sustain a consequent loss in the sense of reality. This is one of the beautiful enigmas of *Don Quixote:* it is simultaneously a work whose authentic subject is literature, yet also a chronicle of a hard, sordid actuality, the declining Spain of 1605–1615. The Knight is Cervantes's subtle critique of a realm that had given him only harsh measures in return for his own patriotic heroism at Lepanto. Don Quixote cannot be said to have a double consciousness, but rather the multiple consciousness of Cervantes himself, a writer who knows the cost of confirmation. I do not believe that the Knight can be said to tell lies, except in the Nietzschean sense of lying against time, and time's grim "It was." To ask what it is that Don Quixote himself believes is to enter the visionary center of his story.

It is the superb descent of the Knight into Montesinos's Cave (Part II, Chapters 22–24) that constitutes Cervantes's longest reach toward hinting that the Woeful Face is aware of its self-enchantment. And yet we never will know if Hamlet ever touched clinical madness, or if Don Quixote was himself persuaded of the absurd wonders he beheld in the Cave of Enchantment. The Knight too is only mad north-northwest, and when the wind blows from the south he is as canny as Hamlet, Shakespeare, and Cervantes.

By descending to the Cave, Don Quixote parodies the journey to the underworld of Odysseus and Aeneas. Lowered by a rope tied around him, the Knight is hauled up less than an hour later,

apparently in deep slumber. He insists that he has sojourned below for several days, and describes a surrealistic world, for which the wicked enchanter Merlin is responsible. In a crystal palace, the celebrated knight Durandarte lies in a rather vociferous state of death, while his beloved Belerma marches by in tears, with his heart in her hands. We scarcely can apprehend this before it turns into outrageous comedy. The Enchanted Dulcinea, supposedly the glory sought by Don Quixote's quest, manifests as a peasant girl, accompanied by two other girls, her friends. Seeing the Knight, the immortal Dulcinea runs off, yet sends an emissary to her lover, requesting immediate financial aid:

> "But of all the grievous things I saw and noted, the one that caused me most sorrow was that as Montesinos was saying these words to me, one of the companions of the unfortunate Dulcinea approached me from the side, without my seeing her, and with her eyes full of tears, in a low, troubled voice, she said to me:
>
> " 'My lady Dulcinea of Toboso kisses the hands of your grace, and implores your grace to let her know how you are; and, because she is in great need, she also entreats your grace most earnestly to be so kind as to lend her, accepting as security this new cotton underskirt that I have here, half a dozen reales or whatever amount your grace may have, and she gives her word to return them to you very soon.'
>
> "I was astounded and amazed at this message, and turning to Señor Montesinos, I asked:
>
> " 'Is it possible, Señor Montesinos, that distinguished persons who are enchanted suffer from need?' To which he responded:

"'Your grace can believe me, Señor Don Quixote of La Mancha, that what is called need is found everywhere, and extends to all places, and reaches everyone, and does not excuse even those who are enchanted; and since Señora Dulcinea of Toboso has sent someone to ask you for six reales, and the pledge is good, it seems, then you must give them to her, for she undoubtedly is in very great difficulty.'

"'Her security, I shall not take,' I responded, 'nor shall I give her what she asks, because I have no more than four reales.'

"I gave these to her (they were the ones that you, Sancho, gave me the other day so that I could give alms to the poor whom I met along the road)."

This curious blend of the sublime and the bathetic does not come again until Kafka, another pupil of Cervantes, would compose stories like "The Hunter Gracchus" and "A Country Doctor." To Kafka, Don Quixote was Sancho Panza's daemon, or genius, projected by the shrewd Sancho into a book of adventure unto death:

Without making any boast of it, Sancho Panza succeeded in the course of years, by devouring a great number of romances of chivalry and adventure in the evening and night hours, in so diverting from him his demon, whom he later called Don Quixote, that his demon thereupon set out in perfect freedom on the maddest exploits, which, however, for the lack of a preordained object, which should have been Sancho Panza himself, harmed nobody. A free man, Sancho Panza philosophically followed Don

Quixote on his crusades, perhaps out of a sense of responsibility,
and had of them a great and edifying entertainment to the end of
his days.

In Kafka's marvelous interpretation, the authentic object of
the Knight's quest is Sancho Panza himself, who as an auditor
refuses to believe Don Quixote's account of the Cave. And so I circle back to my question: does the Knight believe his own story? It
makes little sense to answer either "yes" or "no," and so the question must be wrong. We cannot know what Don Quixote and
Hamlet believe, since they do not share in our limitations. Don
Quixote knows who he is, even as the Hamlet of Act V comes to
know what can be known.

Cervantes stations his Knight quite close to us, while Hamlet
always is remote, and requires mediation. Ortega y Gasset remarks
of Don Quixote, "Such a life is a perpetual suffering," which holds
also for Hamlet's existence. Though Hamlet tends to accuse himself of cowardice, he is as courageous, metaphysically and in action,
as Don Quixote: they compete as literary instances of moral valor.
Hamlet does not believe the will and its object can be brought
together: "Our thoughts are ours, their ends none of our own."
That is the Player-King enacting *The Mousetrap,* Hamlet's revision
of the (nonexistent) *Murder of Gonzago.* Don Quixote, who refuses
such despair, nevertheless suffers it.

Thomas Mann loved *Don Quixote* for its ironies, but then Mann
could have said, at any time, "Irony of ironies, all is irony." We
behold in Cervantes's vast scripture what we already are. Dr.
Samuel Johnson, who could not abide Jonathan Swift's ironies,

easily accepted those of Cervantes; Swift's satire corrodes, while Cervantes's allows us some hope. Johnson felt that we required some illusions, lest we go mad. Is that part of Cervantes's design?

Mark Van Doren, in a very useful study, *Don Quixote's Profession,* is haunted by the analogues between the Knight and Hamlet, which to me seem inevitable. Here are the two characters, beyond all others, who seem always to know what they are doing, though they baffle us whenever we try to share their knowledge. It is a knowledge unlike that of Sir John Falstaff and Sancho Panza, who are so delighted at being themselves that they bid knowledge to go aside and pass them by. I would rather be Falstaff or Sancho than a version of Hamlet or Don Quixote, because growing old and ill teaches me that being matters more than knowing. The Knight and Hamlet are reckless beyond belief; Falstaff and Sancho have some awareness of discretion in matters of valor.

We cannot know the object of Don Quixote's quest unless we ourselves are Quixotic (note the capital Q). Did Cervantes, looking back upon his own arduous life, think of it as somehow Quixotic? The Woeful Face stares out at us in his portrait, a countenance wholly unlike Shakespeare's subtle blandness. They match each other in genius, because more even than Chaucer before them, and the host of novelists who have blended together their influences since, they gave us personalities more alive than ourselves. Cervantes, I suspect, would not have wanted us to compare him to Shakespeare or to anyone else. Don Quixote says that all comparisons are odious. Perhaps they are, but this may be the exception. We need, with Cervantes and Shakespeare, all the help we can get in regard to ultimates, yet we need no help at all to enjoy them.

Each is as difficult and yet available as is the other. To confront them fully, where are we to turn except to their mutual power of illumination?

8

In what sense are Don Quixote and Hamlet and Falstaff's plays—Henry IV, Part 1 and Part 2—wisdom literature? In this chapter's second section, on Shakespeare, I will suggest that *King Lear,* with its echoes of The Wisdom of Solomon, is overtly in the wisdom tradition. Hamlet and Don Quixote, Falstaff and Sancho Panza represent something new in the tradition, since all of these are at once surprisingly wise and dangerously foolish. Of the four, only Sancho is a survivor, because his folk cunning is far stronger than his illusive attachment to his knight's dream. Falstaff, the Socrates of Eastcheap, has the wisdom of his "Give me life," but also the great unwisdom of his love for Prince Hal. Prince Hamlet, intelligent beyond intelligence, embraces annihilation, making darkness his bride. Don Quixote is the wisest of the wise, but even he yields to the reality principle, and so dies a Christian death.

SHAKESPEARE

Nothing explains Shakespeare, or can explain him away. Historicizing him, old- or new-style, expires rapidly, since the same cultural factors are equally apt and inapt for his contemporaries, a large

company of rival poet-dramatists. Nor are the various totalizing approaches—Marxist, Freudian, feminist, what you will—other than reductive. Those who fall back upon language are left with language, and even Wittgenstein contributed nothing but evasion by naming Shakespeare "a creator of language." And yet Lewis Carroll, James Joyce, and others, or Ben Jonson and Edmund Spenser in Shakespeare's age, also were creators of language.

The best speculators upon Shakespeare included Emerson, who saw that somehow one person had written the text of modern life, and Carlyle, who flatly asserted Shakespeare's capaciousness of intellect, larger and subtler than Plato's or Hegel's. If the ancient quarrel between poetry and philosophy inspired Plato's sad and hopeless expulsion of Homer from his idealized Republic, Hegel declined the discredited polemic and granted that Shakespeare's characters were "free artists of themselves." In Hegel's wake, A. C. Bradley named Falstaff, Hamlet, Iago, and Cleopatra as the freest of the free.

The wisest among Shakespeare's critics were Dr. Johnson and William Hazlitt, who plainly realized that the Shakespearean difference was in the portrayal of persons. Though that is a perpetual beginning, it will not take us far enough. Dante and Cervantes give us persons, with Cervantes developing his sad-faced Knight and Sancho on a scale that Hamlet and Falstaff cannot match, since ultimately there is no one for them to talk to, or play to, except themselves. And yet Cervantes has only two persons, and everyone in Dante has been judged and fixed, beyond change. Survey all of literature, and Shakespeare has only one true forerunner and peer: Geoffrey Chaucer.

Chaucer's ironies, though they touch the abyss in the Pardoner, could not create Lear, the breakthrough in all literature (except the Bible) into the transcendental and extraordinary. The Shakespearean difference is akin to the dialectics of creation in the Lurianic Kabbalah. Shakespeare withdraws and contracts himself, until his energies overflow and devastate the vessels he has prepared to incarnate them. Both in comedy and tragedy there is a breaking of forms and of persons, and we have to contemplate Shylock and Lear, whose negative energies can be fulfilled only through self-annihilation. The humiliation of Malvolio in *Twelfth Night*, and the equivocation of the fiend that lies like truth, and breaks Macbeth, seem other versions of this pattern of catastrophe-creation. Though directors and critics snatch at gleanings of restitution, presumably to take place in the audience, the ablest of Shakespearean actors implicitly seem to know better. Shakespeare is the Godlike author that James Joyce and Goethe hoped to approximate, the alienated Creator who pares his fingernails even as his creation is ruined by its own richness. We have had only one such author, who out-Yahwehs Yahweh, which remains the scandal that is Shakespeare.

We read, I think, to repair our solitude, though pragmatically the better we read, the more solitary we become. I cannot regard reading as a vice, but then also it is not a virtue. Thinking in Hegel is one thing; in Goethe, it is quite another. Hegel is not a wisdom writer; Goethe is. The deepest motive for reading has to be the quest for wisdom. Worldly wisdom is rarely wise, or even prudential. Shakespeare, grandest of entertainers, also is the wisest of teachers, though the burden of his teaching may be nihilism,

which is the lesson of *King Lear*. I am not a joyous nihilist, since I am a schoolteacher by profession.

King Lear was first played at the Globe on the day that *Don Quixote* was published. Writing about Cervantes, I have followed the pattern first set by Turgenev, comparing the Knight to Hamlet. Here I desire a more difficult analogy, between the madness of Don Quixote and the shattering derangement of Lear.

Critics long have recognized that Lear's tragedy is a pagan play directed to a Christian audience. After reading David Daniell's *The Bible in English* (2003), I am prepared to modify my view that Shakespeare and the Bible have less in common than most scholars assert, but only in the sense that William Tyndale shares with Chaucer the eminence of being one of the prime precursors of Shakespeare's inventiveness. What Shakespeare read in the Geneva Bible New Testament, or we in the King James Version, was William Tyndale, with some modifications. About half of the Hebrew Bible (no Jew should call it the Old Testament) is also essentially Tyndale's, in the Geneva and King James versions. David Daniell is accurate in showing how Tyndale's language of "elemental simplicity" provided a strong model for Shakespeare's visions of suffering, particularly in *King Lear*. I also am sympathetic to Daniell's demonstration that Shakespeare's stances are far more Protestant than Catholic, and yet (if we can ascertain Shakespeare's own spirituality at all) there are aspects of it that are not Christian. Hamlet's apotheosis is more an annihilation than a revelation. We have no word that is appropriate for Shakespeare: he evades every categorization available to us.

Many critics have associated the Book of Job and *King Lear*,

yet I now find more influences upon the play in Koheleth (Ecclesiastes), The Wisdom of Solomon, and Proverbs. Mindful of King James I, who liked being compared to Solomon, Shakespeare associates Lear with the aged Solomon, supposed speaker of the Hebrew wisdom literature, the Book of Job excepted. Echoes of Job enter Lear's drama, but Elizabethans severely distinguished the Book of Job from the works attributed to Solomon the Wise. In his *Defence of Poesie,* Sir Philip Sidney, with superb aesthetic judgment, identifies the great biblical poets as "David in his Psalms; Solomon in his Song of Songs, in his Ecclesiastes, and his Proverbs; Moses and Deborah in their hymns," while giving a separate eminence to "the writer of Job." Shakespeare evidently would have added the Apocryphal Wisdom of Solomon, and the parables of Jesus.

The Shakespearean critic Arthur Kirsch first suggested that Ecclesiastes is far closer to *King Lear* than the Book of Job could be:

> *The depiction of suffering in* King Lear *has often been compared to the Book of Job, which, of course, focuses upon the suffering of an individual; and the protraction of Job's suffering as well as his protests against it do indeed suggest the magnitude of Lear's heroic characterization. But there is no Satan at the beginning of* King Lear, *nor a whirlwind from which God speaks at the end to make the play's extraordinary sense of heartfelt pain even intellectually explicable. In its overall conception as well as in much of its ironic texture,* King Lear *is closer to Ecclesiastes.*

The skepticism of Ecclesiastes, Kirsch observes, may have been reinforced by Shakespeare's reading of John Florio's version of

Montaigne, available to Shakespeare in manuscript, Florio having been the Earl of Southampton's secretary. And yet Montaigne, in his pragmatic wisdom, stands apart from the nihilism of the eighty-year-old (and more) "Solomon as Preacher" in Ecclesiastes and the equally despairing Lear, who regains Cordelia only to lose her again to death. "Vanity of vanities, all is vanity" is equated with the dread formula of *King Lear:* nothing begets nothing. The enormous emptiness of Koheleth reverberates all through Shakespeare's darkest drama, which is also his wisest, surpassing even *Hamlet.*

I cannot recall ever reading (or listening to) an account of Shakespeare's wisdom. And yet this most inventive of all writers, ever, is also the supreme creator of wisdom literature. Samuel Johnson, poet of the Ecclesiastes-like "The Vanity of Human Wishes," would not have agreed. Wisdom, for Johnson, had to be moral. We owe to Johnson, still Shakespeare's best critic, the alarming judgment that I urge us to turn inside out:

> [Shakespeare] *sacrifices virtue to convenience, and is so much more careful to please than instruct, that he seems to write without any moral purpose.*

Johnson knew better. What is the "moral purpose" of Ecclesiastes? Biblical "wisdom literature," as I stressed in my first chapter, is profoundly skeptical as to when and where God's purposes can be known. The devout Johnson, who surely identified moral purpose with God's will, could have had no illusions that Job and

Solomon wrote only to instruct. In his own writings, Johnson clearly indicates a sense that human life is everywhere a condition in which much is to be endured and little to be enjoyed. That is the cosmos of *King Lear*, the most tragic of all Shakespearean tragedies.

The Apocrypha's Wisdom of Solomon, which I discussed briefly in this book's first chapter, is a prime work of the Hellenistic Judaism of Alexandria, influenced by Platonism, and yet firmly within the Covenant, as was Philo of Alexandria. Shakespeare, reading the Wisdom of Solomon in the Geneva Bible, evidently was so moved by one passage in it (7:1–6) that he has Lear echo it quite directly in one of the tragedy's most shattering interludes, the confrontation between the insane king and the blind Gloucester that attains its apotheosis in IV.vi.174–81:

> *I myself also am a mortal man, like to all, and the offspring of him that was first made of the earth,*
>
> *And in my mother's womb was fashioned to be flesh in the time of ten months, being compacted in blood, of the seed of man, and the pleasure that came with sleep.*
>
> *And when I was born, I drew in the common air, and fell upon the earth, which is of like nature, and the first voice which I uttered was crying, as all others do.*
>
> *I was nursed in swaddling clothes, and that with cares.*
>
> *For there is no king that had any other beginning of birth.*
>
> *For all men have one entrance into life, and the like going out.*
>
> *Wherefore I prayed, and understanding was given me: I called* upon God, *and the spirit of wisdom came to me.*

LEAR. *If thou wilt weep my fortunes, take my eyes;*
I know thee well enough; thy name is Gloucester;
Thou must be patient; we came crying hither:
Thou know'st the first time that we smell the air
We wawl and cry. I will preach to thee: mark.

[Lear takes off his crown of weeds and flowers.]

GLOU. *Alack, alack the day!*

LEAR. *When we are born, we cry that we are come*
To this great stage of fools.

The King James text here is identical with that in the Geneva Bible. I keep brooding upon just why Shakespeare makes so explicit an employment of Solomon's lament at just this moment in Lear's agony, and increasingly come to believe that Lear is meant to be a near-identity with the aged Solomon, at the end of the Hebrew king's half-century reign. Both monarchs are well past eighty, and Lear's division of the kingdom takes place also with Solomon's realm, but only after Solomon's death. Is this an allusion to the sly tale of Solomon's pragmatic wisdom in determining the true mother by suggesting that the disputed infant be divided between them? Lear's motivation in tearing apart his kingdom is also an exercise (fearfully mistaken) in ascertaining whether Cordelia, whom he loves best, truly matches his love.

Solomon as preacher of Ecclesiastes is as mortal as Job, but rarely as kingly concerning death's reality as he is in the seventh chapter of The Wisdom of Solomon, where he addresses his peers, the other monarchs. In Chapter 6, he warns them that "a sure trial

shall come upon the mighty." The epigraph for *King Lear*, had Shakespeare employed that later literary device, well might be:

> And when I was born, I drew in the common air, and fell upon the earth, which is of like nature, and the first voice I uttered was crying, as all others do.

Lear's echo far surpasses the sublime pathos of this source:

> . . . *we came crying hither:*
> *Thou know'st the first time we smell the air*
> *We wawl and cry.*

Since "all men then have one entrance unto life, and the like going out," Lear's godson and successor, Edgar, joins in echoing Solomon when he tells his suicidal father, the despairing Gloucester, that men must endure their going hence even as their coming hither. Lear's eloquence, transcending even the Preacher's in Ecclesiastes, becomes overwhelming when he himself assumes the role of preacher, with only the blind Gloucester and the disguised Edgar as his congregation:

> *When we are born, we cry that we are come*
> *To this great stage of fools.*

The frequent fury of Lear, so akin to the worst moments of Yahweh, is replaced here by a searing pathos: "This great stage of

fools" is set up in the Globe, and Shakespeare wants to remind us that he has made "fools" mean not only court jesters, like Lear's extraordinary Fool, but one's best-beloved, Cordelia. Yet here the word takes the particular imprint of "victims": we all are death's fools, later or sooner.

Is Lear's (and Shakespeare's) wisdom only what Freud was to call "reality testing," the full acceptance of mortality? Set aside all soft readings of *King Lear:* no one in this drama is, or can be, redeemed. The biblical allusions in the play do not render it a Christian work. Whatever Shakespeare himself believed, his grandest achievements cannot be reconciled with either Catholicism or Protestantism, or with any creed or ideology whatever. Shakespeare did not write the poems of his climate, and Ben Jonson was superbly accurate when he proclaimed that Shakespeare was not for an age (Elizabethan-Jacobean) but for all time. The universalism of *King Lear* is neither Christian nor pagan: the fall of the father-god-king who needs and wants more love than anyone can receive is a familial malady, in nearly all times, cultures, and countries. To recognize and accept it is the beginning of Shakespeare's surpassing wisdom. Shakespeare, for reasons we cannot know, never depicted the death of the mother. In Lear, he gave us the definitive vision of the death of fatherhood.

2
—

I cannot find anywhere in Shakespeare a representation of wisdom as constituting part of the labor of redemption. Prospero, the anti-

Faust of *The Tempest,* is perhaps the wisest personage in the plays, except for Hamlet and, in another register, Falstaff. Hamlet's incommensurable intellect thinks the Prince into the truth of annihilation, and all of Falstaff's wit cannot save the fat knight from Henry V's cold humiliation of his rejected mentor, who had been more the Socrates than the Solomon of Eastcheap. Stripped of the Hermetic art, Prospero finds only the merely political redemption of restoration to power in "my Milan, where/Every third thought shall be my grave."

Where then, in Shakespeare, shall wisdom be found? The answer, I fear, is in the emptied-out cosmos of *King Lear* and of *Macbeth.* Though *King Lear* is set in a pagan Britain, *Macbeth* supposedly takes place in a medieval and therefore Catholic Scotland, but there are many more biblical allusions in Lear's tragedy than in Macbeth's night-world of the Weird Sisters and Hecate. A negative wisdom emanates from both dramas, prophesying Schopenhauer and Freud, Proust and Beckett, visionaries of a delusive Eros and a jealous Thanatos.

No single character either in *King Lear* or in *Macbeth* can utter any wisdom that is not immediately qualified by dramatic irony. Hamlet and Falstaff, Iago and Cleopatra: these four are free artists of irony, but Lear and his Fool, Edgar and Edmund, Lady Macbeth and Macbeth all are mastered by a dynamics of irony that prevails everywhere in their dramatic circumstances. Though Shakespeare has no private gnosis, unlike his contemporary Giordano Bruno, who was "terribly burned" (James Joyce's phrase) by the Italian Catholic Church, a darker, still more negative intuition haunts

both of these apocalyptic tragedies. As my subject is wisdom and literature, and Shakespeare *is* literature, I feel compelled to hazard a description of Shakespearean nihilism (to call it that, for now).

History has many instances of nihilistic thinkers and poets before Nietzsche greeted nihilism itself as an uncanny visitor in his Europe. The *Iliad* and Ecclesiastes are in part destructive of values we regard as belonging both to Platonic and Judaic norms, which combined in the transition from Saint Paul to Saint Augustine. *Don Quixote* is a work as comprehensive as to defy categorization, but it permits perspectives as bleak as those made available by *King Lear* though never as terrifying as are implicit in *Macbeth*. The Hebraic Blessing, which promised more life into a time without boundaries, and which culminated both in Hillel and in Jesus, is conspicuously absent from *Don Quixote,* and is in another realm altogether from Lear's and Macbeth's kingdoms.

No one is free in *King Lear* and in *Macbeth,* and only Sancho is free in *Don Quixote,* where the sad-faced knight is confined by his quest until he is freed by an awakening to sanity that all too rapidly transmutes into a sanctified death. Shakespeare, to use James Joyce's word, is "richer" than Dante, Chaucer, Cervantes, because he is even more various than these masters. *Hamlet* is unlimited, in ways not matched even by *King Lear.* I myself am puzzled, even bewildered, by the paradox of Shakespeare's wisdom being so negative when his art is so wealthy beyond wisdom. Falstaff's vitalism generates as much meaning by excess and overflow as Hamlet's consciousness does, and the same contrast emerges again between Cleopatra's energy and Iago's negativity, both of which allow fresh meaning to get started. One could not say that Shakespeare's wis-

dom is in abeyance until he creates Lear, Edgar, and the Macbeths, but I venture that wisdom intensifies in the godlike Solomonic king, and in Macbeth, the great usurper, ancestor of Melville's Captain Ahab in *Moby-Dick*, Faulkner's Sutpen in *Absalom, Absalom!* and Cormac McCarthy's Judge Holden in *Blood Meridian*. The American Hamlet was intended to be Melville's *Pierre*, a blunder, partly compensated for by the wonderful American Falstaff of Philip Roth's *Sabbath's Theater*.

Chroniclers of nihilism, or the road to Nietzsche's transvaluation of all values (God is dead, everything is permitted), tend to emphasize the philosophical tradition, in which the will takes the place of a normative God who has sent down standards for truth and ethics. Michael Allen Gillespie, in his useful *Nihilism Before Nietzsche* (1995), traces the sequence that goes from the early-fourteenth-century William of Ockham through Montaigne, Francis Bacon, Descartes, Rousseau, Kant, and Fichte on to the idealism of the German Romantics: Jacobi, Jean Paul, Tieck, and even Goethe and Hegel, who became what they beheld in opposing Romantic nihilism. Hegelians of the Left—Marx and the Russians culminating in Lenin and Trotsky—carried nihilism into terrorism and class revolution; but Schopenhauer returned to Fichte's Romantic idealism, and thus begat the Dionysiac Nietzsche, who is now claimed by antinihilists and nihilists alike.

Shakespeare is not mentioned in Gillespie's study, but the German Romantics were Shakespeareans, and *Hamlet* is the ancestral work for all Romanticism, Continental and British. Dostoevsky learned his ways of representing Russian nihilists from Shakespearean portrayals of freedom. If there *is* a God in Shakespeare,

He hides in the human will, which finds itself free to evade all ideas of order, and proves not to be free at all. Most Shakespearean scholars, whether Old or New Historicists, decline to see this Shakespeare plain, and prefer to approve either Christian or materialist necessity or imposing constraints upon Hamlet and Falstaff, Macbeth and Cleopatra, Iago and Lear, who cannot keep their freedom even as they die, but not because of constraints. Shakespeare precedes Descartes in transferring God's infinite freedom to men and women, who cannot sustain it, while exiling God somewhere far away in an omnipotent perfection not available to us. God is too good for us, and His remoteness intensifies the dramatic possibilities of representing lives.

In *Cymbeline*, a continuous Shakespearean self-parody, Jupiter descends in Act V, Scene IV, producing a risible travesty of divine intervention. So dead is the verse that it has to be intentional, punishing both audience and poet. We are given Shakespeare's subtle indication (akin to Bacon's) that the human will is unsponsored and free, though Bacon's optimism is totally absent in Hamlet, the supreme protagonist of an absolute will. David Daniell (page 382) aptly invokes Plato's quarrel with Homer as background to Hamlet's (and Shakespeare's) will-to-speculation:

> *In spite of Plato, poetry was on God's side after all, because God himself wrote poetry, as the Bible had newly shown. Freshly inventing thoughts, forms, styles and even words, was part of a poet being, as Sidney said, a 'maker' and, as the Bible also showed, could be both unfettered and endless. Hamlet, his mind racing with suggestions, is not threatened with heresy.*

Nietzsche could have pondered the Bible more deeply, to find there Hamlet's and Lear's nihilism in Job, Ecclesiastes, and the Wisdom of Solomon. Not at all an uncanny guest, nihilism had always been part of poetic tradition, both Homeric and biblical.

3
———

Inventive beyond any other writer, Shakespeare took nihilism beyond all limits in *Macbeth,* where the protagonist's hallucinatory imagination usurps even his own will. The actor Henry Irving, who had played both Hamlet and Macbeth, remarked in 1896 that Macbeth was "the greatest part that Shakespeare has ever drawn." That seems just: Hamlet represents Shakespeare's cognitive power, while Macbeth is Shakespeare's own poetic imagination.

Macbeth, so much of which takes place at night, is also metaphorically the darkest of Shakespeare's dramas, and calls into question any freedom of the will. Is the play's wisdom dependent on the suggestion that Macbeth could have performed any differently? Freud preferred *Macbeth* to the rest of Shakespeare, presumably because he brooded on what seems overdetermination in Shakespeare's hero-villain. Rather desperately, the great interpreter decided that Macbeth and Lady Macbeth were "like two disunited parts of a single individuality, and perhaps they are the divided images of a single prototype." Unfortunately that divests Lady Macbeth of her extraordinary individuality, and complicates more than it explains. What kind of wisdom does Shakespeare manifest in *Macbeth*? Job and Ecclesiastes, and a wealth of other biblical

associations in *King Lear,* are not present in *Macbeth.* Shakespeare recoiled from composing *King Lear* and *Macbeth* by breaking out from their cosmological emptiness into the large world of *Antony and Cleopatra,* where East struggles against West for universal dominion. More even than *Hamlet* is, *Macbeth* is a journey into the interior, where Macbeth's is the heart of darkness.

A good performance of *Macbeth,* if you can find it, is likely to seem more fearful than wise. Nietzsche, in his *Daybreak* (section 240), praised the play for its absence of moral judgments, an observation that I think would be accurate throughout Shakespeare. Rather than discoursing on good and evil, Shakespeare is always more interested in why we cannot sustain our own freedom. As with Falstaff, the plays can offend only the virtuous, since Shakespeare prophesies Blake's proverb: "Energy is Eternal Delight." Can energetics be wisdom? Balzac clearly thought so, and so did Cervantes. Yet the vitality of Macbeth is very different from the ferocious force of Balzac's Vautrin, the exuberant drive of Don Quixote, and the agonistic wit of Sir John Falstaff. All of these possess a difficult wisdom of survival, while Macbeth pragmatically is doom-eager. Lear cannot cease demanding love, in such excess that it wears out, and destroys or psychically maims, all who worship his person and authority. Macbeth, with his attempted murder of Fleance, Banquo's son, and actual slaying of Macduff's children, seeks freedom by canceling the future. This is far crazier than Achilles' destroying so many in the *Iliad* as a vain protest against his own mortality. And yet Shakespeare's wisdom approximates Homer's: to see through violence to its sources cannot heal vio-

lence, but it can lead to a personal refusal of fight, or a retreat from it, both in Homer and in Shakespeare. There are poets addicted to violence: Christopher Marlowe, whom Shakespeare must have known, and a number of Continental poets from Villon to Rimbaud.

Goethe remarked of Shakespeare that each of his plays "revolves around an invisible point which no philosopher has discovered or defined and where the characteristic quality of our being, our presumed free will, collides with the inevitable course of the whole." Later, in his ultimate tribute, "No End to Shakespeare," Goethe distinguishes between ancient and modern literature. In ancient literature, the conflict is between moral obligation and its fulfillment, while in modern literature the agon is between desire and fulfillment. In Goethe's judgment, Shakespeare is unique in that he fuses ancient and modern with surpassing exuberance: "In his plays, obligation and desire clearly try to counterbalance each other." I cannot dispute Goethe's wisdom, though I think he errs when he concludes that "Shakespeare always sees to it that desire remains at a disadvantage." That is not Macbeth, whose desire to maintain kingship destroys innocents and Lady Macbeth, and finally himself.

Wisdom in literature cannot be separated from the representation of desire, of which eros is only one component among others. Desire, as Plato's Socrates argued, at last must be an opening to transcendence, however secularized this becomes in Shakespeare. There is very little Platonism or even Neoplatonism in Shakespeare, though Frances Yates argued eloquently but with little evidence for Shakespeare's Hermetism, reflecting the

supposedly major influence of the fascinating Giordano Bruno upon the poet-dramatist.

George Wilson Knight, whom I knew in my now distant youth, luminously remarked in *The Wheel of Fire* (originally published in 1930) that Macbeth displays "an ecstasy of courage" at the close. Knight even partly redeems Macbeth from any accusation of evil:

> *He has won through by excessive crime to an harmonious and honest relation with his surroundings. He has successfully symbolized the disorder of his lonely guilt-stricken soul by creating disorder in the world, and thus restores balance and harmonious contact.*

I recall reading this, with some wonder, in 1949, and then questioning Wilson Knight about it in 1951, when we first met. He defended his splendidly outrageous observations as an instance of communion between life and death, since he believed in literal rather than figurative immortality. I cannot locate such belief anywhere in Shakespeare, though Wilson Knight's idiosyncratic, rather Nietzschean stance was invariably refreshing. At least he had set moral good and evil aside, and had liberated himself from much conventional condemnation of Macbeth. One thinks of Wallace Stevens finding an idea of order in a great disorder, and of Hamlet's endless scorn for Elsinore as being inadequate for the struggle his immense consciousness requires him to stage.

Shakespeare is so large a form of thought and language, of persons in spiritual turmoil, and of intimations of transcendence

blocked by realities that we scarcely have begun to understand and to absorb him, despite the arrogance of critical-scholarly groupings. We are slow to apprehend the dialectics of his wisdom. Shakespearean irony has much to do with Chaucerian saying of one thing while meaning another, and has few traces of Socratic professed ignorance. Philosophers and theologians did not influence Shakespeare. Ovid was an endless resource, Marlowe a self-destructive rival to be gleaned and then outdone, the Bible a stock of common references, but Chaucerian characterization was the true model, with Falstaff created as a contemporary who could have ridden side by side with the Wife of Bath, prompting her to absolute self-realizations.

When Macbeth overhears himself, he tends to be confirmed in his augmenting murderousness, but Lear is bewildered and doubts his own identity. That is crucial to Shakespearean wisdom: Macbeth has force but no inner authority, while Lear is the image of lost yet legitimate authority, the figure of the benign and kingly father transformed into a raging and ineffectual god. A theomorphic king, like Solomon, has become too human a god.

King Lear as a play despairs of nearly all relationships between parents and children, and turns against Solomon by denying any wisdom to old age. *Macbeth,* at hardly half the length, goes farther into the abyss, and destroys its protagonist because his infinite imagination, unlike Hamlet's intellect, deforms consciousness each time it expands awareness. No one wants to see Lear die, but Shakespeare imposes the death upon us, to Tolstoy's fury. I suspect we look forward to watching Macduff unseam Macbeth onstage,

but Shakespeare will not have it so. He has invested his own power of phantasmagoria in Macbeth, and has made us identify with the usurper, and does not want us to view the moment of dying, since something vital in Shakespeare then also dies. Lear's death is more universal, far more persuasive than Nietzsche's Death of God, since Lear dies of joy, profoundly deluded by his conviction that Cordelia has been resurrected to more life.

THE GREATEST

IDEAS ARE

THE GREATEST

EVENTS

CHAPTER 4

MONTAIGNE AND

FRANCIS BACON

MONTAIGNE

The personal essay is Montaigne's, as the drama is Shakespeare's, the epic is Homer's, and the novel forever Cervantes's. That the first of essayists remains much the best has less to do with his formal originality (though that is considerable) than with the overwhelming directness of his wisdom. He asks us implicitly and incessantly: Are your thoughts of any value if they stay within you? His answer, in clear anticipation of Nietzsche, is no. Thoughts are events. Montaigne's pleasures for the reader are ultimately difficult, but immediately available, like Shakespeare's. He asks you to be a vigorous reader, and his modesty is a mask.

As with Bacon, Montaigne was legally trained, but hardly a lawyer in his perspectives. In a useful study, *Montaigne's Deceits* (1971), Margaret McGowan demonstrates the extent to which

Montaigne's art of persuasion is a mode of indirect communication: I would want to distinguish Montaigne's "deceits," rhetorical devices for capturing the reader, from the ironies of Plato's Socrates, albeit Socrates is Montaigne's prime hero, and also separate them from the flamboyant heteronyms, fictive authors of Kierkegaard's treatises and Fernando Pessoa's poems. Montaigne is not primarily an ironist, unless you want to think of Shakespeare as the supreme of ironists, surpassing even Socrates by creating Falstaff, tavern sage who is the pragmatist of what might be termed immanent irony.

I recall vividly passing through a personal crisis of depression that began when I turned thirty-five, in the middle of the journey. It lasted about a year, during which I read backward and forward everything that Emerson and Freud had written, finally choosing the Concord sage as lifetime guide, because he speaks to me so directly, more so even than Freud. I did not read deeply in Montaigne until a year later, and found there the indubitable source of Emerson's direct mode of address. Not even Emerson, Montaigne's declared disciple, engages the reader as capaciously as Montaigne does: his immediacy always startles again by its freshness. What Montaigne gives you goes beyond wisdom, if so secular a transcendence is acceptable to you. It is as though Hamlet confronted you, with actual concern for your enlightenment, or the expansion of your own consciousness. Hamlet does not much care for us, which paradoxically provokes affection for him in many. Shakespeare, as always, conceals himself; we can only surmise his rela-

tion to Hamlet, yet never get beyond surmise. Montaigne, though he seems to have aided in Shakespeare's creation of Hamlet, does not share the prince's or the dramatist's disinterestedness. He persuades the reader that he cares, primarily by arousing the reader's deep interest in Montaigne himself. Of Montaigne's inwardness, finally we learn almost everything, because he allows his earlier rhetorical stratagems to fall away, as he increases both in self-knowledge and in mastery of his essayistic art.

2

Montaigne, together with Shakespeare, is the great figure of the European Renaissance. His essay "Of Books" is marked by a genial irony that is deeply skeptical of the Humanist program that he rather offhandedly endorses:

> Let people see in what I borrow whether I have known how to choose what would enhance my theme. For I make others say what I cannot say so well, now through the weakness of my language, now through the weakness of my understanding. I do not count my borrowings, I weigh them. And if I had wanted to have them valued by their number, I should have loaded myself with twice as many. They are all, or very nearly all, from such famous and ancient names that they seem to identify themselves enough without me. In the reasonings and inventions that I transplant into my soil and confound with my own, I have sometimes deliberately not indicated the author, in order to hold in check the

temerity of those hasty condemnations that are tossed at all sorts of writings of men still living, and in the vulgar tongue, which invites everyone to talk about them and seems to convict the conception and design of being likewise vulgar. I want them to give Plutarch a fillip on my nose and get burned insulting Seneca in me. I have to hide my weakness under these great authorities. I will love anyone that can unplume me, I mean by clearness of judgment and by the sole distinction of the force and beauty of the remarks. For I who, for lack of memory, fall short at every turn in picking them out by knowledge of their origin, can very well realize, by measuring my capacity, that my soil is not at all capable of producing certain too rich flowers that I find sown there, and that all the fruits of my own growing could not match them.

[*Translated by* DONALD FRAME]

One finds here cunning, humor, tact, and a deliciously bland disarming of one's critics. Montaigne at this time (1578–1580) is well under way to his final stance, where high humanism yields to the common life (and the common reader). This is very different from Ben Jonson's saying of reading that it "maketh a full man," borrowing from Bacon's essay "Of Studies." Burly Ben Jonson pugnaciously scorns Montaigne's use of quite immediate reading:

Some that turn over all books, and are equally searching in all papers; that write out of what they presently find or meet, without choice. By which means it happens that what they have discredited and impugned in one week, they have before or after

extolled the same in another. Such are all the essayists, even their
master Montaigne. These, in all they write, confess still what
books they have read last, and therein their own follow so much,
that they bring it to the stake raw and undigested; not that the
place did need it neither, but that they thought themselves fur-
nished and would vent it.

Jonson was personally and intellectually close to Bacon, and
his purpose in this deprecation of Montaigne is to exalt Bacon as
rival essayist. Bacon's essays certainly do not "confess still what
books they have read last," but Montaigne loved Greek and Latin
wisdom (Plato, Plutarch, Seneca, Vergil), and Bacon wanted an
older wisdom, partly Solomon's but largely his own. Yet Bacon's
project achieved only fragments of what he desired; Montaigne's
Essays are as complete as Shakespeare's plays and poems now
appear to be. Not unlike Shakespeare's protagonists, Montaigne
changes because he reads what he himself has written, while never
allowing himself to forget that the final form of change is death.

The conduct of life matters to Montaigne: he does not study
death, abandoning that to the philosophers and the theologians.
At the center of seven lectures, *Representative Men* (1850), Emerson
placed "Montaigne; or, the Skeptic." It is a superb and accurate
tribute:

The sincerity and marrow of the man reaches to his sentences. I
know not anywhere the book that seems less written. It is the lan-
guage of conversation transferred to a book. Cut these words,
and they would bleed; they are vascular and alive. One has the

*same pleasure in it that we have in listening to the necessary
speech of men about their work, when any unusual circumstance
gives momentary importance to the dialogue. For blacksmiths
and teamsters do not trip in their speech; it is a shower of bullets.
It is Cambridge men who correct themselves, and begin again at
every half sentence, and, moreover, will pun, and refine too
much, and swerve from the matter to the expression. Montaigne
talks with shrewdness, knows the world, and books, and himself,
and uses the positive degree: never shrieks, or protests, or prays:
no weakness, no convulsion, no superlative: does not wish to
jump out of his skin, or play any antics, or annihilate space or
time; but is stout and solid; tastes every moment of the day; like
pain, he rarely mounts or sinks; likes to feel solid ground, and
the stones underneath. His writing has no enthusiasms, no aspiration; contented, self-respecting, and keeping the middle of the
road. There is but one exception,—in his love for Socrates. In
speaking of him, for once his cheek flushes, and his style rises to
passion.*

"Cut these words, and they would bleed; they are vascular and
alive." That is the best observation I know on Montaigne. And yet
there is very little else on Montaigne in Emerson's wonderful lec-
ture. Sometimes it reminds me of D. H. Lawrence's *Study of Thomas
Hardy*, which just barely discusses Hardy, who with Walt Whitman was Lawrence's forerunner, as Montaigne was Emerson's.
Lawrence hymns vitalism, and Emerson charts the mutations of
skepticism and belief. But then, Hardy and Montaigne both defy
much of what passes for literary criticism. Hardy, even in his late

poems, is too dark to be a wisdom writer, unless you regard Schopenhauer as the ultimate wisdom, while Montaigne is wholly a wise mentor, strengthening us to live our lives. Montaigne's motto well might be "You shall know the truth, and the truth will make you wise." I suspect that Emerson finally was much darker and more skeptical than Montaigne, and perhaps came to believe that nothing could render us wise.

I will turn to Emerson later in this book, in apposition with Nietzsche, who both loved and was chagrined by the only American precursor he knew. Walt Whitman might have been better for Nietzsche, whose Zarathustra does not sustain comparison with the rhapsode who composed and chanted *Song of Myself.* Nietzsche was haunted by Emerson's wistful notion that nature "becomes perfect *just now,*" echoed in Zarathustra's high-noon experience: "Did not the world become perfect just now?" Neither Emerson nor Nietzsche would have persuaded Montaigne to "think of the earth." "Think of yourself" is Montaigne's way, pursuing ceaselessly man's nature.

Montaigne's wisdom is not biblical: Christ is mentioned only nine or ten times in the *Essays,* while Socrates is cited in well over a hundred instances. Though Montaigne, unlike Emerson and Nietzsche, takes care not to be post-Christian, he is pragmatically un-Christian. God and Christ exist, but they are so distant and beyond us that they cannot be our concern. A perfect test of this, and a lesson in different wisdoms, is the anxious relation to Montaigne of Blaise Pascal, whose *Pensées* give the impression that the *Essays* were an immortal wound to his own contemplation of Christianity.

3

Pascal never loses his capacity to offend as well as to edify. Contrast his very different effects upon Paul Valéry and T. S. Eliot. Here is Valéry:

> *I hate to see a man using artifice to turn others against their lot, when they are in it in spite of themselves and are doing what they can to make the best of it; to see a man trying to persuade others that they must expect the worst, must always keep in mind the most intolerable notion of their predicament, and be alert to whatever is most unbearable in it—which is precisely the notion of suffering and risk, and anxiety about the risk—using the notion of eternity as an almighty weapon, and developing it by the artifice of repetition.*

This is to accuse Pascal of being an obscurantist rhetorician, rather resembling the T. S. Eliot of the religious prose writings. Here is Eliot on Pascal:

> *But I can think of no Christian writer, not Newman even, more to be commended than Pascal to those who doubt, but who have the mind to conceive, and the sensibility to feel, the disorder, the futility, the meaninglessness, the mystery of life and suffering, and who can only find peace through a satisfaction of the whole being.*

I suspect that Valéry and Eliot are saying much the same thing, the difference being the rival perspectives toward Pascal of a secu-

lar intellectual and a Christian polemicist. Pascal essentially is a polemicist, rather than a religious or meditative writer. The *Pensées* ultimately are not less tendentious than the *Provincial Letters*. A Christian polemicist in our time ought to find his true antagonist in Freud, but nearly all do not; they either evade Freud, or self-defeatingly seek to appropriate him. Pascal's Freud was Montaigne, who could not be evaded or appropriated, and who scarcely can be refuted. But Pascal's case of influence-anxiety, in regard to Montaigne, was hopelessly overwhelming. Eliot, putting the best case for Pascal, insisted that Montaigne simply had the power to embody a universal skepticism, in which Pascal necessarily shared, though only to a limited degree. Doubtless Eliot attributed to Montaigne one of the essayist's plethora of authentic powers, but a secretly shared (and overcome) skepticism hardly can account for the full scandal of Montaigne's influence upon Pascal. Tables of parallel passages demonstrate an indebtedness so great, extending to figuration, examples, syntax, actual repetition of phrases, that Pascal would be convicted of plagiarism in any American school or university, with their rather literal notions of what constitutes plagiarism. The frequent effect in reading Pascal is that he begins to seem an involuntary parody of his precursor. This is particularly unfortunate whenever Pascal overtly denounces Montaigne, since sometimes we hear the pious son castigating the unbelieving father in the father's inescapable accents.

It has been surmised that Pascal jotted down his *Pensées* with his copy of Montaigne's *Essays* always lying open before him. Whether this was literally true or not, we may say that Montaigne was for Pascal quite simply a presence never to be put by. Eliot

speaks of Montaigne's readers as being "thoroughly infected" by him, and certainly Pascal must have known inwardly the anguish of contamination. What are we to do with Pensée 358, one example out of many:

> Man is neither angel nor brute, and the unfortunate thing is that he who would act the angel acts the brute.

That would have been admirable, had it not been lifted from the best essay every written, Montaigne's "Of Experience," where it is expressed with rather more force and insight:

> They want to get out of themselves and escape from the man. That is madness: instead of changing into angels, they change into beasts; instead of raising themselves, they lower themselves.

It is an ancient commonplace, but Montaigne plays variations on his sources, since his sense of self is his own. What is distressing is that Pascal does not evade or revise Montaigne but simply repeats him, presumably unaware of his bondage to his skeptical precursor. Since Pascal's mode is polemic, and Montaigne's is rumination and speculation, the rhetorical edge is different; Pascal emphasizes moral action, while Montaigne centers on moral being. Yet the reader is made uncomfortable, not because Pascal has appropriated Montaigne but because Pascal has manifested a paucity of invention. Voltaire and Valéry would seem to be confirmed. Pascal writes as a pragmatic enemy of Montaigne, and this necessarily makes Pascal, as Valéry said, into an enemy of humankind. We are

in a difficult situation enough, without being castigated by Pascal merely for being what we have to be. Do we still need Pascal? We read Montaigne as we read Shakespeare and Freud. How can we read Pascal?

Nietzsche insisted upon finding in Pascal an antithetical precursor, and shrewdly located Pascal's major error in the famous "wager":

> He supposes that he proves Christianity to be true because it is necessary. This presupposes that a good and truthful providence exists which ordains that everything necessary shall be true. But there can be necessary errors!

Later Nietzsche observed, "One should never forgive Christianity for having destroyed such men as Pascal." Yet Nietzsche also remarked, in a letter to Georg Brandes, that he almost loved Pascal for having been "the only *logical* Christian." The true link between the two was in their greatness as moral psychologists, a distinction they share with Montaigne and with Kierkegaard, and in another mode with Swift. Pascal's strong swerve away from Montaigne, which transcends his guilt of obligation to a naturalistic and skeptical master, is manifested in the development of a new kind of religious irony. Montaigne urges relativism because we are opaque to ideas of order other than our own, but this is precisely Pascal's motivation for our necessary surrender to God's will. Since God is hidden, according to Pascal, our condition is not less than tragic. A hidden God is doubly an incoherence for us; intolerable if he exists, and equally intolerable if he does not. We are thus

reduced to an ironic quietism, in which we are best off doing nothing in regard to worldly realities. We reject the order of society so thoroughly that pragmatically we can accept it totally.

The extraordinary ironies of *Provincial Letters* are founded upon this Pascalian stance that allows him to chastise the Jesuits for worldliness while defending society against them:

> *What will you do with someone who talks like that, and how will you attack me, since neither my words nor my writings afford any pretext for your accusation of heresy and I find protection against your threats in my own obscurity? You feel the blows of an unseen hand revealing your aberrations for all to see. You try in vain to attack me in the persons of those whom you believe to be my own allies. I am not afraid of you either on behalf of myself or of anyone else, as I am attached to no community and no individual whatsoever. All the credit you may enjoy from the world; I fear nothing from it, I desire nothing of it; by God's grace I need no one's wealth or authority. Thus, Father, I entirely escape your clutches. You cannot get hold of me however you try. You may well touch Port-Royal, but not me. Some have indeed been evicted from the Sorbonne, but that does not evict me from where I am. You may well prepare acts of violence against priests and doctors, but not against me who am without such titles. You have perhaps never had to deal with anyone so far out of your range and so well fitted to attack your errors, by being free, without commitments, without allegiance, without ties, without connexions, without interests; sufficiently*

acquainted with your precepts and determined to drive them as
far as I may believe myself obliged by God to do, without any
human consideration being able to halt or check my pursuit.

Implicit in this superbly polemical paragraph is the unassailable
rhetorical position of the ironic quietist, beyond this world yet its
only true defender. One calls this "unassailable" in Pascal's stance,
because his rhetoric and psychology are so intimately related to his
cosmology, and the three indeed are one. We have fallen into figuration, psychic division, and the eternal silence of the infinite spaces,
and all these ought to terrify us equally. Sara Melzer usefully emphasizes Pascal's difference from negative theology, to which I would
add Gnosticism, as the most negative of all theologies. God's oth-
erness, the Pascalian version of which is hiddenness, has nothing in
common with the alien God of the Gnostics and the Hermeticists.
For Pascal, the hiddenness leads to the wager of faith, rather than
to a negation of all tropes, terms for order, and scientific postulates.

If this is error, it is at least one of the necessary errors, psychologically speaking. Pascal never found his way out of the shadow
of Montaigne, not, I think, because Montaigne spoke also for Pascal's own skepticism, but because Montaigne was too authentic a
self and too strong a writer to need wagers of any kind. A paragraph like this, from the *Apology for Raymond Sebond*, must have
been a permanent reproach to Pascal:

Furthermore, it is here in us, and not elsewhere, that the powers
and actions of the soul should be considered. All the rest of its

perfections are vain and useless to it; it is for its present state that all its immortal life is to be paid and rewarded, and for man's life that is solely accountable. It would be an injustice to have cut short its resources and powers; to have disarmed it, and to pass judgment and a sentence of infinite and perpetual duration upon it, for the time of its captivity and imprisonment, its weakness and illness, the time when it was forced and constrained; and to stop at the consideration of so short a time, perhaps one or two hours, or at worst a century, which is no more in proportion to infinity than an instant; in order, from this moment of interval, to decide and dispose definitively of its whole existence. It would be an inequitable disproportion to receive eternal compensation in consequence of so short a life.

Against this, Pascal's eloquence and psychic intensity must fall short, even in the most notorious of the *Pensées:*

When I consider the short duration of my life, swallowed up in the eternity before and after, the little space which I fill, and even can see, engulfed in the infinite immensity of spaces of which I am ignorant, and which know me not, I am frightened, and am astonished at being here rather than there; for there is no reason why here rather than there, why now rather than then. Who has put me here? By whose order and direction have this place and time been allotted to me? Memoria hospitis unius diei prætereuntis. [205]

The eternal silence of these infinite spaces frightens me. [206]

"It is here in us, and not elsewhere, that the powers and actions of the soul should be considered." Montaigne remains in our mind, Pascal in our heart. Freud, the Montaigne of our era, reminded us that the voice of reason was not loud but would not rest until it gained a hearing. Montaigne's voice is never-resting, while Pascal's voice is restless. As Montaigne's involuntary and perpetual disciple, Pascal always knew which voice was stronger.

4

"What do I know?" is the most famous of Montaigne's questions. He knew himself, as most of us (myself included) never do. Pascal's God is hidden; Montaigne's is remote. Pascal is tormented; Montaigne is serene in his freedom to learn wisdom by studying himself. Catholicism, for him, is beyond skepticism, as Pascal and Eliot declined to understand, presumably because they needed to find wisdom there. And yet neither could evade Montaigne: there is a desperation in Eliot's lament that battling Montaigne is akin to throwing hand grenades into a fog. Once again, you cannot contain Shakespeare or Montaigne: they contain you.

The *Essays,* in Donald Frame's superb translation, take up some 850 large pages. If you read them straight through, and ponder what is offered, then something in you will be permanently changed. You may be no wiser or better, but you will know well a great charismatic, a personality that rivals the Shakespearean originals: Falstaff, Hamlet, Cleopatra. Is there any other writer (except perhaps Dante, Whitman, and Tolstoy) so large in spirit as is

Montaigne? Shakespeare, Emerson remarked, will reveal himself only to the Shakespeare in us, but Montaigne all but totally will award his self-knowledge even to the abyss each carries within us.

We learn that Hamlet neither wants us nor needs us. Montaigne, in the mode of Falstaff, desires to ward off melancholia. Wisdom heals melancholy, if only we can allow our grief and mourning to be assuaged. Montaigne expresses love only for his father (not for his mother, his wife, his daughter) and for his single friend, Étienne de La Boétie, dead at thirty-two, after six years of close friendship with Montaigne. The great essayist, thirty when he lost La Boétie, never risked another friendship. Though the turbulence of politics frequently absorbed him, generally as a mediator between Catholics and Protestants in the French civil wars of religion, Montaigne longed for reading and writing in solitude, which across twenty years made the *Essays* possible.

The hero of the most crucial of the *Essays* is always Socrates, both Plato's and Xenophon's, but the distinction matters little, because Montaigne's Socrates is finally his own, as here in the magnificent essay "Of Physiognomy":

> *Socrates makes his soul move with a natural and common motion. So says a peasant, so says a woman. His mouth is full of nothing but carters, joiners, cobblers, and masons. His are inductions and similes drawn from the commonest and best-known actions of men; everyone understands him. Under so mean a form we should never have picked out the nobility and splendor of his admirable ideas, we who consider flat and low all ideas*

that are not raised up by learning, and who perceive richness only in pomp and show. Our world is formed only for ostentation; men inflate themselves only with wind, and go bouncing around like balls. This man did not propose to himself any idle fancies: his aim was to furnish us with things and precepts that serve life really and more closely:

> *To keep the mean, to hold our aim in view,*
> *And follow nature.*
>
> LUCAN

He was also always one and the same, and raised himself, not by sallies and dispositions, to the utmost point of vigor. Or, to speak more exactly, he raised nothing, but rather brought vigor, hardships, and difficulties down and back to his own natural and original level, and subjected them to it. For in Cato we see very clearly that his is a pace strained far above the ordinary; in the brave exploits of his life and in his death we feel that he is always mounted on his high horse. The other walks close to the ground, and at a gentle and ordinary pace treats the most useful subjects; and behaves, both in the face of death and in the thorniest trials that can confront us, in the ordinary way of human life.

It happened fortunately that the man most worthy to be known and to be presented to the world as an example should be the one of whom we have the most certain knowledge. We have light on him from the most clear-sighted men who ever lived;

the witnesses we have of him are wonderful in fidelity and competence.

It is a great thing to have been able to impart such order to the pure and simple notions of a child that, without altering or stretching them, he produced from them the most beautiful achievements of our soul. He shows it as neither elevated nor rich; he shows it only as healthy, but assuredly with a very blithe and clear health. By these vulgar and natural motives, by these ordinary and common ideas, without excitement or fuss, he constructed not only the best regulated but the loftiest and most vigorous beliefs, actions, and morals that ever were. It is he who brought human wisdom back down from heaven, where she was wasting her time, and restored her to man, with whom lies her most proper and laborious and useful business. See him plead before his judges, see by what reasonings he rouses his courage in the hazards of war, what arguments fortify his patience against calumny, tyranny, death, and his wife's bad temper. There is nothing borrowed from art and the sciences; even the simplest can recognize in him their means and their strength; it is impossible to go back further and lower. He did a great favor to human nature by showing how much it can do by itself.

Plato's Socrates serves the transcendental Good, while Xenophon's teaches endurance, heroism, and all other soldierly virtues. Montaigne's Socrates rescues human wisdom from heavenly exile, and returns her to share our labors. Divine wisdom is larger than we can absorb. A wealth already ours is activated by this Socrates. He brings us neither dialectics nor virtue, but a state of the

spirit that is a unique strength, directed toward itself. Such strength, and not fear of the god, is the beginning of wisdom. The secret of Montaigne is in this unnamed strength, which is a kind of natural directness in the way the common people live and die. They accept themselves, and they and Socrates taught Montaigne to do the same.

Is that a wisdom that can be linked to the reading of the strongest literature? You don't need to appoint yourself defender of canonical literature to show others that period pieces and commercial rubbish cannot yield any wisdom, let alone the strength that is the wisdom Montaigne exalts. There is a substance in us that prevails, Wallace Stevens insists, and its vivid portrayals require no defense. But if Montaigne possesses a secret, he wants it revealed to his most vigorous readers. Where shall we seek it except in "Of Experience," the essay he chose to close his book?

5
—

"In the experience I have of myself I find enough to make me wise, if I were a good scholar." Montaigne's ironies tend to be clear; this is not one of them. In this most intimate of his essays, he details his diet and his digestion, his table habits, and states his credo:

> We are great fools. "He has spent his life in idleness," we say; "I
> have done nothing today." What, have you not lived? That is
> not only the fundamental but the most illustrious of your occu-
> pations. "If I had been placed in a position to manage great

affairs, I would have shown what I could do." Have you been
able to think out and manage your own life? You have done the
greatest task of all. To show and exploit her resources Nature
has no need of fortune; she shows herself equally on all levels
and behind a curtain as well as without one. To compose our
character is our duty, not to compose books, and to win, not bat-
tles and provinces, but order and tranquility in our conduct. Our
great and glorious masterpiece is to live appropriately. All other
things, ruling, hoarding, building, are only little appendages and
props, at most.

Certainly this is Xenophon's Socrates, but the emphasis makes
him Montaigne's own, and leads on to another of the essayist's
triumphs:

There is nothing so beautiful and legitimate as to play the man
well and properly, no knowledge so hard to acquire as the knowl-
edge of how to live life well and naturally; and the most bar-
barous of our maladies is to despise our being.

As secular wisdom this may well be the most cogent, if it can
yield to the common reader's interpretation. Ragged Socrates,
grotesque and hemmed in by circumstance, possesses absolute
self-knowledge, and his stance of professed ignorance cannot be
his own, but is Plato's supreme fiction, beautifully exploited in
Phaedo, which with *Symposium* seems to me Plato's aesthetic glory
at its outer limit. Even the greatest of Hebrew heroes, David,
ancestor of Jesus, knows his total dependence on God. The prophet

Samuel had given David a blessing in order to confer royal status, a blessing finally confirmed by Yahweh himself. The great writer who gave us II Samuel portrays the agony of David despising himself, which always reminds me of Hamlet's malady of believing simultaneously that he is everything and nothing in himself. There Hamlet departs from Montaigne and returns to the translator William Tyndale's David. All of us have known and still must know those hours when we despise our being. Montaigne, if he is to become our teacher, urges us to dismiss those hours as "the most barbarous of our maladies."

Montaigne's sublimity rises to its own interpretation of the cure for this worst of maladies in the final passage of the *Essays*, the conclusion to "Of Experience":

> They want to get out of themselves and escape from the man. That is madness: instead of changing into angels, they change into beasts; instead of raising themselves, they lower themselves. These transcendental humors frighten me, like lofty and inaccessible places; and nothing is so hard for me to stomach in the life of Socrates as his ecstasies and possessions by his daemon, nothing is so human in Plato as the qualities for which they say he is called divine. And of our sciences, those seem to me most terrestrial and low which have risen the highest. And I find nothing so humble and so mortal in the life of Alexander as his fancies about this immortalization. Philotas stung him wittily by his answer. He congratulated him by letter on the oracle of Jupiter

Ammon which had lodged him among the gods: "As far as you are concerned, I am very glad of it; but there is reason to pity the men who will have to live with and obey a man who exceeds and is not content with a man's proportions."

Since you obey the gods, you rule the world.

HORACE

The nice inscription with which the Athenians honored the entry of Pompey into their city is in accord with my meaning.

You are as much a god as you will own
That you are nothing but a man alone.

AMYOT'S PLUTARCH

It is an absolute perfection and virtually divine to know how to enjoy our being rightfully. We seek other conditions because we do not understand the use of our own, and go outside of ourselves because we do not know what it is like inside. Yet there is no use our mounting on stilts, for on stilts we must still walk on our own legs. And on the loftiest throne in the world we are still sitting only on our own rump.

The most beautiful lives, to my mind, are those that conform to the common human pattern, with order, but without miracle and without eccentricity. Now old age needs to be treated a little more tenderly. Let us commend it to that god who is the protector of health and wisdom, but gay and sociable wisdom:

Grant me but health, Latona's son,
And to enjoy the wealth I've won,
And honored age, with mind entire
And not unsolaced by the lyre.

HORACE

A wisdom both cheerful and sociable is neither biblical nor Platonic, but prophesies both Sancho Panza and Falstaff. This is wisdom both literary and pragmatic. If we observed literary birthdays as Catholics do saints' days, I would mark February 28 on my calendar. That is the day in 1553 on which Montaigne was born, near Bordeaux. Of all French authors, at least until Proust, Montaigne remains the wisest and the most universal.

FRANCIS BACON

In Bacon, as in Montaigne, philosophy is not a Platonic preparation for death. Though some of their scholars describe Montaigne and Bacon as Catholic and Protestant respectively, I find that to be a difference that makes no difference. The skepticism and self-acceptance of Montaigne dominate his essays, while Bacon's idiosyncratic balance between a newly molded rationalism and an untraditional esotericism is not particularly Christian. The poet Shelley's passion for Bacon reflects the visionary of *Prometheus Unbound*'s customary accuracy in seeking out precursors. In his death fragment, *The Triumph of Life,* Shelley allows Rousseau (another admirer of Bacon) the

ultimate praise of the English aphorist and speculator, supreme empiricist and overthrower of Aristotle, who

> . . . still had kept
> The jealous keys of truth's eternal doors
>
> If Bacon's spirit . . . had not leapt
> Like lightning out of darkness; he compelled
> The Proteus shape of Nature's as it slept
>
> To wake & to unbar the caves that held
> The treasures of the secrets of its reign—.

In *A Defence of Poetry*, Shelley insisted that Plato and Bacon were poets:

> An observation to the regular mode of the recurrence of harmony in the language of poetical minds, together with its relation to music, produced metre, or a certain system of traditional forms of harmony and language. Yet it is by no means essential that a poet should accommodate his language to this traditional form, so that the harmony, which is its spirit, be observed. The practice is indeed convenient and popular, and to be preferred, especially in such composition as includes much action: but every great poet must inevitably innovate upon the example of his predecessors in the exact structure of his peculiar versification. The distinction between poets and prose writers is a vulgar error. The distinction between philosophers and poets has been antici-

pated. Plato was essentially a poet—the truth and splendour of his imagery, and the melody of his language, are the most intense that it is possible to conceive. He rejected the measure of the epic, dramatic, and lyrical forms, because he sought to kindle a harmony in thoughts divested of shape and action, and he forbore to invent any regular plan of rhythm which would include, under determinate forms, the varied pauses of his style. Cicero sought to imitate the cadence of his periods, but with little success. Lord Bacon was a poet. His language has a sweet and majestic rhythm, which satisfies the sense, no less than the almost superhuman wisdom of his philosophy satisfies the intellect; it is a strain which distends, and then bursts the circumference of the reader's mind, and pours itself forth together with it into the universal element with which it has perpetual sympathy. All the authors of revolutions in opinion are not only necessarily poets as they are inventors, nor even as their words unveil the permanent analogy of things by images which participate in the life of truth; but as their periods are harmonious and rhythmical, and contain in themselves the elements of verse; being the echo of the eternal music. Nor are those supreme poets, who have employed traditional forms of rhythm on account of the form and action of their subjects, less capable of perceiving and teaching the truth of things, than those who have omitted that form. Shakespeare, Dante, and Milton (to confine ourselves to modern writers) are philosophers of the very loftiest power.

Subtly (as is his wont) Shelley subverts Plato's restatement of "the ancient quarrel between poetry and philosophy." One of

Bacon's two "poems" cited by Shelley is the famous second essay, "Of Death," in what is now Bacon's most popular work, the beautiful *Essays or Counsels, Civil and Moral*, definitively enlarged in 1625. Like most of Bacon's essays, it is condensed and gnomic, occupying only three brief paragraphs. Few meditations upon death open so eloquently:

> *Men fear Death, as children fear to go in the dark; and as that natural fear in children is increased with tales, so is the other. Certainly, the contemplation of death, as the wages of sin and passage to another world, is holy and religious; but the fear of it, as a tribute due unto nature, is weak. Yet in religious meditations there is sometimes mixture of vanity and of superstition. You shall read in some of the friars' books of mortification, that a man should think with himself what the pain is if he have but his finger's end pressed or tortured, and thereby imagine what the pains of death are, when the whole body is corrupted and dissolved; when many times death passeth with less pain than the torture of a limb: for the most vital parts are not the quickest of sense. And by him that spake only as a philosopher and natural man, it was well said, 'Pompa mortis magis terret, quam mors ipsa'. Groans and convulsions, and a discoloured face, and friends weeping, and blacks, and obsequies, and the like, shew death terrible.*

The Roman moralist Seneca is the chief source here, but the precursor being battled is Montaigne, who had dismissed Seneca's writing on death in the great "Of Physiognomy" (*Essays* III, 12),

the penultimate statement preceding Montaigne's masterpiece, the final "Of Experience." Whereas Seneca advises us to anticipate the worst, Montaigne, grand as Shakespeare's Hamlet (Montaigne's student), tells us:

If you don't know how to die, don't worry; Nature will tell you what to do on the spot, fully and adequately. She will do this job perfectly for you; don't bother your head about it.

Ben Jonson argued that his friend Bacon was Montaigne's superior as an essayist, which is about as plausible as preferring Jonson to Shakespeare. Bacon is a superb essayist and Jonson wrote magnificent comedies in *Volpone* and *The Alchemist,* but *The Complete Essays of Montaigne* and Shakespeare's totality of plays and poems are literary universes. Bacon and Jonson are wisdom writers in a narrower sense.

We have an enormous number of outward facts about Shakespeare, but of his inwardness we know only what we can glean from his work. Montaigne, as has been shown, is totally self-revelatory, while the outspoken Ben Jonson is almost as open. Bacon, despite his public career as a statesman, remains enigmatic. Few who study his life and works come to love him or them. Scholars are not even in agreement as to how Bacon is to be categorized. Is he a philosopher? I would prefer to call him a sage, like Emerson (totally antithetical to Bacon), or rather more like Freud (an intense admirer of his English forerunner). Sages can be pleasant or unpleasant: Bacon was perhaps as unpleasant as he was brilliant, original, and incapable of loving anyone. Abstractly, Bacon loved the future,

in which technology would liberate mankind. Inundated as we now are by information technology, one wonders if Bacon's dream has not turned into nightmare.

Montaigne's public life did not end when he retreated into his chosen lonely tower to study, and to compose his essays, but even the French civil wars between Catholics and Protestants were only distractions for him. Bacon, unlike Montaigne, craved political power, and finally achieved it, only to fall from the high place of glory into disgrace. Enigmatic as his public career became, he remained always the most idiosyncratic of thinkers, a kind of visionary empiricist and dissimulating Epicurean, invariably living and imagining luxuriously, both well beyond his means. Dead at sixty-five, Bacon was over 20,000 pounds sterling in debt, a vast sum in 1626. His widow, married only for her money, and apparently never touched by him, waited fewer than three weeks before marrying his principal servant. According to John Aubrey's lively *Brief Lives* (1681), she rendered her second husband "deaf and blind, with too much of Venus," thus reacting to twenty years of sexual frustration.

Bacon's political career justifies Alexander Pope's characterization of him as "the wisest, brightest, meanest of mankind." The youngest son of Sir Nicholas Bacon, a highly placed adviser to Queen Elizabeth, Francis studied first at Cambridge, and then was educated in law at Grays Inn. At twenty, he was in Parliament, and would have attained high rank at Elizabeth's court had he not displeased her by speaking out against increased royal taxes in 1593. After publishing a first version of his *Essays* in 1597, he served as government prosecutor in the trial that condemned the Earl of

Essex to death. Since Bacon had received enormous financial patronage from Essex, this state service was humanly rather dubious, and helped establish the pattern that ultimately ruined the lavishly overspending politician.

Under King James I, the most learned ever of all English monarchs, Bacon rose rapidly, until in 1618 he became Lord Chancellor, and was created Baron Verulam. By 1621, Bacon was apparently secure in power, and was created Viscount St. Alban, but later that year was himself convicted of taking bribes on a grand scale. Stripped of the Lord Chancellorship, he was fined 40,000 pounds, briefly imprisoned, and then pardoned back to private life.

In the five years remaining to him, Bacon wrote copiously, both in Latin and in his inimitable English. A third, final edition of the superb *Essays* (now enlarged to fifty-eight) came forth in 1625, the year before his death. By then he had a European reputation for his originality and power as a thinker and eloquent aphorist, a wisdom writer widely acclaimed. In England, his literary achievement was canonized by a sequence of great writers, commencing with his friends Thomas Hobbes and Ben Jonson and going on through Dr. Johnson and Alexander Pope to the Romantic tradition of Samuel Taylor Coleridge, Thomas De Quincey, William Hazlitt, and, most fervently, Shelley. Of the Victorian prophets, John Ruskin had a particular reverence for Bacon.

Bacon's prose is extraordinarily wrought, and I find that my memory possesses some of the essays as fully as if they were lyric or meditative poems. The second essay, "Of Death," I have cited already. Here is the opening of the crucial sixth essay, "Of

Simulation and Dissimulation," followed by its self-revelatory final paragraph:

> Dissimulation is but a faint kind of policy or wisdom; for it asketh a strong wit and a strong heart to know when to tell truth, and to do it. Therefore it is the weaker of politiques that are the great dissemblers.

> The great advantages of simulation and dissimulation are three. First, to lay asleep opposition, and to surprise. For where a man's intentions are published, it is an alarum to call up all that are against them. The second is, to reserve to a man's self a fair retreat. For if a man engage himself by a manifest declaration, he must go through or take a fall. The third is, the better to discover the mind of another. For to him that opens himself men will hardly shew themselves adverse; but will (fair) let him go on, and turn their freedom of speech to freedom of thought. And therefore it is a good shrewd proverb of the Spaniard, 'Tell a lie and find a truth.' As if there were no way of discovery but by simulation. There be also three disadvantages, to set it even. The first, that simulation and dissimulation commonly carry with them a shew of fearfulness, which in any business doth spoil the feathers of round flying up to the mark. The second, that it puzzleth and perplexeth the conceits of many, that perhaps would otherwise co-operate with him; and makes a man walk almost alone to his own ends. The third, and greatest, is, that it depriveth a man of one of the most principal instruments for action; which is trust and belief. The best composition and temperament

is to have openness in fame and opinion; secrecy in habit; dis-
simulation in seasonable use; and a power to feign, if there be no
remedy.

Bacon was one of the masters of dissimulation, as Montaigne was also, though in a different mode, slyer than Bacon's. Montaigne's modesty, as I have indicated, was a mask or rhetorical "deceit," part of his originality at indirect communication. Bacon has no modesty, yet his dissimulation is darker than Montaigne's Socratic irony. Who among us would desire a friend, lover, companion, or spouse whose temperament is reputed as frank, yet who is secretive, well seasoned at lying, and a strong feigner, acting out life and death as a play? Montaigne does not see his own life as theater, but Bacon has a touch of Hamlet in him. Like Hamlet's, Bacon's open hand can modulate swiftly into a clenched fist. If Montaigne wants to persuade you, it is not by argument or authority, but through insinuation. Bacon is not so tendentious as Saint Augustine or Sigmund Freud, but the philosopher-scientist was firmly convinced that he had both truth and wisdom to communicate.

Anne Righter Barton, one of the best Shakespearean critics, defends Bacon from the chorus of denigrators he has attracted among modern academics. She joins Shelley in seeing Bacon as a prose poet, whose style was "responsive to the slightest demands made upon it," and she accurately praises the variety of his prose, which made him an artist almost despite himself. His isolation, drive to persuade, fear of time's ravages, and sensory images are the factors she cites as crucial to his achievement. Like Freud,

another master of persuasive prose, Bacon was a kind of conquistador in his life's enterprise. Yet Bacon was, more than Freud, a dramatist of ideas, and had affinities with Shakespearean wisdom.

Bacon's authentic genre was wisdom writing, which tends to rely on aphorisms, where Bacon was most himself. Anne Righter Barton, knowing that Bacon wished totally to reorient learning, shrewdly calls him a "ghostly anti-Hamlet." The aphorisms of Hamlet consistently are ironic: they do not say what they mean, and frequently do not mean what they appear to say. Bacon, except when he dissimulates, can be quite desperate in conveying his wisdom, whereas Hamlet does not much care. Hamlet rarely keeps a secret for very long: his wisdom is that all perspectives are at home in him. Bacon pursued a secret wisdom, to be revealed only as it suited him. Where Dr. Johnson humanely considered love to be the wisdom of fools and the folly of the wise, Bacon considered it to be destructive of wisdom. His apparent homosexuality may have been an element in that avoidance of passion.

Of all his contemporaries, Ben Jonson valued Bacon the most. What Jonson made of Bacon's close affinity with Machiavelli, we do not know. Bacon's judgment of the common people was far more negative than Machiavelli's, whose spirit was generous and humane, despite Renaissance caricatures. It seems fair to observe that Bacon was not at all benign.

2

The wisdom of Montaigne, as we saw earlier in this chapter, has everything to do with how we ought to live: self-knowledge leads to self-acceptance, accurate self-expectations, and goodness toward the self and others. There, I essentially followed Donald Frame, Montaigne's definitive translator.

The wisdom of Bacon is far more equivocal, and no scholar has offered us an adequate summary of it. To be told by Bacon himself that human sovereignty lies in knowledge is a beginning, and certainly Bacon is a sage of learning. But to what end? He had a lifelong attachment to the Proverbs of Solomon, and they reverberate throughout his work. But where Proverbs 8:22–31 gives us wisdom as a woman in close relation to God, that sequence is not particularly Baconian. Elsewhere, the Proverbs frequently suggest Bacon, and explain why his visionary *New Atlantis* is ruled by the precepts of its founder, King Solamona. The wise who come after him follow his tradition, yet achieve authority through their own wisdom.

King Solamona's wisdom, like Bacon's, is founded on *secrecy.* Bensalem, the utopia of New Atlantis, is a closed society, rather like that of the Mormon hierarchy of Salt Lake City, which preserves its own secrets, as Joseph Smith and Brigham Young, the Solamonas of the Latter-day Saints, shrewdly advised.

In The Advancement of Learning, Book Two, Bacon admires the aphorisms or Proverbs of Solomon, and gives a cento of his own

favorites among them. They are the implicit ground rules of Salomon's House, founded as the center of power by Solamona, who thus inaugurates both an Academy and a benevolent tyranny, on the model of Plato's Republic. We ought to expect this: New Atlantis returns us to Plato's fable of Atlantis in *Timaeus* and *Critias*. The first Atlantis was overwhelmed by the waves; New Atlantis will see people dominate nature and make themselves literally immortal. Bacon's wisdom becomes that of a post-Christian Magus; the instauration of a New Age will restore the Wisdom of the Ancients, who preceded the Greeks and the Hebrews. Wisdom, for Bacon, is both scientific and irrational, and will withstand Time.

Despite the intricate surface of his *Essays,* Bacon is as magical as Shakespeare's Prospero. At heart, Francis Bacon is a mythologue, like an aspect of Plato, though he labors to replace Plato with the Bible, Bacon's Bible we might call it. For Bacon's wisdom is esoteric though essentially original and in no way mystical. He is a technocrat, and a prophet of what has happened to us in our Age of Information. Knowledge is the only good, which is not to say that Bacon would have us drown in the ocean of the Internet. Championing the sophists against Plato and Aristotle, as Bacon does, is for him not an abandonment of the goods of the soul. Bacon wishes to heal violence, in the age of religious warfare between Protestants and Catholics. His wisdom is humanist, and more than a little plangent, since he too inherits Erasmus's sense of the pathos of Humanism, always badly in need of defense.

The common reader's access to Bacon is through the *Essays,* to which I will return. But the more inquiring spirits among readers should turn to *The Wisdom of the Ancients* (1609), thirty-one idio-

syncratic interpretations of classical fables, and to what could be called Bacon's polemical epitome, the famous "Idols of the Mind," one hundred and thirty packed aphoristic numbered paragraphs from Book I of the *Novum Organum* (1620). Many editions of the essays have appendices giving selections from both sequences, and readers will see again Shelley's justice in naming Bacon as a great prose poet.

In *The Wisdom of the Ancients,* Bacon's fables commence with Cassandra and end with the Sirens, while notably including Orpheus, Daedalus, Dionysus, and Prometheus along the way. C. W. Lemmi, in *The Classic Deities in Bacon* (1933), stresses the esoteric sources of the great scientific philosopher, finding them particularly in alchemy. As Lemmi itemizes Bacon's debts, the distance between Bacon and the Hermetic philosopher Giordano Bruno begins to wane. Hermetic doctrines of transmutation crowd Bacon's fables. Paracelsus and Raymond Llull infiltrate *The Wisdom of the Ancients,* as indeed they should, since Bacon's wisdom is both esoteric and secretive, rather than rhetorically disguised, like Montaigne's or that of Plato's Socrates.

The most revelatory of *The Wisdom of the Ancients* is "Prometheus or the State of Man," in which Bacon alters the traditional story. Instead of stealing fire from Heaven for the sake of mankind, Prometheus is accused by Jupiter of attempting to rape Minerva, Goddess of Wisdom and daughter of the High God. On this account, Prometheus is Bacon's foretype, though Bacon will not quite say so:

I must now return to a part which, that I might not interrupt the connexion of what precedes, I have purposely passed by. I mean that last crime of Prometheus, the attempt upon the chastity of Minerva. For it was even for this offence—certainly a very great and grave one—that he underwent that punishment of the tearing of his entrails. The crime alluded to appears to be no other than that into which men not unfrequently fall when puffed up with arts and much knowledge—of trying to bring the divine wisdom itself under the dominion of sense and reason: from which attempt inevitably follows laceration of the mind and vexation without end or rest. And therefore men must soberly and modestly distinguish between things divine and human, between the oracles of sense and of faith; unless they mean to have at once a heretical religion and a fabulous philosophy.

Whether Bacon's religion was heretical cannot be answered, but certainly his fabulous philosophy attempted "to bring the divine wisdom itself under the dominion of sense and reason." Yet his identification with Prometheus, unlike Shelley's, is ambivalent. Perhaps we never can see Bacon plain. Our best hope for doing so is in the sequence of aphorisms, *Idols of the Mind,* that make up Book I of the *Novum Organum:*

1

There are four classes of Idols which beset men's minds. To these for distinction's sake I have assigned names—calling the first class Idols of the Tribe; *the second,* Idols of the Cave; *the*

third, Idols of the Market-place; *the fourth*, Idols of the Theatre.

2

The formation of ideas and axioms by true induction is no doubt the proper remedy to be applied for the keeping off and clearing away of idols. To point them out, however, is of great use, for the doctrine of Idols is to the Interpretation of Nature what the doctrine of the refutation of Sophisms is to common Logic.

3

The Idols of the Tribe have their foundation in human nature itself, and in the tribe or race of men. For it is a false assertion that the sense of man is the measure of things. On the contrary, all perceptions as well of the sense as of the mind are according to the measure of the individual and not according to the measure of the universe. And the human understanding is like a false mirror, which, receiving rays irregularly, distorts and discolours the nature of things by mingling its own nature with it.

4

The Idols of the Cave are the idols of the individual man. For every one (besides the errors common to human nature in general) has a cave or den of his own, which refracts and discolours the light of nature; owing either to his own proper and peculiar nature; or to his education and conversation with others; or to the reading of books, and the authority of those whom he esteems

and admires; or to the differences of impressions, accordingly as they take place in a mind preoccupied and predisposed or in a mind indifferent and settled; or the like. So that the spirit of man (according as it is meted out to different individuals) is in fact a thing variable and full of perturbation, and governed as it were by chance. Whence it was well observed by Heraclitus that men look for sciences in their own lesser worlds, and not in the greater or common world.

5

There are also Idols formed by the intercourse and association of men with each other, which I call Idols of the Market-place, on account of the commerce and consort of men there. For it is by discourse that men associate, and words are imposed according to the apprehension of the vulgar. And therefore the ill and unfit choice of words wonderfully obstructs the understanding. Nor do the definitions or explanations wherewith in some things learned men are wont to guard and defend themselves, by any means set the matter right. But words plainly force and overrule the understanding, and throw all into confusion, and lead men away into numberless empty controversies and idle fancies.

6

Lastly, there are Idols which have immigrated into men's minds from the various dogmas of philosophies, and also from wrong laws of demonstration. These I call Idols of the Theatre, because in my judgment all the received systems are but so many stage-plays, representing worlds of their own creation after an unreal

164

and scenic fashion. Nor is it only of the systems now in vogue, or only of the ancient sects and philosophies, that I speak; for many more plays of the same kind may yet be composed and in like artificial manner set forth, seeing that errors the most widely different have nevertheless causes for the most part alike. Neither again do I mean this only of entire systems, but also of many principles and axioms in science, which by tradition, credulity, and negligence have come to be received.

But of these several kinds of Idols I must speak more largely and exactly, that the understanding may be duly cautioned.

Bacon's aphorisms, here at their most mature, generate an aura of wisdom, relying on an internalization of the biblical rejection of idols, and also upon the Platonic dismissal of shadows in the myth of the Cave in the *Republic*. That did not save Plato from Bacon's Christian condemnation as "groveling before . . . confused idols." Bacon, surprisingly, desires to enter into the Kingdom of Heaven, and needs to cast out all idols in order to be welcomed there. He is not exactly Jeremiah the Prophet, but rather a secularist seeking to appropriate biblical categories for his private ends. His Idols of the Mind are not false gods impersonating Yahweh but the false knowledge of men who have not yet studied Bacon. His attack upon the Idols is a persuasive redefinition of Christianity, and not the outcry of a repentant Christian returning to the Gospel and the Prophets. To accuse Bacon of bad faith would be redundant; he is nothing but bad faith. He knows it, and does not bother to shrug it off.

That does not prevent his fourfold division of Idols from being strikingly wise and pragmatically useful. Who among us is free of

the worship of Idols of the Tribe, the Cave, the Market-place, the Theatre? The Tribe is all men and women. We are not the measure of all things, but their dupes. The Cave is personal, a den closed in upon itself, cut off from the common world. The Market-place of commerce we know too well. And the Theatre is not the arts, not the dramas of Shakespeare, but whatever theories are fashionable at a particular time.

Comparing Bacon as a wisdom writer with Montaigne can be destructive to Bacon, but who since the Bible and Plato's Socrates, and then Cervantes and Shakespeare, can sustain that comparison? Freud believed that only he could overcome the immense difficulties of self-analysis; he forgot Montaigne. Readers of Bacon now tend not to see him as a liberator of human potential, as Shelley and Rousseau did. The great instaurator chooses not to know himself, at least in his writings, and his Prometheanism lacks pathos. Though his style cannot contaminate you, its variety is enormous, almost always brilliantly aphoristic. Very few readers I encounter love Francis Bacon, and his modernity is by now a weary concept. Progress, his driving ideal, gives us one technology after another, but less and less self-knowledge.

CHAPTER 5

SAMUEL JOHNSON

AND GOETHE

DR. SAMUEL JOHNSON

At one point in his Conversations with Eckermann, Goethe asks his Boswell, Eckermann, to read his contemporary Johnson's *Rasselas* for him. I cannot recall a single mention of Goethe by Johnson. All that the two sages have in common is the vast scale of intimate knowledge we possess of both their lives. Perhaps Napoleon and Freud are the only other figures we know in such detail.

A conversation between Johnson and Goethe is all but inconceivable. Perhaps a gathering of Shakespeare, Plato, and Oscar Wilde, put together in Eternity, could create it. Shakespeare would convey the inability of the English critic and the German poet to listen to each other, while Plato would mold the irony of the encounter, and Wilde suggest the wasted wit.

Though I myself have loved and tried to imitate Dr. Johnson

since my adolescence, Goethe is an endless wonder to me, an authentic miracle of literary fecundity at its most absolute. Johnson still seems to me the best of all literary critics, while Goethe is the unmatchable poet of Old Europe. Johnson would have been a great poet, except that he believed English poetry had achieved formal perfection with Alexander Pope, which, from a Neoclassical stance, is true. As a critic, Johnson ranked Shakespeare and Milton with Homer, but he did not love them as he did Pope. Goethe acknowledged Shakespeare to be a vastness beyond him, but rejoiced that nothing before the Goethean advent in the German language could inhibit him in any regard. Except for Shakespeare, the miracle of quite another language, Goethe reigned alone upon Olympus. The pugnacious Johnson, as his "Vanity of Human Wishes" demonstrates, perhaps might have outshone Pope, but he so revered the workmanship of his precursor that he largely gave up poetry, and developed instead his own extraordinary style: an orotund sublimity superbly adequate for conveying wisdom.

Johnson's literary criticism and Goethe's poetry are secondary for me here; I wish to contrast them as wisdom writers, which means primarily as moral aphorists, where they totally diverge. Goethe was an instinctive pagan, believing in his own daemonic endowment and spontaneously manifesting the "joyful wisdom" that Nietzsche so desperately sought to attain. The Johnsonian wisdom is somber and mordant, in the mode of Ecclesiastes. Though he exalted (and pretty well invented) "the common reader" rendered yet more famous by Virginia Woolf, Johnson hated solitude, which to me seems crucial now if reading is to survive at all. The demigod Goethe, universally revered as literature

itself, enjoyed whatever solitude he commanded, since the world came to his feet whenever summoned.

2
—

Johnson, sincerely a Christian sage, set himself against cant, now the curse both of the universities and of the media. For a decade, 1746–1756, he was a lexicographer, and his *Dictionary* labors taught him to despise the slogans of politics and allied ideologies. Cant at our moment is best exemplified by those who decry anyone opposing tax cuts for the wealthiest as proponents of "class war-fare," and by academic resenters who dismiss all cognitive and aesthetic standards as masks for "racism" and "sexism." Johnson serves me as almost a last resource against the madness of ranting against such mindless provocations. He teaches the long view: "All censure of a man's self is oblique praise. It is in order to show how much he can spare."

Johnson disliked mere history and loved biography, thus anticipating Emerson's "There is no history, only biography." He also was averse to prose that adhered to plain fact, not as opposed to fiction but rather language that avoided elaboration. W. K. Wimsatt, Jr., in his admirable *The Prose Style of Samuel Johnson* (1941), says that the Johnsonian aim was "to multiply words, to use various expressions, to deal not in things but in thoughts about things." Johnson expresses this splendidly in *Rambler* No. 3:

The task of an author is, either to teach what is not known, or to recommend known truths by his manner of adorning them; either to let new light in upon the mind, and open new scenes to the prospect, or to vary the dress and situation of common objects, so as to give them fresh grace and more powerful attractions, to spread such flowers over the regions through which the intellect has already made its progress, as may tempt it to return, and take a second view of things hastily passed over or negligently regarded.

I cannot think of a better counsel for wisdom writing: it must be *rich,* which is why Shakespeare, richest of all stylists, is also the wisest of authors. In the Preface to his great *Dictionary,* Johnson uttered a nostalgia for what he knew had never been, a fusion of idea and thing:

I am not yet so lost in lexicography, as to forget that words are the daughters of earth, and that things are the sons of heaven. *Language is only the instrument of science, and words are but the signs of ideas: I wish, however, that the instrument might be less apt to decay, and that signs might be permanent, like the things which they denote.*

This is the lament of all lexicographers, eloquently summoned up by Robert Burchfield, in his *Unlocking the English Language* (1989). Dr. Samuel Johnson, lion of literary critics and lexicographers alike, taught us that the essence of poetry is invention, in the sense of discovery. Robert Burchfield, Johnsonian lexicographer, teaches

us that invention also is the essence of language, though this is a teaching that does not altogether console him or us:

> *The English language is now at an uneasy stage of its develop-*
> *ment and expansion: the sheer voluminousness and complexity*
> *of the network of the language throughout the English-speaking*
> *world place almost insuperable obstacles in the path of those*
> *whose job it is to set down an accurate record of all of its*
> *varieties.*

Burchfield, though wary of a future in which lexicographers may be replaced by clerks, refuses to be the elegist of his craft. If the reader seeks Borgesian parables of the last lexicographer, that quest must be fulfilled elsewhere. Politics and social movements shadow the lexicographer as they do the literary critic, and Burchfield accepts new pressures on his enterprise, sometimes ruefully, but always with a stoic grace. His balanced defense of the lexicographer caught between bitter camps is manifested most forcefully in the essay "The Turn of the Screw: Ethnic Vocabulary and Dictionaries," where the key words are *"Jew, Palestinian, Arab, Pakistan, Turk, Asiatic, Muhammadan,* and *Negro."* With a sad dignity, Burchfield murmurs that "dictionaries cannot be regulative in matters of social, political, and religious attitudes." As a literary critic, I want to assert as much for criticism, if it is to remain the realm of aesthetic description and judgment, but like Burchfield I sense the encroachments of our Age of Resentment.

As the editor of the four-volume *Supplement to the Oxford English Dictionary* (final volume published in 1986), Burchfield gave

nearly thirty years to his Johnsonian task, and emerged from it
with a Johnsonian literary humanism enhanced. He is a historical
philologist, which is to be a dissident in an era dominated by
descriptive linguistics. A critic who takes (as I do) a historical view
of rhetoric, as opposed to the theory of Paul de Man, is bound to
be attracted by Burchfield's principles. What vanishes in deconstructive criticism is the pragmatic distinction between denota-
tion, or naming, and connotation, or association, upon which
poetry depends. Saussure sets a bar between signifier and signified,
but then cannot tell us on which side of the bar connotation is to
be discovered. Without a sense of connotation, the reader would
be tone-deaf, and all figurative language would become a form of
irony, as it does in de Man's formulations. One of the uses of
Burchfield's meditations is to restore an understanding of trope
that is diachronic. The skilled lexicographer shows us that the
irony of one age is the noble synecdoche of another, and helps us
also in seeing how the prestige of metaphor rises and falls with
that of sublimation, as we move from one age to another.

Burchfield's most fascinating essay, for me, is the dryly wicked
performance "The Genealogy of Dictionaries," which might be
retitled "The Anguish of Contamination Among Lexicographers,"
or even "The Anxiety of Influence in the Making of the *Oxford English Dictionary Supplements*." But Burchfield's emphasis is properly
on his precursors: Dr. Johnson, Noah Webster, and J. A. H. Murray
(crucial editor of the *Oxford English Dictionary*). Himself a medieval-
ist, Burchfield sagely reminds us that plagiarism is a relatively
modern legalism:

Medieval European authors took it as axiomatic that their main purpose was to "translate" or adapt the great works of their predecessors. The word plagiarism *itself is first recorded in 1621, but the association of* plagiarism *with guilt and furtiveness came rather later.*

One could notice that Chaucer himself delights in giving credit to fictive authorities, while slyly translating Dante and Boccaccio, but it remains true that all strong literature is a kind of theft. Emerson cheerfully affirmed that "the Originals were not original," and literary originality generally has little to do with origination. Burchfield traces the "path of descent" from the *American College Dictionary* (1947) down to its British and Australian derivatives, and the more surprising reliance of *Webster's Third New International* upon the *OED*. By the time he has shown us Dr. Johnson quietly cannibalizing one Nathan Bailey, Burchfield is ready to suggest that we "take the word *plagiarism* right out of the subject as an unnecessarily delicate consideration in the provision of information for mankind." The word "delicate" is crucial there, and so is "information." If you are going to unlock the language, whether through philology or criticism, you need to take help wherever you can get it.

Contrasting his project to that of his direct precursor Murray, Burchfield remarks that Murray averaged one quotation per century for any given meaning of a word, whereas the *Supplements* aim for at least one quotation per decade. This raises the image of future supplements giving one quotation for each year for meaning, and

suggests that dictionaries beyond that may touch their apocalypse, with fresh quotations being required each month as meanings swerve toward the end of our time. Beyond even that will be the quotation per day, and lexicographers will have to accept the choice of extinction or madness. Unlocking the English language will become equivalent to rebuilding the Tower of Babel, a Kafkaesque exercise without restraint, a Borgesian excursion into an endlessly upward-mounting labyrinth.

Burchfield's book is too cheerful and pragmatic for such a vision, and that is certainly part of its value. Rereading it tends to put me into an elegiac mood, which is very contrary to Burchfield's purposes. But I suspect that my mood is more than personal, and that Burchfield, like Dr. Johnson, Noah Webster, and J. A. H. Murray, belongs to the Giant Race before the Flood. A great dictionary, in another decade or so, is likely to seem a grand monument rising out of the compost heap of a universal electronic culture. We will resort to that monument in the way that the librarians worked at the Museion in Hellenistic Alexandria, hoping to preserve what needs to be preserved, in the coming times of the Fire and the Flood, knowing that conservation needs to be the mode of our New Alexandrianism.

Johnson would not be happy with my prophecy, but if alive now might agree with it. In his Preface to his *Dictionary,* he had anticipated that the language could not be arrested from the tendency to decay:

When we see men grow old and die at a certain time one after another, from century to century, we laugh at the elixir that promises to prolong life to a thousand years; and with equal justice may the lexicographer be derided, who being able to produce no example of a nation that has preserved their words and phrases from mutability, shall imagine that his dictionary can embalm his language, and secure it from corruption and decay, that it is in his power to change sublunary nature, or clear the world at once from folly, vanity, and affectation.

Kevin Hart, commenting on this in *Samuel Johnson and the Culture of Property* (1999), affirms that Johnson sees the English language "as a complex organism, both living and dying." Fanatically learned as he was, Johnson brooded hard upon that "dying" as the final form of linguistic change. But then, it took all his wisdom to confront mortality.

3
—

What precisely is the nature of Johnson's wisdom? *Rasselas,* which Goethe might have dismissed had he himself read it, always moves me by its wisdom. I have just reread it, and enjoyed it as much as before, in what may be some dozen readings across the last half-century. Its full title is *The History of Rasselas, Prince of Abissinia,* and it purports to be a prose quest-romance, but is picaresque only in its narrative procedures. As most of the little book's exegetes

remark, the story—to term it so—is a thread upon which an extra-ordinary number of powerful *adagia* are precariously arranged in series. Johnson once remarked that he looked forward to a time when all conversation would be an exchange of aphorisms. Ironically, Oscar Wilde, of whom Johnson would have been wary, knows only that world in his plays and narratives. Lady Bracknell, my own favorite in *The Importance of Being Earnest,* enunciates everything in rolling periods, her style essentially a parody of Johnson's, just as she and the great critic both can sound like travesties of Sir John Falstaff, who competes with Hamlet as the supreme wit in Shakespeare. I go on preferring Falstaff to Hamlet, even after having lost nearly a hundred pounds.

Rasselas leaves his palace in the happy valley, where he is discontent, and sets off with the learned Imlac, and with his own sister, the princess Nekayah, to experience the universe. Little happens, but much is said, with Imlac, Johnson's surrogate, expressing continuously a superb cascade of wisdom, both pragmatic and theoretic. Goethe also packs his narrative fictions with marvelous apothegms, yet the reader senses that the magnificent poet possessed such quantities of them that they needed to be embedded somewhere. They emerge from the same burning fountain that his poetry exuberantly overflows. Johnson's maxims are more experiential than Goethe's, or perhaps I should refine that by observing that the German sage gives us the benefits of the experience of being Goethe, while Johnson, who lived in the streets of London when he first came up to the city, relies on his experience of life.

Imlac is Johnson-as-critic, as here in Chapter 10, where he discourses upon poetry:

The business of a poet, said Imlac, is to examine, not the individual, but the species; to remark general properties and large appearances: he does not number the streaks of the tulip, or describe the different shades in the verdure of the forest. He is to exhibit in his portraits of nature such prominent and striking features, as recall the original to every mind; and must neglect the minuter discriminations, which one may have remarked, and another have neglected, for those characteristicks which are alike obvious to vigilance and carelessness.

But the knowledge of nature is only half the task of a poet; he must be acquainted likewise with all the modes of life. His character requires that he estimate the happiness and misery of every condition; observe the power of all the passions in all their combinations, and trace the changes of the human mind as they are modified by various institutions and accidental influences of climate or custom, from the spriteliness of infancy to the despondence of decrepitude. He must divest himself of the prejudices of his age or country; he must consider right and wrong in their abstracted and invariable state; he must disregard present laws and opinions, and rise to general and transcendental truths, which will always be the same: he must therefore content himself with the slow progress of his name; contemn the applause of his own time, and commit his claims to the justice of posterity. He must write as the interpreter of nature, and the legislator of mankind, and consider himself as presiding over the thoughts and manners of future generations; as a being superiour to time and place.

His labour is not yet at an end: he must know many languages

and many sciences; and, that his stile may be worthy of his thoughts, must, by incessant practice, familiarize to himself every delicacy of speech and grace of harmony.

How many poets fulfill these comprehensive requirements of Imlac/Johnson? There is only Shakespeare, who would have rejected this emphasis on "right and wrong in their abstracted and invariable state." Imlac's rhetoric is Johnson's and not Shakespearean:

Human life is every where a state in which much is to be endured, and little to be enjoyed.

Memorable and mordant, this is the heart of Imlac's philosophy. Is it also Johnson's? In company, no, but solitude enhanced Johnson's darker wisdom. His prayers, of which we have almost a hundred, are poignant meditations on Christian endurance, marked equally by faith and by suffering. Johnson declined to become a devotional writer, like Pascal, whom he admired, perhaps because he sensed that his own powers were cognitive and poetic, rather than strictly spiritual. In his prayers he endlessly chastises himself for not studying and writing incessantly, and yet I remind myself daily of his response to Boswell's probing as to a book never commenced: "Sir, a man is not obliged to do all that he can."

Johnson, a self-thwarted poet, suffered deeply from what he called "the dangerous prevalence of imagination," the title of Chapter 44 of *Rasselas*. There Imlac speaks of the wavering demarcation between creative power and madness, anticipating the fate of Nietzsche:

Perhaps, if we speak with rigorous exactness, no human mind is in its right state. There is no man whose imagination does not sometimes predominate over his reason, who can regulate his attention wholly by his will, and whose ideas will come and go at his command. No man will be found in whose mind airy notions do not sometimes tyrannise, and force him to hope or fear beyond the limits of sober probability. All power of fancy over reason is a degree of insanity; but while this power is such as we can controll and repress, it is not visible to others, nor considered as any depravation of the mental faculties: it is not pronounced madness but when it comes ungovernable, and apparently influences speech or action.

To indulge the power of fiction, and send imagination out upon the wing, is often the sport of those who delight too much in silent speculation. When we are alone we are not always busy; the labour of excogitation is too violent to last long; the ardour of enquiry will sometimes give way to idleness or satiety. He who has nothing external that can divert him, must find pleasure in his own thoughts, and must conceive himself what he is not; for who is pleased with what he is? He then expatiates in boundless futurity, and culls from all imaginable conditions that which for the present moment he should most desire, amuses his desires with impossible enjoyments, and confers upon his pride unattainable dominion. The mind dances from scene to scene, unites all pleasures in all combinations, and riots in delights which nature and fortune, with all their bounty, cannot bestow.

In time some particular train of ideas fixes the attention, all other intellectual gratifications are rejected, the mind, in

weariness or leisure, recurs constantly to the favourite conception, and feasts on the luscious falsehood whenever she is offended with the bitterness of truth. By degrees the reign of fancy is confirmed; she grows first imperious, and in time despotick. Then fictions begin to operate as realities, false opinions fasten upon the mind, and life passes in dreams of rapture or of anguish.

This, Sir, is one of the dangers of solitude, which the hermit has confessed not always to promote goodness, and the astronomer's misery has proved to be not always propitious to wisdom.

The struggle of Dr. Johnson against madness was incessant; his profound melancholia was never far away, in an era when mental illness afflicted many of the best poets: William Collins, Christopher Smart, William Cowper among them. Johnson feared dying and death, despite his devout Christianity, yet he feared a cognitive breakdown even more, particularly of melancholy mixed with guilt. Imlac, in Chapter 46, expounds this Johnsonian anxiety:

No disease of the imagination, answered Imlac, is so difficult of cure, as that which is complicated with the dread of guilt: fancy and conscience then act interchangeably upon us, and so often shift their places, that the illusions of one are not distinguished from the dictates of the other. If fancy presents images not moral or religious, the mind drives them away when they give it pain, but when melancholick notions take the form of duty, they lay hold on the faculties without opposition, because we are afraid to

exclude or banish them. For this reason the superstitious are often
melancholy, and the melancholy almost always superstitious.

Though Johnson is so well chronicled, between Boswell and
rival biographers, surmise is necessary to illuminate his sense of
guilt, though his strong belief in original sin could be answer
enough. He was a widower, and a survivor; *Rasselas* famously was
written in a week to defray the expenses of his mother's funeral.
His father died in 1731, and his wife, Elizabeth, in 1752. When his
mother died, in 1759, the childless Johnson was left with no immediate family, at the age of fifty. He was to live another twenty-five
very active years, his mind more powerful than ever at seventy-
five, and his anxieties unappeased. His augmenting wisdom is the
total antithesis of Goethe's serenity. Contrast to Johnson's "dangerous prevalence of the imagination" Goethe's "Imagination is
only ordered and structured by poetry. There is nothing more
awful than imagination devoid of taste." Madness and bad taste do
not inhabit the same sphere of discourse.

If Johnson and Goethe touch at all, it must be in their mutual
sense that wisdom depended upon "knowledge of the heart." Was
either of them ever in love? Johnson had a deep attachment, well
after the death of his wife, to Mrs. Hester Thrale, but it was familial. Goethe suffered from his long, unfulfilled relationship to Char-
lotte von Stein, but one suspects that gratification would have
cooled him very rapidly.

The passional life is not a central concern for Johnson, while
for Goethe its principal use was to provide a succession of Muses.

Goethe would not, like Johnson, have inscribed on the dial plate of his watch "The night cometh, when no man can work" (John 9:4). His maxims and reflections are not self-chastising, and he is overtly elitist, always aware of his own greatness as nature's favorite son. Johnson, hungry for imagination and yet fearing it, had a very contrary awareness of his place in nature. Though this difference between Goethe and Johnson is psychological, it shades into the distinction between an instinctual pagan and a troubled Christian.

4
___

Johnson had a particular regard for his series of periodical essays *The Rambler,* which I strongly share. His masterworks of literary criticism are his commentaries on Shakespeare and his *Lives of the Poets,* but *The Rambler* is his crucial contribution to wisdom literature.

The Rambler (1750–1752) represents Johnson at his most vigorous and fecund, in his early forties. As Mr. Rambler, Johnson cheerfully termed himself "dictatorial," yet his authority is too amiable for that word. Before 1760, the novelist Tobias Smollett permanently named Johnson as the "great CHAM of literature," custodian of the literary canon. A constant strain in *The Rambler* concerns the sorrows and hazards of writing as a career. I do not hear much Johnsonian anxiety in this; rather a curiously comic realism that I recommend to all who write:

> *But, though it should happen that an author is capable of excelling, yet his merit may pass without notice, huddled in the*

variety of things, and thrown into the general miscellany of life. He that endeavours after fame by writing, solicits the regard of a multitude fluctuating in pleasures, or immersed in business, without time for intellectual amusements; he appeals to judges prepossessed by passions, or corrupted by prejudices, which preclude their approbation of any new performance. Some are too indolent to read any thing, till its reputation is established; others too envious to promote that fame, which gives them pain by its increase. What is new is opposed, because most are unwilling to be taught; and what is known is rejected, because it is not sufficiently considered, that men more frequently require to be reminded than informed. The learned are afraid to declare their opinion early, lest they should put their reputation in hazard; the ignorant always imagine themselves giving some proof of delicacy, when they refuse to be pleased: and he that finds his way to reputation, through all these obstructions, must acknowledge that he is indebted to other causes besides his industry, his learning, or his wit.

That chastening wisdom, from *Rambler* No. 2, is enhanced throughout the series, sometimes laced with what Johnson called "naked criticism" or literary criticism proper. I remember most vividly from *The Rambler* its closing essay, No. 208, where the writer is warned against condemning himself to compose on a fixed day, when it is as likely as not that he will have:

an attention dissipated, a memory overwhelmed, an imagination embarrassed, a mind distracted with anxieties, a body

*languishing with disease; he will labour on a barren topic till it
is too late to change it; or . . . diffuse his thoughts into wild exuberance, which the pressing hour of publication cannot suffer
judgment to examine or reduce.*

Sometimes I grin ruefully when murmuring these words to
myself, waking up at four on a cold October morning, and knowing that by five I must return to writing, and that by nine I must
leave for the cardiac rehabilitation gym. The thought of Johnson,
perhaps settling down to write the next *Rambler* after groggily
wolfing his breakfast, helps to get me started.

In 1753–1754, *The Rambler* was followed by the *Adventurer*
series, really further *Rambler*s. At the end of the decade, Johnson
changed tone in the final series of periodical essays, *The Idler*
(1758–1760), during which he turned fifty. Lighter on their surface,
the *Idler* essays tend to be pure wisdom literature. A few days
after his mother died, Johnson wrote his most memorable essay
(No. 41), a three-page rival to Freud's dark essay "Mourning and
Melancholia." I cannot recall Freud mentioning Johnson, who
nevertheless was a precursor, nearly as much as Schopenhauer.
Freud insisted he had never read Schopenhauer (or Nietzsche), but
that seems unlikely.

Johnson, mourning his mother and all his dead friends, at once
affirms the reality of total loss yet also accepts the Christian hope
(fantasy, in Freud's judgment) of reunion:

*Nothing is more evident than that the decays of age must termi-
nate in death; yet there is no man, says Tully, who does not*

believe that he may yet live another year; and there is none who does not, upon the same principle, hope another year for his parent or his friend, but the fallacy will in time be detected; the last year, the last day must come. It has come and is past. The life which made my own life pleasant is at an end, and the gates of death are shut upon my prospects.

The loss of a friend upon whom the heart is fixed, to whom every wish and endeavour tended, is a state of dreary desolation in which the mind looks abroad impatient of itself, and finds nothing but emptiness and horror. The blameless life, the artless tenderness, the pious simplicity, the modest resignation, the patient sickness, and the quiet death, are remembered only to add value to the loss, to aggravate regret for what cannot be amended, to deepen sorrow for what cannot be recalled.

These are the calamities by which Providence gradually disengages us from the love of life. Other evils fortitude may repel, or hope may mitigate, but irreparable privation leaves nothing to exercise resolution or flatter expectation. The dead cannot return, and nothing is left us here but languishment and grief.

Yet such is the course of nature, that whoever lives long must outlive those whom he loves and honours. Such is the condition of our present existence, that life must one time lose its associations, and every inhabitant of the earth must walk downward to the grave alone and unregarded, without any partner of his joy or grief, without any interested witness of his misfortunes or success.

Misfortune, indeed, he may yet feel, for where is the bottom of the misery of man? But what is success to him that has none to

enjoy it? Happiness is not found in self-contemplation; it is per-
ceived only when it is reflected from another.

We know little of the state of departed souls, because such
knowledge is not necessary to a good life. Reason deserts us at
the brink of the grave, and can give no further intelligence. Revela-
tion is not wholly silent: "There is joy in the angels of heaven over
one sinner that repenteth"; and surely this joy is not incommuni-
cable to souls disentangled from the body, and made like angels.

Let hope therefore dictate, what revelation does not confute,
that the union of souls may still remain; and that we who are
struggling with sin, sorrow, and infirmities, may have our part
in the attention and kindness of those who have finished their
course and are now receiving their reward.

Johnson is very close to Ecclesiastes and Proverbs, and in their
wake he tends not to associate mourning with melancholia, from
which he perpetually suffered. Melancholia is stimulated by grief,
according to Freud, because all love relationships have some degree
of ambivalence, which comes forward through the provocation of
loss. There is an affect in Johnson's *Idler* No. 41 that has little to do
with ambivalence; one hears an extraordinary pathos in the reverberation of "The dead cannot return, and nothing is left us here
but languishment and grief." This in turn emanates from the wisdom of "Happiness is not found in self-contemplation; it is perceived only when it is reflected from another." Whether the
Christian wisdom concerning hope for afterlife that concludes
Idler No. 41 is equally persuasive depends on creed. "Philosophy
may infuse stubbornness, but religion only can give patience."

5

Why was Johnson so adept at aphorisms? Unlike William Blake and Nietzsche, he was conservative and royalist: Blake had fierce disdain for him. There is nothing in Johnson that has the firepower of the Proverbs of Hell in Blake's *The Marriage of Heaven and Hell*. Johnson would have been outraged by Blake's proverb "The tygers of wrath are wiser than the horses of instruction." In turn, Blake might have accepted "Love is the wisdom of fools and the folly of the wise," but he would have erupted at "The only end of writing is to enable the reader better to enjoy life, or better to endure it." Those were not alternatives for Blake but moral evasions. For him, the end of writing was to hasten the apocalypse of imagination.

All aphorists are ironic, but no writer's irony is quite another's. Even Johnson's ironies are prudential; one of Blake's Proverbs of Hell replies, "Prudence is a rich ugly old maid courted by Incapacity." Blake and Nietzsche communicate urgency: each is a visionary trying to teach us a freedom from false and habitual perspectivism. Johnson, who rejected all cant, was a classical realist. Nothing much could be said in conversation between Johnson and Kierkegaard, whose central concern was the impossibility of becoming a Christian in any ostensibly Christian society. But between Johnson and prophets like Blake or Nietzsche, nothing could be said at all.

A sensitive reader in the early twenty-first century is probably going to prefer the aphoristic wisdom of Blake or of Nietzsche to

Johnson's Ecclesiastes-like sense of the vanity of human wishes. And yet Johnson is a great teacher, particularly at a time when the "common reader," whom he exalted, is beginning to vanish, and when the mediaversity barely teaches most students to read better books, or to read them more closely. Johnson came to wisdom writing through literary criticism, and then went back to criticism again. Goethe primarily was a poet, and of all poets since Shakespeare could be judged the wisest. But no literary critic ever, whether before Johnson or since, gives what Johnson offers all of us. He can *sound* dogmatic, but has no literary dogma, and distrusts all systems of interpretation. His love of Falstaff, disreputable but sublimely diverting, is an index to Johnson's humanity. He would not have agreed with me that Falstaff was the Socrates of Eastcheap, and yet he learned from Falstaff one of the secrets that makes Shakespeare supreme among all writers: "Give me life," Falstaff observes amid the carnage at the battle of Shrewsbury, and he speaks also for Samuel Johnson, whose wisdom indeed is Falstaffian in its affirmation of life despite the vanity of all our desires.

GOETHE

Though Goethe was a cosmos in himself, with astonishing literary scope, his highest excellence is as a lyric and meditative poet. Perhaps he would have placed his *Faust* foremost; I myself never weary of rereading its outrageous Second Part. I will glance at his poetry later in this section, but primarily I want to explore Goethe's wisdom, as a sage antithetical to Dr. Samuel Johnson.

Though he scattered pungent aphorisms throughout his writings, Goethe preferred to call them "maxims." As first Goethean text here I will employ the very useful and available *Maxims and Reflections* (1998), translated by Elisabeth Stopp and edited by Peter Hutchinson. Goethe never gathered his wisdom literature in a single volume, and he might have been pleased by the Stopp-Hutchinson collection, which preserves the geniality and grace that he brought to the wisdom tradition of the Bible and Montaigne.

There is rather little in common between Ecclesiastes, a somber and fierce vision of reality, and Goethe's serene contemplations of our condition. Montaigne's full acceptance of the common life differs in temper from Goethe's ideal of *Bildung,* the self-development of the elite individual. *Bildung,* once a prime educational motive both on the Continent and in the America of Emerson, seems now to be an obsolete project. Its last major literary proponent was Goethe's disciple Thomas Mann, whose *The Magic Mountain* charted the ironic *Bildung* of Hans Castorp, caught between two opposed mentors, the Italian liberal Humanist Settembrini, and the Jesuit-Jewish Naphta, permanently reactionary. Mann ironically keeps stressing how ordinary Castorp is, but the youthful hero of *The Magic Mountain* would be remarkable in any group at any time. Like Mann himself, Hans Castorp is a Goethean seeker, in the mold of Goethe's Wilhelm Meister. "The highest degree of culture" is the Goethean aspiration, bequeathed not only to Thomas Mann but also to Sigmund Freud.

In *Wilhelm Meister's Journeyman Years,* Goethe includes a maxim that E. R. Curtius, the major German scholarly critic of the twentieth century, identifies as the true standpoint of the sage of Weimar:

Moderation and a clear sky are Apollo and the Muses.

There are not many wisdom writers who offer us a clear sky. Goethe, amiably eclectic, observed that "Researching into nature we are pantheists, writing poetry we are polytheists, morally we are monotheists." The Austro-Hungarian poet-dramatist Hugo von Hofmannsthal once observed that Goethe could replace all of culture and still give you an entire education. In the English-speaking world of the nineteenth century, that was true: Carlyle and Emerson agreed on this, despite their severe differences. In the early twenty-first century, we can no longer speak of Goethe as educator. Interpreters of nature now are biophysicists, and not people of letters. Goethe's "scientific researches" are seen these days as the study of metaphors, while Freud's "science" is a vast figurative structure constituting a strong poem, with no more general authority than is possessed by Goethe or by William Blake. Goethe, Blake, Freud have become prophets of sensibility or wisdom teachers. Their common motto might be Blake's:

Wisdom is sold in the open market where none comes to buy
Or in the withered field where the farmer ploughs for bread
in vain.

At such a time, Goethe's maxims convey an unintended pathos:

If you want to deny that nature is a divine organ, you might as
well deny all revelation. [810]

So out of fashion is this Spinoza-like pantheism that such a reflection is obsolete. And yet many of the Goethean aphorisms cannot lose their relevance:

When two people are really happy about one another, one can generally assume that they are mistaken.

Goethe does not quite have the particular bite of Kierkegaard:

When two people fall in love and begin to feel they are made for one another, then they should break off, for by going on they have everything to lose and nothing to gain.

The irony of Kierkegaard is more savage than Goethe could allow himself, since the difficulty of becoming a Christian in an ostensible Christian society meant nothing to the pagan Goethe. Renunciation, termed a "piercing virtue" by Emily Dickinson, is Goethe's mature project, but itself is converted by him into a complex kind of *Bildung*.

Two volumes have been published of a great biography, *Goethe: The Poet and the Age,* by Nicholas Boyle (1991, 2000), with another to come. The best definition of Goethean "renunciation" is Boyle's:

Renunciation is the negative image of desire. Once Goethe has recognized it as the moral attitude required of him by the most decisive public event in his lifetime [the French Revolution], he is

free to respond to events by deploying in a new form—inverted, intensified, and idealized—the energies which made his earlier poetry possible. As in Schiller's account of the elegy, in his essay On Naïve and Sentimental Poetry, *the desired object can now be represented in literature either to be lost, though unforgotten, in the past, or to be inaccessible, though secure, in an ideal future; as in Mme de Staël's more realistic view, the proper theme of the mature poet can now be 'having loved'.*

But renunciation of the hope of possessing the object is also renunciation of the self which hopes to possess. Kant has not only shown that the Supreme Good cannot be found here and now, though it may be allowed to beckon to us from the end of history; he has also shown that the self which collects together all experience cannot itself be experienced but is at best a 'regulative idea': we must think of ourselves 'as if' we were, or had, a self. It was a profound error of Schiller, and others in his time and class, to think that Kant's postulates and ideas could somehow be made manifest, shown to us by a sufficiently skillful manipulator of appearances, so that out of the corner of the eye, in the moment of action, we might catch a glimpse of the freely acting Person.

Boyle analyzes this view of renunciation as a freedom from outdated literary conventions, in the age of the French Revolution. Central symbolic characters are no longer necessary, and any distinction between the private feelings of the author and those of his public vanishes, thus idealizing the audience. Even plot can be

renounced, and poems and stories turned into wisdom literature, into what Kierkegaard ironically called "edifying discourses." Wisdom in Goethe is an acknowledgment that what matters most is the open mystery, what can be suggested but not stated. Nietzsche was to exalt the will's revenge against time's pronouncement "It was." Goethe seeks no revenge, but accepts pastness as a condition of the good. The present is renounced, or surrendered to time.

Pragmatically, in terms of living our life, that means giving up desire. Is wisdom then only another renunciation of desire? Boyle's Goethe progresses from being the poet of desire to being the poet of renunciation. What then is "desire" in Goethe? Thomas Mann, in his late "Fantasy on Goethe," sees renunciation as the casting-out of the dream of an entirely personal fulfillment. In 1828, Goethe, approaching eighty, told Eckermann (his Boswell):

> Man must be ruined again! Every extraordinary man has a certain mission to accomplish. If he has fulfilled it, he is no longer needed upon the earth in the same form, and Providence uses him for something else. But as everything here below happens in a natural way, the dæmons keep tripping him up till he falls at last.

Goethe is fascinatingly perverse in his playing with belief. Not a Christian, he still longs for a literal immortality, as Tolstoy and Ibsen did, and as Shakespeare wisely did not. Heine's "There is a God and his name is Aristophanes" directly derives from Goethe's charmed conviction that "the stage of Aristophanes is also a sacred

place." Only irony for Goethe makes wisdom available to us. Such wisdom is hardly the biblical wisdom of Dr. Johnson or the regenerated skepticism of Montaigne. I am not at all certain that Goethe's wisdom is still available to us, whether we are European or American.

Is Goethe's wisdom subtle (like Emerson's or that of Plato's Socrates) or just intolerably tricky, like Peer Gynt's? Underestimating Goethe is always a mistake: his revenge is to haunt you. He loved Shakespeare, however jealously, because he sensed that only Shakespeare, and Goethe, knew everything. One might add Cervantes and Tolstoy. Goethe credits Shakespeare with the original insight that the function of stage drama is to expand the audience's imaginative and cognitive powers, but only by hindering them. That, according to Goethe, is why there is "no end to Shakespeare."

2
—

Before we allow Goethean "renunciation" to irritate us, we ought to confront its greatest manifestation, the "Trilogy of Passion" elegies that he completed in 1824, inspired by the sublime absurdity of a poet in his seventies falling in love with a girl of nineteen, Ulrike von Levetzow, who sensibly declined his offer of marriage. Renouncing the ecstasy of loss is redundant in what seems to many, myself included, the finest of Goethe's lyrical poems, the "Marienbad Elegy," which centers the "Trilogy." This extraordinary work refuses irony and defies translation, but the close prose ver-

sion of David Luke eloquently conveys the authenticity of the poet's erotic anguish. Goethe, on a deep level, knows that an antipoetic disaster would have ensued had Ulrike accepted him, aside from the grotesquerie of a seventy-four-year-old groom with a nineteen-year-old bride:

I am far from you now. This present minute—what does it demand? I cannot tell. It offers me many good and lovely things; they are only a burden, which I must renounce. An irresistible longing drives me hither and thither; unending tears are my only counsel.

Flow on then, tears, and flow unquenchably—though you could never still this fire within me! Already my heart is torn by a terrible frenzy, by a hideous life-and-death struggle. There may be herbs that can heal the body's pain, but one's mind lacks the power to will or to decide, or to grasp the very idea of being without her. A thousand times it evokes within itself her image, which is sometimes slow in coming and sometimes snatched away—now indistinct and now radiantly clear. How can this yield the slightest comfort, this ebb and flow, this going and coming?

Leave me here, faithful comrades! leave me alone amid rocks and marsh and moss! Hold to your course! To you the world lies open, the earth is wide, the heavens splendid and great; examine, investigate, collect details, and slowly spell out Nature's mystery.

I have lost the whole world, I have lost myself—I who but lately was the darling of the gods. They put me to the test, they

gave me Pandora with her abundant store of blessings and
greater abundance of danger. They pressed me to the bountiful
lips—they sunder me from them, and destroy me.

These are the last five of twenty-three six-line stanzas, and
they carry with them, in context, the ecstatic surge of what precedes them. Were the "Marienbad Elegy" mere self-therapy, its
wisdom would not touch the universal, as it does. The equivalent
in German was not to come again until Freud composed his
"Mourning and Melancholia," a guide to the grief for the beloved
dead, but also for erotic bereavement. Goethe's final stanzas of his
"Elegy" record absolute ruin: "I have lost the whole world, I have
lost myself." We can doubt that Goethe actually was capable of
losing his overwhelming sense of self for a single sentence, yet
within the poem he persuades us of his agony, since Ulrike's rejection is accepted as a death sentence. The girl, who never married,
receives the equivocal role of Pandora, more dangerous because of
her "abundant store of blessings." Again, we distrust the literalism
of a Goethe who finds himself oppressed by images he cannot
conceptualize, since his "Elegy" performs so powerfully exactly
that process. Freud's "work of mourning" follows the example of
Goethe's marvelous formalism. We are at the center of Goethean
wisdom. In Wordsworth, experiential loss is transmuted into imaginative gain, a presage of all poetry since. Goethe, ending a tradition that pragmatically began with Homer, remains more Classical
than Romantic. Passional loss is not poetic enhancement, whether
in Achilles or in Goethe, who once had been the genius of "happiness and astonishment."

3
—

What is it that Goethe adds to the difficult wisdom of Homer, which he completes? The best of modern German scholar-critics, Ernst Robert Curtius, observed that Goethe preferred to be in a state of *heiter*, defined as "light over darkness," or a cloudless sky. That is not exactly Homeric, particularly in the *Iliad*. If, as I have urged, we are to find the whole truth in Homer, rather than in Plato, Goethe is something other than Homeric in the "Marienbad Elegy." He himself was characterized by Emerson as larger than his poetry:

> But, whilst men distinguished for wit and learning, in England and France, adopt their study and their side with a certain levity, and are not understood to be very deeply engaged, from grounds of character, to the topic or the part they espouse,— Goethe, the head and body of the German nation, does not speak from talent, but the truth shines through: he is very wise, though his talent often veils his wisdom. However excellent his sentence is, he has somewhat better in view. It awakens my curiosity. He has the formidable independence which converse with truth gives: hear you, or forbear, his fact abides; and your interest in the writer is not confined to his story, and he is dismissed from memory, when he has performed his task creditably, as a baker when he has left his loaf; but his work is the least part of him. The old Eternal Genius who built the world has confided himself more to this man than to any other. I dare not say that Goethe

ascended to the highest grounds from which genius has spoken.
He has not worshipped the highest unity; he is incapable of a
self-surrender to the moral sentiment. There are nobler strains in
poetry than any he has sounded. There are writers poorer in tal-
ent, whose tone is purer, and more touches the heart. Goethe can
never be dear to men. His is not even the devotion to pure truth;
but to truth for the sake of culture.

Emerson, always more ironic than we expect, is charmed by
Goethe but regards him as "the Writer," while seeing Shakespeare
as "the Poet." Superb lyric poet as Goethe was, his masterwork is
Faust, particularly the Second Part, which Emerson probably would
have rejected as outrageous. Goethe's wisdom always verges on
outrageousness, and I like *Faust II* best for its excesses, whereas
Goethe's overtly Homeric epic, *Hermann and Dorothea,* is now very
hard to get through. Most of *Faust II* is parody, and it works, but as
a parodist of Homer, Goethe fails. Homeric irony is subtle and
frightening; *Hermann and Dorothea* is bland in comparison. Depri-
vation rouses Wordsworth to greatness, as in *The Ruined Cottage.*
Goethe, though he made the wisdom of renunciation uniquely his
own, hardly could tolerate any total loss.

Can we distinguish Goethe's pagan kind of renunciation from
its Christian analogues? As an elitist, Goethe is very far from Christian humility:

Man can only live together with his own kind and not with them
either; for in the long run he cannot bear the thought that anyone
is like him. [1405]

Like Emerson, Goethe rejects both creed and prayer. One of his most fascinating late maxims is endless to meditation, and sets the pattern by which Hamlet has become the Christ of the intellectuals:

> That Christ perished in Hamlet-like fashion, and, worse, because he called men around him when he dropped, while Hamlet perished only as an individual. [1305]

Posthumously published, this reflection hardly shows a Goethe who is reconciled with Christianity. Nicholas Boyle is careful to emphasize that Goethe's faith, insofar as it existed, always remained subtly personal. I think that it defies summary because Goethe was his own Christ, and needed no other Messiah. The mysterious "wholeness" of Goethe's personality was threatened with extinction by Christianity. Whatever else Goethe had to renounce—to time, circumstance, or the French Revolution, or his own aging—he would not renounce his uniqueness.

4
—

With Goethe, one has to keep circling in order to define what "renunciation" could mean. He would never renounce any possibility of his own higher development, or accept any compromise in his consciousness of himself. His last conversation with Eckermann on religion pictures a God constantly active in such higher natures as Mozart, Raphael, and Shakespeare. Pragmatically, for all its moral

colorings, Goethe's last reflections on religion reduce it to an aesthetic vitalism, akin to Wallace Stevens's early "Sunday Morning":

> Yet I look upon all four Gospels as thoroughly genuine; for there is in them the reflection of a greatness which emanated from the person of Jesus, and which was of as divine a kind as ever was seen upon earth. If I am asked whether it is in my nature to pay Him devout reverence, I say—certainly! I bow before Him as the divine manifestation of the highest principle of morality. If I am asked whether it is in my nature to revere the Sun, I again say—certainly! For he is likewise a manifestation of the highest Being, and indeed the most powerful that we children of earth are allowed to behold. I adore in him the light and the productive power of God; by which we all live, move, and have our being—we, and all the plants and animals with us. But if I am asked whether I am inclined to bow before a thumb-bone of the Apostle Peter or Paul, I say—'Spare me, and stand off with your absurdities!'

Goethe's regard for Christ is that of one great nature for another. Clear away the moral rhetoric, and wholeness is the only criterion. "Narcissism" would be an unfriendlier characterization of the Goethean sense of self-completion. Since he himself felt that he had moved from "the poetry of desire" to that of renunciation, a kind of counterpoetry, Goethe could believe that he had undergone a *kenosis,* the emptying-out of the divine nature that St. Paul ascribed to Christ. Goethe's wisdom, if it is to be useful to us as it was for Ibsen, Gide, and Mann, has to be seen as a persuasive

redefinition of wisdom, one that finds the specifically aesthetic element in the Bible's wisdom literature.

Tradition divides the Hebrew Bible into Torah (mistranslated as the Law), the Prophets, and the Writings (including wisdom), but all three contain elements of wisdom. Within the Hebrew canon, the prophet Ezekiel (33:30–33) is told by God that the people will receive him as a singer rather than as admonisher:

> Also, thou son of man, the children of thy people still are talking against thee by the walls and in the doors of the houses, and speak one to another, every one to his brother, saying, Come, I pray you, and hear what is the word that cometh forth from the LORD.
>
> And they come unto thee as the people cometh, and they sit before thee as my people, and they hear thy words, but they will not do them: for with their mouth they show much love, but their heart goeth after covetousness.
>
> And, lo, thou art unto them as a very lovely song of one that hath a pleasant voice, and can play well on an instrument: for they hear thy words, but they do them not.
>
> And when this cometh to pass, (lo, it will come,) then shall they know that a prophet hath been among them.

Poetry goes one way here, and prophecy another. Walter Reed, in his *Dialogues of the Word* (1993), interprets this differently, following the Russian critic Bakhtin and saying that "it is only in the communicative paradigm of wisdom . . . that the Bible begins to acknowledge its own aesthetic dimensions." But does one regard

the Psalms and the Song of Solomon, or the war song of Deborah and Barak, and the Song of Miriam at the Red Sea, as other than poems of the highest power? They recognize their own glory, as when Deborah cries out in triumph, "O my soul, thou hast trodden down strength" (Judges 5:21), where the Hebrew in fact reads, "O my soul, tread them down with strength."

"Aesthetic" is a Greek word meaning "perceptive," and the example of Homer and the Greeks meant more to Goethe than the Bible did, particularly since his youthful quest had been to free art from Christianity. The poetry of desire, in the earlier Goethe, had sought to transmute nature into the happiness of art. The wisdom of renouncing that transmutation is convincingly traced by Boyle to the effect of the French Revolution and of Napoleon on Goethe. Aesthetic education, the dream of Goethe's *Bildung*, fades into the light of common day, and Germany cannot become either a second Athens or a second Renaissance Italy. Romanticism and Christian reaction against it were neither of them alternatives for Goethe. The way onward could only be a poetry of renunciation.

5
—

Goethe is one of the best antidotes I know for our current ideologies of Resentment, which have now pretty well destroyed aesthetic education in the English-speaking world. I am not suggesting a renunciatory criticism to match his poetics of renunciation. The disturbances of 1967–1970 were not exactly on the scale of the French Revolution, and yet they have made a culture of *Bildung*

impossible. Goethe does not *find* me as Dr. Johnson does, and yet both of them are wisdom teachers for the current age. The Christian Johnson and the pagan Goethe come together in their appreciation of Shakespeare, who wrote neither the poetry of desire nor the poetry of renunciation. Call Shakespeare's the poetry of all climes and climates, and of all seasons of the soul.

CHAPTER 6

EMERSON AND

NIETZSCHE

EMERSON

Born on May 26, 1803, Emerson is closer to us than ever, on his two hundredth birthday. In the United States, we continue to have Emersonians of the Left (the post-Pragmatist Richard Rorty) and of the Right (a swarm of libertarian Republicans, who exalt President Bush the Second). The Emersonian vision of Self-Reliance inspired both the humane philosopher John Dewey and the first Henry Ford (circulator of *The Protocols of the Learned Elders of Zion*). Emerson remains the central figure in American culture, and informs our politics, as well as our unofficial religion, which I regard as more Emersonian than Christian, despite nearly all received opinion on this matter.

In the domain of American literature, Emerson was eclipsed during the era of T. S. Eliot, but was revived in the middle 1960s

and is again what he was in his own time, and directly after: the dominant sage of the American imagination. I recall sadly the American academic and literary scene of the 1950s, when Emerson was under the ban of Eliot, who had proclaimed, "The essays of Emerson are already an encumbrance." I enjoy the thought of Eliot reading my favorite sentence in the essay "Self-Reliance":

As men's prayers are a disease of the will, so are their creeds a disease of the intellect.

It delights me that, in the twenty-first century, there is an abundance in Emerson to go on offending, as well as inspiring, multitudes. "O you man without a handle!" was the exasperated outcry of his disciple, Henry James, Sr., father of William the philosopher-psychologist and Henry the novelist. Like Hamlet, Emerson has no handle, and no ideology. And like another disciple, the greatest American poet, Walt Whitman, Emerson was not bothered by self-contradiction, since he knew he contained endless multitudes: "a foolish consistency is the hobgoblin of little minds."

Almost all post-Emersonian writers of real eminence in American literature are either passionately devoted to Emerson or else are moved to negate him, rather ambiguously in the stances of Hawthorne and Melville, but fiercely in the case of Poe and most Southerners after him. (Emerson shrugged Poe off as "the jingle man.") At every lunch that I happily shared with the poet-novelist Robert Penn Warren, he would denounce Emerson as the Devil. Warren was anything but dogmatic, whether on literary or spiritual matters, but he blamed Emerson for the murderous John

Brown and for most of what was destructive in American culture. C. Vann Woodward, a historian of extraordinary distinction, told me many times that Emerson could not be forgiven for the essay "History," which never ceases to give me joy with its opening sentence: "There is no history, only biography." Whenever I met the fiery and gifted poet-critic Allen Tate, he would assure me again that Emerson was "evil" and deserved damnation, if any damnation was still available.

On the other side, there is the testimony of Walt Whitman, celebrating Emerson as the explorer who led us all to "the shores of America." Thoreau and Emily Dickinson can be said to evade Emerson, but only after absorbing him, while Robert Frost was the most exuberant of all affirmers of Emerson. There are too many to cite: no single sage in English literature, not Dr. Johnson nor Coleridge, is as inescapable as Emerson goes on being for American poets and storytellers.

Emerson at his best was an authentic poet, though not of the stature of the major American poets: Whitman, Dickinson, Frost, Wallace Stevens, Eliot, Hart Crane, Robert Penn Warren, Elizabeth Bishop, James Merrill, A. R. Ammons, John Ashbery. The prose of Emerson—essays, journals, lectures—is his triumph, both as eloquence and as insight. After Shakespeare's prose, it matches anything else in the language: Swift, Johnson, Burke, Hazlitt. As an essayist, Emerson professedly follows Montaigne, and Montaigne's precursors: Plato, Plutarch, Seneca. Montaigne and Shakespeare were, for Emerson, the two writers always with him.

Why did Emerson have a unique influence on both his con-

temporaries and those who wrote later? Originally a Unitarian minister, Emerson abandoned his post because he knew only the God within, which he defined as the best and oldest part of his self. He became a wisdom writer, practicing what could be called interior oratory, but also a public lecturer. Many of his essays began as journal entries, were transformed into lectures, and then were refined for publication.

As a lecturer, and as a writer, Emerson manifested a remarkable conversionary power, very different in kind from evangelical salvations. The leap in awareness that Emerson offered is not radically new, and is related to the effect Shakespeare has on us, allowing us to see what already is there yet which would not be available except for Shakespeare's mediation. I am suggesting that Emerson is not an Idealist or Transcendental philosopher, but an experiential essayist, like Montaigne, and so more a dramatist of the self than a mystic:

> That is always best which gives me to myself. The sublime is excited in me by the great stoical doctrine, obey thyself. That which shows God out of me, makes me a wart and a wen. There is no longer a necessary reason for my being.

Emerson suggests that we give ourselves to ourselves, that each of us can be cosmos rather than chaos. Autonomy ought to be our aim, though Emerson intends a healing of the self, rather than alienation from society. Even such a self-mending reveres transition, rather than any final state of the individual. One of the central passages in Emerson is from the essay "Self-Reliance":

Life only avails, not the having lived. Power ceases in the instant of repose; it resides in the moment of transition from a past to a new state, in the shooting of a gulf, in the darting to an aim. This one fact turns all riches to poverty, all reputation to shame, confounds the saint with the rogue, shoves Jesus and Judas equally aside. Why, then, do we prate of self-reliance? Inasmuch as the soul is present, there will be power not confident but agent. To talk of reliance is a poor external way of speaking. Speak rather of that which relies, because it works and is.

Nothing is more American, whether catastrophic or amiable, than that Emersonian formula concerning power: "it resides in the moment of transition from a past to a new state, in the shooting of a gulf, in the darting to an aim." Throughout his own lifetime, Emerson was ambiguously on the Left, but then the crusade against slavery, and the South, overdetermined his political choices. Much as I love Emerson, it is important to remember always that he valued power for its own sake. If he is a moral essayist, the morality involved is not primarily either humane or humanistic.

As I grow older, I find Emerson to be strongest in the essays of *The Conduct of Life*, published in late 1860, several months before the South began the Civil War by firing upon Fort Sumter. Something vital in Emerson began slowly to burn out afterward in the emotional stress of the war, perhaps because his hatred of the South intensified. *Society and Solitude* (1870) manifests a falling off, even more apparent in *Letters and Social Aims* (1875). His last five years, from 1877 on, saw an end to his memory and his cognitive

abilities. But in *The Conduct of Life,* written in his middle fifties, he establishes a crucial last work for Americans, in particular through a grand triad of essays: "Fate," "Power," and "Illusions." "Power" is the center, and might have been composed last week, in its shrewd sense of Americans, so little changed a century and a half later:

> *One comes to value this* plus *health, when he sees that all diffi-culties vanish before it. A timid man listening to the alarmists in Congress, and in the newspapers, and observing the profligacy of party,—sectional interests urged with a fury which shuts its eyes to consequences, with a mind made up to desperate extremities, ballot in one hand, and rifle in the other,—might easily believe that he and his country have seen their best days, and he hardens himself the best he can against the coming ruin. But, after this has been foretold with equal confidence fifty times, and govern-ment six per cents have not declined a quarter of a mill, he dis-covers that the enormous elements of strength which are here in play, make our politics unimportant. Personal power, freedom, and the resources of nature strain every faculty of every citizen. We prosper with such vigor, that, like thrifty trees, which grow in spite of ice, lice, mice, and borers, so we do not suffer from the profligate swarms that fatten on the national treasury. The huge animals nourish huge parasites, and the rancor of the disease attests the strength of the constitution. The same energy in the Greek Demos drew the remark, that the evils of popular govern-ment appear greater than they are; there is compensation for them in the spirit and energy it awakens. The rough and ready style*

which belongs to a people of sailors, foresters, farmers, and mechanics, has its advantages. Power educates the potentate. As long as our people quote English standards they dwarf their own proportions. A Western lawyer of eminence said to me he wished it were a penal offence to bring an English law-book into a court in this country, so pernicious had he found in his experience our deference to English precedent. The very word 'commerce' has only an English meaning, and is pinched to the cramp exigencies of English experience. The commerce of rivers, the commerce of railroads, and who knows but the commerce of air-balloons, must add an American extension to the pond-hole of admiralty. As long as our people quote English standards, they will miss the sovereignty of power; but let these rough riders,—legislators in shirt-sleeves,—Hoosier, Sucker, Wolverine, Badger,—or whatever hard head Arkansas, Oregon, or Utah sends, half orator, half assassin, to represent its wrath and cupidity at Washington,—let these drive as they may; and the disposition of territories and public lands, the necessity of balancing and keeping at bay the snarling majorities of German, Irish, and of native millions, will bestow promptness, address, and reason, at last, on our buffalo-hunter, and authority and majesty of manners. The instinct of the people is right. Men expect from good whigs, put into office by the respectability of the country, much less skill to deal with Mexico, Spain, Britain, or with our own malcontent members, than from some strong transgressor, like Jefferson, or Jackson, who first conquers his own government, and then uses the same genius to conquer the foreigner. The senators who dissented from Mr. Polk's Mexican war, were not those who knew better, but those who,

*from political position, could afford it; not Webster, but Benton
and Calhoun.*

I have quoted this long paragraph partly for its perpetual relevance, and partly for its Emersonian self-revelation and exuberant
amoralism. This cultural nationalism, invariably directed against
the English, has no illusions as to what Emerson will go on to call
(quite cheerfully) "the power of lynch law, of soldiers and pirates,"
of bullies of every variety. These roughs represent the power of
violence, only a slightly lower order, for Emerson, of the violence
of power:

> *Those who have most of this coarse energy,—the 'bruisers,' who
> have run the gauntlet of caucus and tavern through the county
> or the state, have their own vices, but they have the good nature
> of strength and courage. Fierce and unscrupulous, they are usu-
> ally frank and direct, and above falsehood. Our politics fall into
> bad hands, and churchmen and men of refinement, it seems
> agreed, are not fit persons to send to Congress. Politics is a dele-
> terious profession, like some poisonous handicrafts. Men in power
> have no opinions, but may be had cheap for any opinion, for any
> purpose,—and if it be only a question between the most civil and
> the most forcible, I lean to the last. These Hoosiers and Suckers
> are really better than the snivelling opposition. Their wrath is at
> least of a bold and manly cast. They see, against the unanimous
> declarations of the people, how much crime the people will bear;
> they proceed from step to step, and they have calculated but too
> justly upon their Excellencies, the New England governors, and*

upon their Honors, the New England legislators. The messages of the governors and the resolutions of the legislatures, are a proverb for expressing a sham virtuous indignation, which, in the course of events, is sure to be belied.

Fundamentally, America in 1860 and America now are little different. Our current bruisers are distinctly not "frank and direct, and above falsehood," because they come from the corporate world, but certainly they know "how much crime the people will bear," and much of the opposition we can muster is, alas, "sniveling." An uncanny ironist, as a prophet must be, Emerson is archetypically American in his appreciation of power:

In history, the great moment is, when the savage is just ceasing to be a savage, with all his hairy Pelasgic strength directed on his opening sense of beauty:—and you have Pericles and Phidias,—not yet passed over into the Corinthian civility. Everything good in nature and the world is in that moment of transition, when the swarthy juices still flow plentifully from nature, but their astringency or acridity is got out by ethics and humanity.

The "moment of transition" again is emphasized: power is always at the crossing. Americans can read Emerson without reading him: that includes everyone in Washington, D.C., now pressing for power in the Persian Gulf (I write this sentence on February 24, 2003). I return to the paradox of Emerson's influence: Peace

Marchers and Bushians alike are Emerson's heirs in his dialectics of power.

I am much happier thinking about Emerson's effect on Whitman and Frost, Wallace Stevens and Hart Crane, than his effect on American geopolitics, but I fear that the two arenas finally are difficult to sever. What matters most about Emerson is that he is the theologian of the American religion of Self-Reliance, which comes at a high cost of confirmation. Every two years the Gallup organization conducts a poll on religion. The somewhat disconcerting central facts do not change: ninety-three percent of Americans say that they believe in God, and eighty-nine percent affirm that God loves them on a personal and individual basis. Even in Ireland, those who believe are not that prevalent, and no other country in the world (that I know of) is a land where almost nine out of ten have so intimate a relationship with God.

I am persuaded that Emerson, a master ironist, would be uneasy at such progeny, but his knowledge of the God within certainly contributed to this aspect of the American Religion. Among his early poems, abandoned by him in manuscript, there are startling intimations of the American wildness in religion, a fusion of Enthusiasm and a native gnosticism:

> I will not live out of me
> I will not see with others' eyes
> My good is good, my evil ill
> I would be free—I cannot be
> While I take things as others please to rate them

I dare attempt to lay out my own road
That which myself delights in shall be Good
That which I do not want,—indifferent,
That which I hate is Bad. That's flat
Henceforth, please God, forever I forego
The yoke of men's opinions. I will be
Lighthearted as a bird & live with God.
I find him in the bottom of my heart
I hear continually his Voice therein
And books, & priests, & worlds, I less esteem
Who says the heart's a blind guide? It is not.
My heart did never counsel me to sin
I wonder where it got its wisdom
For in the darkest maze amid the sweetest baits
Or amid horrid dangers never once
Did that gentle Angel fail of his oracle
The little needle always knows the north
The little bird remembereth his note
And this wise Seer never errs
I never taught it what it teaches me
I only follow when I act aright.
Whence then did this Omniscient Spirit come?
From God it came. It is the Deity.

It is not meter but a meter-making argument that validates a poem, according to Emerson. There is more than a meter-making argument in this fragment. It has the authentic accent of the American Religion. As the voice of Emerson, it fascinates me, but

causes anxiety when I imagine it being uttered by my Pentecostal, Southern Baptist, and Mormon contemporaries. As a devout Emersonian, I nevertheless admit that, in forming the mind of America, he prophesied a crazy salad to go with our meat. He spoke of himself as an endless experimenter, with no past at his back. Old Europe was rejected by him, in favor of the American Adam. Semiliterate as the Bush bunch are, their vision of the Evening Land imposing ideas of order upon the universe has an implied link to Emersonianism.

To do justice to the Sage of Concord, I will abandon politics and religion in the remainder of this chapter to address his literary qualities. With Emerson as benign father of the Americanism of American literature, only a Southern author should quarrel. No other critic has stressed so productively the use of literature for life. There are hundreds of Emersonian aphorisms that reverberate for me, but none more than this, embedded in the first paragraph of "Self-Reliance":

> *In every work of genius we recognize our own rejected thoughts:*
> *they come back to us with a certain alienated majesty.*

Several of our best living writers have quoted that to me, and I have been quoting it to my students these last four decades. "I read for the lustres," Emerson remarked, and he filled his notebooks with them, drawing particularly upon Plutarch's *Moralia* and Montaigne's *Essays*. Doubtless there are many other ways to

read, but I like best Emerson's way, which is to take back what is your own, wherever you may find it.

"All power is of one kind, a sharing of the nature of the world": that is another of Emerson's sayings, and is subject to dark interpretations in a United States determined to share in the nature of all the world. But Emerson, however he may be employed now, loathed the American imperialism of the Mexican War, and would be sublimely ironic at any of our later conquests.

Emerson looked frail, but he was a survivor. The family malady was tuberculosis, and Emerson had to endure the loss of his first wife, Ellen; of his brothers Edward and Charles; and of his young son, Waldo (to scarlet fever). These were all he had loved best, but a strong stoicism prevailed in him. For all his ailments, Emerson's travels and exertions as a lecturer rival Charles Dickens's theatrical readings, and those killed Dickens. A passion for teaching self-trust drove Emerson through an astonishing public career, in which he became a kind of Northern institution of one, rather than the icon of Transcendentalism. Though his books sold well, Emerson's fame and influence came as a popular lecturer, a kind of displacement of his earlier role as an exemplary Unitarian minister.

The United States has nothing now that approximates the wandering public lecturers of its nineteenth century. Emerson cheerfully would deliver a series, often of ten or twelve orations, for good fees, in city after city, and on very diverse topics: the philosophy of history, human life, human culture, representative men (which became a book), mind and manners, antislavery, American

civilization, or whatever he willed. Sometimes he would deliver from seventy to eighty lectures in a year, in locales spread widely throughout Canada and the United States (always excluding the South). Wherever he went, Emerson encountered sold-out houses of enthusiastic auditors. Contemporaries who attended testify to the sage's charismatic presence: serene, restrained, yet invariably intense, and spiritually formidable.

As a wisdom writer, Emerson essentially was in the oral tradition, and yet he had to be Plato to his own Socrates. Though myself an Emersonian, I wonder whether the essay of Plutarch and of Montaigne was his appropriate genre. Emerson seems most himself in his marvelous journals, begun on January 25, 1820, under the auspicious title "The Wide World." He was sixteen, and already himself, and continued the journals faithfully until 1875, when they start to trail off, as his mind wanders away from him.

An extraordinary work of self-creation, Emerson's fifty-five years of journals are his authentic greatness, insofar as his writing could convey the apparent miracle of his voice. I have read through the journals many times, and though I have a somewhat preternatural verbal memory, I frequently have difficulty in relocating particular passages that have affected me strongly. But then it is hard to find many of the crucial passages in Emerson's essays, since they blend together in the mind. Often I go looking for what I think is in "Self-Reliance," only to encounter it in "Spiritual Laws" or some other essay. One understands why Formalist critics, like Allen Tate and Robert Penn Warren, Cleanth Brooks, and John

Crowe Ransom, felt that Emerson was formless, quite aside from their Southern hatred for a Concord sage who had told his audiences that John Brown's execution had made the gallows as "glorious as the cross."

Emersonian freedom (his synonym for it is "wildness") is not primarily a formlessness, as it becomes in Allen Ginsberg and other claimants to the heritage of the greatest of Emerson's disciples, Walt Whitman. Selections from the journals do not work as books, though there have been several. Huge as the journals are, they need to be read complete, because Emerson's mind has become the mind of America. I am aware that this is not always a good thing, now that a self-reliant United States bids to become a twenty-first-century version of the Roman Empire. In fairness again to the prophetic Emerson, he vehemently opposed the admission of Texas to the Union, and wrote and lectured against the Mexican War, the archetype of America's Iraqi wars, and doubtless of wars to come.

Emerson's power of contamination was unique even in his own century, and even writers who backed away from him could not fail to absorb his stance. Herman Melville attended all of Emerson's lectures in New York City, and uneasily read the *Essays*. He satirizes the sage in *Pierre* and in *The Confidence Man*, but both Ahab and Ishmael in *Moby-Dick* are Emersonians. Hawthorne, a walking companion of Emerson's who silently resisted the prophet of self-reliance, nevertheless makes Hester Prynne, heroine of *The Scarlet Letter*, an Emersonian before Emerson. Henry James, who tried to condescend to his father's friend and master, goes beyond

Hester Prynne in the overtly Emersonian Isabel Archer of *The Portrait of a Lady*. No one, after Emerson, has taken up the burden of the literary representation of Americanness or Americans without returning to Emerson, frequently without knowing it.

"A man is a god in ruins" and "Man is the dwarf of himself": these Emersonian formulations are Hamlet-like in spirit, and can be as self-destructive as Hamlet was. Yet I thrill to Emerson's extravagant summonings to a greatness we do not yet know or understand. He had married twice: tragically but with deep love in the first instance with the doomed Ellen; happily enough but with no fierce passion toward the formidable Lidian. In the unsettling "Illusions" of *The Conduct of Life*, marriage is not exactly idealized:

> We are not very much to blame for our bad marriages. We live amid hallucinations; and this especial trap is laid to trip up our feet with, and all are tripped up first or last.

"Hallucinations" seems a strong word there, but Emerson genially assures us that most of what we live out is illusion:

> We cannot write the order of the variable winds. How can we penetrate the law of our shifting moods and susceptibility? Yet they differ as all and nothing. Instead of the firmament of yesterday, which our eyes require, it is to-day an eggshell which coops us in; we cannot even see what or where our stars of destiny are. From day to day, the capital facts of human life are hidden from our eyes. Suddenly the mist rolls up, and reveals them,

and we think how much good time is gone, that might have been saved, had any hint of these things been shown. A sudden rise in the road shows us the system of mountains, and all the summits, which have been just as near us all the year, but quite out of mind. But these alternations are not without their order, and we are parties to our various fortune. If life seems a succession of dreams, yet poetic justice is done in dreams also. The visions of good men are good; it is the undisciplined will that is whipped with bad thoughts and bad fortunes. When we break the laws, we lose our hold on the central reality. Like sick men in hospitals, we change only from bed to bed, from one folly to another; and it cannot signify much what becomes of such castaways,— wailing, stupid, comatose creatures,—lifted from bed to bed, from the nothing of life to the nothing of death.

The grim charm of Emerson, and his wisdom, are caught imperishably in that characteristic paragraph from the essay "Illusions." How difficult it is to explicate this subtle prose-poetry: is Emerson exalting whim (as he does elsewhere) while warning us that "the laws" are not to be evaded? His reader needs to bring nearly all of him to the consideration of each fresh enigma:

The intellect is stimulated by the statement of truth in a trope, and the will by clothing the laws of life in illusions.

Emerson will not tell us so, but we need to juxtapose this sentence from "Illusions" with the aphorism I quoted earlier from "Self-Reliance":

As men's prayers are a disease of the will, so are their creeds a disease of the intellect.

Prayer, then, is illusory, and creeds are less healthy than tropes or metaphors for "the statement of truth." We ordinarily do not think of Oscar Wilde as an Emersonian, but we should. Wilde's two finest essays, "The Decay of Lying" and "The Soul of Man Under Socialism," both echo "Self-Reliance" and are deeply grounded on its spiritual stance. Just as Emerson inspired (and irritated) Nietzsche, so he profoundly moved Walter Pater's disciple, the sublime Oscar.

To sum Emerson up is all but impossible: he affirms shocking antitheses. And yet I want to conclude this bicentennial birthday salute by finding his best balance in that grand death-march of an essay "Fate," in *The Conduct of Life*:

Nor can he blink the freewill. To hazard the contradiction,— freedom is necessary. If you please to plant yourself on the side of Fate, and say, Fate is all; then we say, a part of Fate is the freedom of man. Forever wells up the impulse of choosing and acting in the soul. Intellect annuls Fate. So far as a man thinks, he is free.

I hear, in the foreground of this, the stance of Hamlet, at once the freest of Shakespeare's "free artists of themselves" and the most fated. Emerson is his own Hamlet, and argues for what he famously

calls "the double consciousness," credited by W. E. B. Du Bois, crucial African-American thinker, as being one of his starting points:

> *One key, one solution to the mysteries of human condition, one*
> *solution to the old knots of fate, freedom, and foreknowledge,*
> *exists, the propounding, namely, of the double consciousness. A*
> *man must ride alternately on the horses of his private and his*
> *public nature, as the equestrians in the circus throw themselves*
> *nimbly from horse to horse, or plant one foot on the back of one,*
> *and the other foot on the back of the other. So when a man is the*
> *victim of his fate, has sciatica in his loins, and cramp in his*
> *mind; a club-foot and a club in his wit; a sour face, and a selfish*
> *temper; a strut in his gait, and a conceit in his affectation; or is*
> *ground to powder by the vice of his race; he is to rally on his rela-*
> *tion to the Universe, which his ruin benefits. Leaving the dæmon*
> *who suffers, he is to take sides with the Deity who secures uni-*
> *versal benefit by his pain.*

Emerson had stated the iron New England law of compensation: "Nothing is got for nothing." Though I am grimly impressed
by this final Emerson, who engendered the poets Edwin Arlington
Robinson and Robert Frost, I am not likely to rally on my relation to
the Universe, which my ruin benefits. That is too much like the very
American maxim "If you can't beat 'em, join 'em." The wording of
that pragmatic maxim is not Emersonian, but the sentiment is.

I come back to the earlier Emerson, who urged self-reliance, a
wisdom more humane though more difficult to realize in our daily
lives. Many among us would reject Emersonian self-reliance as

"elitism." I regard such a reaction as a weak misunderstanding. Self-trust, for Emerson, need not involve any dismissal of common concerns. Primarily it is an admonition that educates us to the enterprise of realizing our full potential, whether or not that realization is always acceptable to the public.

NIETZSCHE

An admirable study by Alexander Nehamas, *Nietzsche: Life as Literature* (1985), argues that Friedrich Nietzsche views life as a literary text, human beings as literary characters, and knowledge as literary criticism. Were Nehamas precisely right, then Nietzsche could not be judged to be a wisdom writer, akin to Emerson. Clearly, as Nehamas intimates, Nietzsche understood his limitations, and made his work available to be interpreted other than philosophically. Wisdom writers are rarely philosophers: Montaigne and Bacon, Johnson and Goethe, Emerson and Nietzsche, Freud and Proust, are not Descartes and Hobbes, Spinoza and Leibniz, Hume and Kant, Hegel and Wittgenstein. The ancient quarrel between poetry and philosophy can never end, and wisdom writing is more poetic than philosophical. Plato, the only philosopher who can compete with Homer, Shakespeare, and Dante, is in a category entirely his own, as I tried to demonstrate in this book's second chapter. His dialogues contest not Homer but the Athenian dramatists, and destroy many of the distinctions between myth-making and philosophy.

Nietzsche's wisdom is very mixed, and probably disturbs more

than it clarifies, since it is not at all prudential, unlike Emersonian wisdom, which Nietzsche surprisingly admired, by way of a strong misreading. David Mikics, in *The Romance of Individualism* (2003), genially attempts to bring together Emerson and Nietzsche as prophets of self-reliance, which indeed is the central concern of the sage of Concord, but hardly of the tragic Nietzsche, whose Zarathustra is a failed comedian. A reading side by side of the Emersonian Walt Whitman's *Song of Myself* and *Thus Spake Zarathustra* produces a precise sense of Nietzsche's aesthetic self-defeat. Emerson, like the earlier Whitman, is too canny and too American to lose his balance. This is not to say that the difference between Emerson and Nietzsche is only a matter of temperament. Emerson is America's Plato, one not much interested in Socrates, who obsessed Nietzsche, as he did Kierkegaard. The vast distance between Emerson and extraordinary Europeans like Nietzsche and Kierkegaard is that Emerson declines any asceticism of the spirit, and so shrugs off both Socrates and Jesus. Either of them would have made Emerson into what he called a secondary man. When Nietzsche lamented the loss of a philosopher in Emerson, he projected his own dilemma on the most formidable of Americans, who had bypassed philosophy by founding the American Religion, which cheerfully dismisses history, without Nietzsche's strenuous struggle with history, a wrestling that the self-proclaimed "philosopher of the future" could not win.

Emerson and Goethe were serene, almost as though they lacked superegos. Renunciation, as a gesture, worked for them, as it did for Freud, who in *Civilization and Its Discontents* (to be considered in my next chapter) made of renunciation and its discomforts a

Punch-and-Judy show, with superego pounding away at ego the more strenuously, the more the wretched ego surrenders its desires. Punched the harder even as it yields all aggressivity, the poor ego cannot escape the sadistic superego's furious injunction: "Stop being so aggressive!" Nietzsche went mad because he could not stop this assault on the part of us that holds us back, could not cease studying the nostalgias even as he cried out for newness. I fear that Nietzsche was destroyed because he was flooded by belatedness. Emerson had no American precursor, and Goethe easily surmounted anyone who had written German poetry before him. Nietzsche, accurately knowing the cultural potency of Emerson and of Goethe, failed at self-reliance. He remains a superb wisdom writer, but this is wisdom at the extreme edge, poised before an abyss into which it must tumble.

2

Nietzsche had too many precursors; Schopenhauer and Wagner caused him more anxiety than Goethe, remote in time, or Emerson, in far-off America. Here I desire only to examine his wisdom at its most mature, rather than analyze his anxieties. As central texts I take *On the Genealogy of Morals* (1887) and one notebook entry from the posthumously published *The Will to Power* (1901). Quotations from both are translated by Walter Kaufmann and R. J. Hollingdale (1967).

Origin and purpose—where we begin and what we attempt to do—for the sake of life, must be kept apart; that fierce admonition is central to Nietzsche. Can they be kept apart, for very long, in an

individual psychology? Nietzsche's true strength was as a psychologist, but he finally asked of us what no psychologist rightfully can expect, since the cyclic return of aim or purpose to origin is not to be evaded, a dark lesson taught by poets and speculators throughout recorded time. Beginnings have more than prestige; they foster the perpetual illusion of freedom, even though the invasion of that illusion generally means dying.

Nietzsche's deepest teaching, as I read it, is that authentic meaning is painful, and that the pain itself is the meaning. Between pain and its meaning comes a memory of pain that then becomes a memorable meaning:

> *"How can one create a memory for the human animal? How can one impress something upon this partly obtuse, partly flighty mind, attuned only to the passing moment, in such a way that it will stay there?"*
>
> *One can well believe that the answers and methods for solving this primeval problem were not precisely gentle; perhaps indeed there was nothing more fearful and uncanny in the whole prehistory of man than his mnemotechnics. "If something is to stay in the memory it must be burned in; only that which never ceases to* hurt *stays in the memory"—this is the main clause of the oldest (unhappily also the most enduring) psychology on earth. One might even say that wherever on earth solemnity, seriousness, mystery, and gloomy coloring still distinguish the life of man and a people, something of the terror that formerly attended all promises, pledges, and vows on earth is still effective: the past, the longest, deepest and sternest past, breathes upon us and rises up in*

us whenever we become "serious." Man could never do without blood, torture, and sacrifices when he felt the need to create a memory for himself; the most dreadful sacrifices and pledges (sacrifices of the first-born among them), the most repulsive mutilations (castration, for example), the cruelest rites of all the religious cults (and all religions are at the deepest level systems of cruelties)—all this has its origin in the instinct that realized that pain is the most powerful aid to mnemonics.

I hesitate to name this as Nietzsche's most fundamental insight, but I myself always remember it first when I think of Nietzsche. That the hurt itself should be the *logos,* the link of meaning that connects character and feeling, is the implicit teaching of all religions, which indeed are "systems of cruelties" as Nietzsche calls them, and I am certain he would have placed Marxism and psychoanalysis among them. But I fear that Nietzsche's insight is darker and more comprehensive than that. It embraces all literature as well, since what *On the Genealogy of Morals* goes on to call "the ascetic spirit" might as well be called "the aesthetic spirit" also, or the ascetic/aesthetic ideal:

That this idea acquired such power and ruled over men as imperiously as we find it in history, especially wherever the civilization and taming of man has been carried through, expresses a great fact: the sickliness of the type of man we have had hitherto, or at least of the tamed man, and the physiological struggle of man against death (more precisely: against disgust with life, against exhaustion, against the desire for the "end"). The ascetic

priest is the incarnate desire to be different, to be in a different place, and indeed this desire at its greatest extreme, its distinctive fervor and passion; but precisely this power of his desire is the chain that holds him captive so that he becomes a tool for the creation of more favorable conditions for being here and being man—it is precisely this power *that enables him to persuade to existence the whole herd of the ill-constituted, disgruntled, underprivileged, unfortunate, and all who suffer of themselves, by instinctively going before them as their shepherd. You will see my point: this ascetic spirit, this apparent enemy of life, this denier—precisely he is among the greatest* conserving *and yes-creating forces of life.*

With singular contempt, and questionable insistence, Nietzsche keeps repeating that, in the case of an artist, ascetic ideals mean nothing whatever, or so many things as to amount to nothing whatever. This repetition is defensive and so is not altogether sincere. It is part of his polemic against his once-idealized Wagner, but it is also the apology of a failed poet who could not acknowledge his failure, as *Zarathustra* dreadfully demonstrates. The desire to be different, to be elsewhere, is the one motive for metaphor in Nietzsche, and perhaps in everyone else as well. If it leads to a Moses, then it leads to a Goethe also. The antithetical spirit in Nietzsche, his own versions of the ascetic and the aesthetic, drives him toward what I venture to call a *poetics of pain*, which has to be read antithetically, as meaning nearly the reverse of what it appears to say:

Art—to say it in advance, for I shall some day return to this sub-
ject at greater length—art, in which precisely the lie is sanctified
and the will to deception has a good conscience, is much more
fundamentally opposed to the ascetic ideal than is science: this
was instinctively sensed by Plato, the greatest enemy of art Europe
has yet produced. Plato versus Homer: that is the complete, the
genuine antagonism—there the sincerest advocate of the
"beyond," the great slanderer of life; here the instinctive deifier,
the golden nature. To place himself in the service of the ascetic
ideal is therefore the most distinctive corruption of an artist
that is at all possible; unhappily, also one of the most common
forms of corruption, for nothing is more easily corrupted than
an artist.

The agon between Plato and Homer here is misread, creatively or strongly, as a struggle between the ascetic and the
aesthetic, rather than as the struggle for aesthetic supremacy Nietzsche elsewhere declared it to be. But Nietzsche's superb irony
anticipates my attempts to "correct" him; what artists have not
shown such *corruption* when they place themselves in the service
of the ascetic ideal? Indeed, what other option have they, or we,
according to Nietzsche? Which is to say: how are we to read the
final section of the *Genealogy*?

Apart from the ascetic ideal, man, the human animal, had no
meaning so far. His existence on earth contained no goal; "why
man at all?"—was a question without an answer; the will for

man and earth was lacking; behind every great human destiny there sounded as a refrain a yet greater "in vain!" This is precisely what the ascetic ideal means: that something was lacking, that man was surrounded by a fearful void—he did not know how to justify, to account for, to affirm himself; he suffered from the problem of his meaning. He also suffered otherwise, he was in the main a sickly animal: but his problem was not suffering itself, but that there was no answer to the crying question, "why do I suffer?"

Man, the bravest of animals and the one most accustomed to suffering, does not repudiate suffering as such; he desires it, he even seeks it out, provided he is shown a meaning for it, a purpose of suffering. The meaninglessness of suffering, not suffering itself, was the curse that lay over mankind so far—and the ascetic ideal offered man meaning! It was the only meaning offered so far; any meaning is better than none at all; the ascetic ideal was in every sense the "faute de mieux" par excellence so far. In it, suffering was interpreted; the tremendous void seemed to have been filled; the door was closed to any kind of suicidal nihilism. This interpretation—there is no doubt of it—brought fresh suffering with it, deeper, more inward, more poisonous, more life-destructive suffering: it placed all suffering under the perspective of guilt.

But all this notwithstanding—man was saved thereby, he possessed a meaning, he was henceforth no longer like a leaf in the wind, a plaything of nonsense—the "sense-less"—he could now will something; no matter at first to what end, why, with what he willed: the will itself was saved.

We can no longer conceal from ourselves what is expressed by all that willing which has taken its direction from the ascetic ideal; this hatred of the human, and even more of the animal, and more still of the material, this horror of the senses, of reason itself, this fear of happiness and beauty, this longing to get away from all appearance, change, becoming, death, wishing, from longing itself—all this means—let us dare to grasp it—a will to nothingness, *an aversion to life, a rebellion against the most fundamental presuppositions of life; but it is and remains a* will! . . . *And, to repeat in conclusion what I said at the beginning: man would rather will* nothingness *than not will.*

To give suffering a meaning is not so much to relieve suffering as it is to enable meaning to get started, rather than merely repeated. What Nietzsche shares most deeply with the Hebrew Bible and with Freud is the drive to find sense in everything, to interpret everything, but here Nietzsche is at his most dialectical, since he knows (and cannot accept) the consequences of everything having a meaning. There could never be anything new, since everything would have happened already; that is the Hebrew Bible's loyalty to Yahweh, its trust in the Covenant, and finally that is Freud's faith in the efficacy of interpretation. And that is Nietzsche's most profound argument with the Hebrew Bible.

"Man . . . suffered from the problem of his meaning" and then yielded to the ascetic ideal, which made the suffering itself into the meaning, and so opened the perspective of guilt. Rather than be void of meaning, man took the void *as* meaning, a taking that saved the will, at a fearful cost. Nietzsche has no alternative but to

accuse the poets of nihilism, an accusation in which he himself did not altogether believe. But his association of memory, pain, and meaning is unforgettable and productive, suggesting as it does an antithetical poetics not yet fully formulated, yet lurking in his forebodings of an uncannier nihilism than any yet known.

3

"We possess art lest we should perish of the truth." If a single apothegm could sum up Nietzsche on the aesthetic, it would be that. Poetry tells lies, but the truth, being the reality principle, reduces to death, our death. To love truth would be to love death. This hardly seems to me, as it does to Gilles Deleuze, a tragic conception of art. The world is rich in meaning because it is rich in error, and strong in suffering, when seen from an aesthetic perspective. Sanctifying a lie, and deceiving with a good conscience, is the necessary labor of art, because error about life is necessary for life, since the truth about life merely hastens death. The will to deceive is not a tragic will, and indeed is the only source for an imaginative drive that can counter the ascetic drive against life. But these antithetical drives, as in Freud's *Beyond the Pleasure Principle,* form the figure of a chiasmus. Nietzsche is scarcely distinguishable from the Pater of *Marius the Epicurean,* who also so mingles the ascetic and the aesthetic that we cannot undo their mutual contamination, at least in the strong poet.

Richard Rorty makes the crucial observation that only the

strong poet, in Nietzsche, is able to appreciate his own contingency, and thus to appropriate it:

The line between weakness and strength is thus the line between using language which is familiar and universal and producing language which, though initially unfamiliar and idiosyncratic, somehow makes tangible the blind impress all one's behavings bear.

Rorty goes on to say that Nietzsche does not avoid an "inverted Platonism—his suggestion that a life of self-creation can be as complete and as autonomous as Plato thought a life of contemplation might be." In some terrible sense, Nietzsche did live his life as though it were a poem, and found a value in the idea of his own suffering, a value not unrelated to his adversary, the ascetic ideal. In his own terms, Nietzsche was one of the corrupted strong poets, but such corruption is indistinguishable from strength, even as the ascetic and the aesthetic spirits do blend together. More even than Pater, Nietzsche is an aesthete, giving everything to perception, and finding valid perception only in the arts. Yet Nietzsche, unlike Pater, has his own kind of uneasy conscience at his own aestheticism.

Does Nietzsche offer any mode of understanding reality that does not depend on literary culture? Clearly not, and that seems to me his difference from all previous psychologists and philosophers. Though he insisted that he was wiser than the poets, he never presented us with that wisdom. If you are going to be the poet of your own life, then you are going to share, at best, the wisdom of the strong poets, and not of the philosophers, theologians,

psychologists, or politicians. I think that Nietzsche's true strength, his originality, was that he did realize the cognitive implication of poetic wisdom. To call our cosmos the primordial poem of mankind, something that we have composed ourselves, sounds like Shelley, but is Nietzsche:

1. We want to hold fast to our senses and to our faith in them— and think their consequences through to the end! The nonsensuality of philosophers hitherto is the greatest nonsensicality of man.

2. The existing world, upon which all earthly living things have worked so that it appears as it does (durable and changing slowly), we want to go on building—and not criticize it away as false!

3. Our valuations are a part of this building; they emphasize and underline. Of what significance is it if entire religions say: "all is bad and false and evil"! This condemnation of the entire process can only be a judgment of the ill-constituted!

4. To be sure, the ill-constituted can be the greatest sufferers and the most subtle? The contented could be of little value?

5. One must understand the artistic basic phenomenon that is called "life"—the building spirit that builds under the most unfavorable conditions: in the slowest manner—A demonstration of all its combinations must first be produced afresh: it preserves itself.

[*THE WILL TO POWER*, 1046 (1884)]

Walter Pater would have had no difficulty in endorsing this; his own emphasis upon sensation and perception as constitutive of his kind of reality would be wholly consonant with Nietzsche, except that Pater is overtly and candidly solipsistic. Nietzsche, rebellious student of Schopenhauer, might not have agreed with his mentor (or with Wittgenstein) that what the solipsist means is right.

What the poet means is hurtful, Nietzsche tells us, nor can we tell the hurt from the meaning. What are the pragmatic consequences for wisdom of Nietzsche's poetics of pain? To ask that is to ask also what I am convinced is the determining question of the canonical: what makes one poem more memorable than another? The Nietzschean answer must be that the memorable poem, the poem that has more meaning, or starts more meaning going, is the poem that gives (or commemorates) more pain. Like Freud's ghastly Primal History Scene (in *Totem and Taboo*), the strong poem repeats and commemorates a primordial pain. Or to be more Nietzschean (and more Paterian), the strong poem constitutes pain, brings pain into being, and so creates meaning.

The pain is the meaning. I find this formulation peculiarly and personally disturbing because, ever since I was a small boy, I have judged poems on the basis of just how memorable they immediately seemed. It is distressing to reflect that what seemed inevitable phrasing to me (and still does) was the result of inescapable pain, rather than of what it seemed to be, bewildering pleasure. But then the Nietzschean Sublime, like the Longinian and the Shelleyan, depends on our surrendering easier pleasures in order to experience more difficult pleasures. Strong poetry is difficult, and

its memorability is the consequence of a difficult pleasure, and a difficult enough pleasure is a kind of pain.

Rorty is right, I think, in associating Nietzsche's wisdom with the acceptance of contingency, to which I would add only that it is very painful to accept contingency, to be the contained rather than the container. The uneasy fusion of the aesthetic and ascetic spirits (I would prefer to call them stances) figures again in Nietzsche's ability to compound with facticity. Stevens's Nietzschean "The Poems of Our Climate" ends with a return to what Nietzsche called the primordial poem of mankind, to what had been so long composed by all of us as a fiction that replaces reality. This is Nietzsche's exaltation of the aesthetic lie, lest we perish of the truth:

> Note that, in this bitterness, delight,
> Since the imperfect is so hot in us,
> Lies in flawed words and stubborn sounds.

———

CHAPTER 7

FREUD AND

PROUST

SIGMUND FREUD

In search of wisdom literature in the twentieth century, I initially found it odd that the two figures who seemed to me incontrovertible should have been the founder of psychoanalysis and the major novelist of the age. Sigmund Freud insisted that he had developed a science that would make a vital contribution to biology, but in that regard he was self-deceived. He became not the Darwin but the Montaigne of his era, a superb moral essayist rather than a revolutionist who overturned our sense of humankind's place in nature. Marcel Proust disputes with James Joyce the eminence of the greatest literary artist of their age, yet Proust is the wisest of storytellers, while Joyce's project was to alter and complete Western literary tradition, and wisdom was secondary to other concerns in Joyce's writing.

Sigmund Freud was born on May 6, 1856, and began his characteristic work in Vienna in 1886, when he opened a private practice for the treatment of hysteria. By 1896, before his fortieth birthday, he had begun to use his personal term, "psychoanalysis," to describe what was at once his mode of therapy and his developing theory of the mind. In 2003, more than a century after Freud began his therapeutic career, it seems incredible that he should have died as much as sixty-four years ago, on September 23, 1939, at a still very active eighty-three. We live more than ever in the Age of Freud, despite the relative decline that psychoanalysis has begun to suffer as a public institution and as a medical specialty. Freud's universal and comprehensive theory of the mind probably will outlive the psychoanalytical therapy, and seems already to have placed him with Plato and Montaigne and Shakespeare rather than with the scientists he overtly aspired to emulate.

This is not to suggest that Freud was primarily a philosopher or a poet, but rather that his influence has been analogous to that of Plato, Montaigne, Shakespeare: inescapable, immense, almost incalculable. In some sense, we are all Freudians, whether we want to be or not. Freud is much more than a perpetual fashion: he seems to have become a culture, our culture. He is at once the principal writer and the principal thinker of our century. If one seeks the strongest authors in the West in our time, most readers would agree on the crucial figures; Proust, Joyce, Kafka, Yeats, Mann, Lawrence, Woolf, Eliot, Rilke, Faulkner, Valéry, Stevens, Montale, Akhmatova, and Beckett certainly would be among them. The essential thinkers might constitute a shorter and more controversial canon, whether of scientists or philosophers, and I will not venture

to list them here. Freud is unique in that he would dominate the second group and successfully challenge even Proust, Joyce, and Kafka in the first. Nor can one match him with any of the religious figures or scholars of the century. His only rivals indeed are Plato, Montaigne, Shakespeare, or even the anonymous primal narrator of Genesis, Exodus, and Numbers, called the J writer, or Yahwist, in biblical scholarship.

It is this unique stature, this pervasive influence of Freud, that now constitutes the overwhelming element in his achievement. Perhaps his effect on us is even more important than the apparently lasting value of his general theory of the mind. Himself the creator of the darkest Western vision of fatherhood since the ancient Gnostics, he has become a generic father figure in Western culture, a fate he would have resented. His Viennese contemporary the satirist Karl Kraus bitterly observed that psychoanalysis itself was the mental illness or spiritual disease of which it purported to be the cure. This remains, I think, the most destructive remark that Freud ever has provoked, because it centers on what is most problematic in his writing and in his therapy, the intimately related ideas of authority and transference.

In the name of *his* science, Freud audaciously usurped authority and triumphantly manifested an originality comparable even to Shakespeare's. Perhaps he subsumed Schopenhauer and Nietzsche in something of the way in which Shakespeare can be said to have absorbed Christopher Marlowe. Iago and Edmund have traces of the Marlovian hero-villain, but *Othello* and *Lear* are universes of language, while *The Jew of Malta* and *Tamburlaine* in comparison seem only local regions of powerful rhetoric. Schopenhauer lurks

uneasily in the Freudian mythology of the drives, and Nietzsche's tracing of the genealogy of morals perhaps haunts Freud's account of our need for punishment, the economics of moral masochism. But we read Marlowe now in the shadow of Shakespeare, and the psychoanalytical acuity of Nietzsche and Schopenhauer appears fitful in direct juxtaposition to Freud's uncanny stories of our unconscious mental processes. "Great havoc makes he among our originalities," Emerson ruefully observed of Plato, and he came near to saying the same of Montaigne and Shakespeare. We must say of Freud: after him there is only commentary.

2

To begin is to be free, and after Freud we are never free of Freud. His peculiar subject was psychic overdetermination or unconscious bondage, or again, the inability to begin fresh rather than repeat. Eros, he taught, is never free but always a repetition, always a transference in authority from past to present. Presumably just this sense of enforced illusion gave Freud his double concept of taboo and transference, two heightened versions of emotional ambivalence, of simultaneous love and hatred invested in the same object to a nearly equal degree, a conflict manifested in that other masterpiece of emotional ambivalence, the Oedipus complex. Love, reliant on the fixations of infantile sexuality for its origins, suffers always from the felt stigma of the narcissistic scar, the infant's first tragic failure in sexual strife or its loss of the parent of the opposite sex to the rival, the parent of the same sex. Already necessarily

neurotic, love thus is usefully vulnerable to the "artificial neurosis" of the psychoanalytic transference, the false Eros induced by Freud and his followers for therapeutic purposes, or as a fresh wound inflicted supposedly to heal a wound.

The analytical transference marks the crisis in Freud's vision of Eros, a crisis that is again the hidden point of Karl Kraus's bitter jest that psychoanalysis itself was the illness for which it pretended to be the cure. By 2004, psychoanalysis in a societal sense has become a kind of universal transference neurosis, and the figure of Freud has assumed a mythological status darkly akin to that of the totemic father who is slain and devoured in the ghastly Primal History Scene of *Totem and Taboo*. As the dead father, Freud is stronger than any living father can be, indeed has blended into the man Moses, a new Moses, to be sure, replacing monotheism, but hardly with the religion of science. The dead ancestor has become a numinous shadow for his adherents, by a Nietzschean irony that haunts many other modern secularisms.

3
—

Michel Foucault once observed that Marxism swims in nineteenth-century thought as a fish swims in the sea. One could not make the same remark about what I suggest we begin to call the Freudian speculation. Though Freud emerged from the Age of Darwin, he is a curiously timeless figure, as old as Jewish memory. His Jewish-ness is far more central to him than he cared to believe and, together with Kafka's, may be retrospectively definitive of what

Jewish culture can still be as this new century develops. Gershom Scholem, who loved Kafka's writings and rather resented Freud's, said of Kafka's that they had for certain readers (like Scholem) "something of the strong light of the canonical, of that perfection which destroys." For certain other readers (like myself), Freud's writings share that quality with Kafka's. Though barely touched by normative Judaism, Freud and Kafka were Jewish writers, just as Scholem was. Someday, perhaps, all three together will be seen as having redefined Jewish culture among them.

Freud, in his overt polemic against religion, insisted on reducing all religion to the longing for the father. This reduction makes sense only in a Hebraic universe of discourse, where authority always resides in figures of the individual's past and only rarely survives in the individual proper. The Greek spirit encouraged an individual agon for contemporary authority, an agon made possible by the example of the Homeric heroes. But if the hero is Abraham or Jacob rather than Achilles or Odysseus, he provides a much more anxious example. Plato was ironically Homeric in entering upon a struggle with Homer for the mind of Athens, but Rabbi Akiba would never have seen himself as struggling with Moses for the mind of Jerusalem. Zeus was not incommensurate with the godlike Achilles. Abraham, arguing with Yahweh on the road to Sodom, haggled over the number of righteous men required to prevent the destruction of the city, but he knew he was nothing in himself when face to face with Yahweh. Yet, in his humane desperation, Father Abraham pragmatically needed to act momentarily as if he were everything in himself. It is Jewish, and not Greek, to vacillate so dizzily between the need to be everything in oneself and the

anxiety of being nothing in oneself. That vertigo is the condition that makes necessary what Freud called defense or repression, the flight from prohibited representations of desire.

But what are the motives for such flight, for the defense of repression? Since Freud defines the drive as that which yields pleasure when fulfilled, what is it that sets it off, by displeasure, repression? I find no overt answer to this crucial question in Freud, whose characteristic dualism was too fundamental for questioning. The only answer is implicit in the dualism, a point shrewdly noted by the Dutch historical psychologist J. H. Van den Berg: "The theory of repression . . . is closely related to the thesis that there is sense in everything, which in turn implies that everything is past and there is nothing new." That is to say, we can understand repression only in a psychic world where everything is absolutely meaningful, where a symptom or a witticism or a verbal slip is so overdetermined that enormous interpretive intensity can and must be applied. Such a world, the realm of the great normative rabbis and of Freud, ensues when everything is over already, when the truly significant has happened once and for all. The time of the fathers, for the rabbis, is akin to Freud's age of infancy, when we are scarred forever.

What for the rabbis was significant memory appears in Freud, under the sign of negation, as unconscious but purposeful forgetting, or repression. But this Freudian negation is precisely Jewish or rabbinical, marked by the Hebraic mode of dualism, which is not a split between mind or soul and body, or between the self and nature, but a subtler dichotomy between inwardness and outwardness. This is prophetic dualism, the stance of Elijah and of the line of his successors from Amos to Malachi. In standing against

the unjust world, Elijah and his disciples proclaim that justice must be established *against the world,* in a deep inwardness of morality that wars against all outwardness whatsoever. But what is this, in the Freudian register, except the moral basis for Freud's only transcendence, which is reality testing, or learning to live with the reality principle? Why, after all, is the psyche at civil war? What does it war with, in itself, except the injustice of outwardness, the repressive vicissitudes of the drives, the neurotic sufferings that rob us of the freedom that yet can give time to time, so that for a moment it might be our time?

4
—

Our inability to characterize Freud accurately without revising him is a true sign of his varied strength. His central ideas—the drives, the defenses, the psychic agencies, the dynamic unconscious—are all frontier concepts, making ghostlier the demarcations between mind and body. Freud's science, psychoanalysis, is neither primarily speculative/poetic nor empirical/therapeutic but is on the border between all prior disciplines. So his concept of negation is a frontier idea also, breaking down the distinction between inwardness and outwardness. In Freudian negation, as in normative Jewish memory, a previously repressed thought, desire, or feeling achieves formulation only by being disowned, so that it is cognitively accepted but still affectively denied. Thinking is freed from its sexual past, even as thinking is desexualized also in the rituals of normative Judaism.

Richard Wollheim brilliantly relates Freud's idea of negation to Freud's difficult realization that the ego is always a bodily ego. So the capacity to assign truth or falsehood to an assertion is traced to a primitive movement of mind, wherein a kind of thought is felt and then either introjected (swallowed up) or projected (spat out). This explains how negation works so as to internalize certain objects of the mind, an internalization that results in the bodily ego. But both "internalized object" and a "bodily ego" are very difficult fictions or metaphors. How after all can a thought become an object, even if that object has been introjected by one's bodily ego? Freud's language here is radically poetic and mythological, akin to the prophetic language of an intensified moral inwardness that itself personifies justice, and that also breaks down the frontiers between the soul and the outward world.

Wisdom is to be found scattered everywhere in Freud, as in Goethe. But one must choose among these riches, and I will center here on the book translated into English as *Civilization and Its Discontents*, composed by Freud in 1929–1930, the year he received the Goethe Prize, and later experienced the sorrow of his mother's death. Freud was seventy-four; three years later Hitler assumed power, and a bonfire was made of Freud's books in Berlin. Five years further on, when Hitler took over Austria, Freud was ransomed by his followers and allowed to go into exile from Vienna to London, where he died a year later.

He had thought of calling this book *Das Unglück in der Kultur* ("Unhappiness in Civilization") but then changed it to *Das Unbehagen in der Kultur*, and suggested that the English translation be entitled "Man's Discomfort in Culture." However, the first English

version, by Joan Riviere (which I still prefer, and will quote from) was called *Civilization and Its Discontents,* printed in London in 1930. This title has entered the language and scarcely can be changed now.

Lionel Trilling, in his Charles Eliot Norton lectures, *Sincerity and Authenticity* (1972), remarked of *Civilization and Its Discontents* that its argument was that the mind, in the process of establishing a cultured social order, "has so contrived its own nature that it directs against itself an unremitting and largely gratuitous harshness." This is what, in my comments on Nietzsche, I termed a Punch-and-Judy show, in which the superego cudgels the ego yet more severely each time the poor ego renounces aggressivity. In *The Future of an Illusion* (1927), Freud had rejected all religion as the product of our need to renounce the sexual drive in order to establish and maintain culture. Our consequent anger at civilization expresses itself as the religious illusion. Not one of Freud's most persuasive treatises, *The Future of an Illusion* has been rightly eclipsed by *Civilization and Its Discontents.* The difference is the astonishing redefinition of our guilt, in the later book. Freudian guilt is *not* remorse for anything we actually have done, but results from our unconscious desire to have murdered the father (as in *Totem and Taboo*). On this unprovable but still disturbing basis, Freud says that we experience guilt in the forms of depression and of anxious expectations:

> *The tension between the strict super-ego and the subordinate ego we call the sense of guilt; it manifests itself as the need for punishment. Civilization therefore obtains the mastery over the dan-*

gerous love of aggression in individuals by enfeebling and dis-
arming it and setting up an institution within their minds to
keep watch over it, like a garrison in a conquered city.

The internalization of authority by the superego is the wisdom of civilization, which in Freud is sharply distinguished from
the wisdom of an individual, a very rare yet possible phenomenon.
There is for Freud, unlike Goethe, no poetry in or of renunciation.
Ambivalence toward authority, and toward the father, governs the
imagination. Freud quotes "The Song of the Harper" from Goethe
as our protest against the heavenly forces of authority:

> *Ye set our feet on this life's road,*
> *Ye watch our guilty, erring courses,*
> *Then leave us, bowed beneath our load,*
> *For earth its very debt enforces.*
>
> [*Translated by* ETHEL COLBURN MAYNE]

Freud's own ambivalence toward the superego can be regarded as
more Jobean than Goethean. The superego is a sadistic tyrant, and
yet also the guardian of civilization. Leviathan in the Book of Job
is God's king over all the children of pride, and yet God answers
Job's questions as to why evil afflicts the virtuous only with a series
of rhetorical questions that affirm the sanctified tyranny of nature
over all of us. We can make no covenant with Leviathan, who at
last will be death, our death. When Freud urges what he calls
"reality-testing," he means that we must learn to accept our mortality, and so finally reject all fictions, except Freud's own.

Literal mortality, as the final form of change, no one can dispute, though Christianity and Islam in all their branches, Eastern religions, and the normative Judaism that Freud declined to inherit all insist on alternative visions of resurrection. Freud dismissed religion as a powerful mythology that would fade out, but he underestimated his opponent. And yet Freud's wisdom is profound, and rarely is as reductive as it seems. His ironies, like Plato's, can be very subtle, and there is a vestige of Platonism in Freud's own myth of a Reality Principle. Freud did not literalize Freud: that has been the work of unimaginative Freudians. *Civilization and Its Discontents* may not be part of a psychotheology, as Levinas and others seem to think, but there are ironies in Freud's conception of the superego that remain to be more fully explored. One of the virtues of Eric Santner's *On the Psychotheology of Everyday Life* (2001) is its uneasiness with reductive accounts of the superego. Santner speaks of "moments . . . when the superego's impossible demands become manifest as bits of nonsense that permeate our being but cannot, not even in any form of recovered memory, be rendered as consistent, meaningful communications." Freud distrusted such mystical moments, ironically terming them "oceanic," but implicitly he relied on them for his insights, as all of us are constrained to do, which is why we go on searching for wisdom.

5

Paul Ricoeur, in his *Freud and Philosophy* (1970), indicated a fundamental flaw in the psychoanalytic theory of religion, which seeks

a direct psychology of the superego. Freud, perhaps out of dis-
taste, avoided any exegesis of writings that describe religious experience. I sometimes wonder what Freud would have made of
William James on this crucial subject. This Freudian lacuna dam-
ages *Future of an Illusion,* yet has little effect on the somber strength
of *Civilization and Its Discontents,* because there is little wisdom in
the first, and surpassing cultural insight in the second. This insight
can be characterized as Freud's own ambivalence toward the superego. Though it behaves like a circus-master punching away at the
Punchinello-ego, the superego nevertheless establishes and main-
tains civilization. Our discomfort with culture will not abandon us,
yet we are unable to survive without it. Cultural guilt has become
far more conscious among us than it tended to be in Freud's
Vienna, indeed so much so that our higher learning of a humanist
kind is ebbing away, almost as a kind of sacrifice for what we take
to be our implication in societal tyrannies and exploitations.
Freud, a wisdom writer rather than a prophet or a teacher of the
law, could not anticipate such a waning. He believed that Goethe's
sense of culture would prevail, but plainly it has not. *Bildung* is not
the concern of education in the English-speaking world. Because
Freud took the project of education for culture as a given, he was
free to analyze the superego's sadism, a freedom he might not now
assume.

Does that render *Civilization and Its Discontents* a Period Piece?
By definition, Period Pieces and wisdom literature are antithetical
to each other. Ecclesiastes and the Book of Job are not likely ever
to seem cultural bric-a-brac. The famous concluding paragraphs
of *Civilization and Its Discontents* retain their cogency in the early

twenty-first century, but even their ironies may not preserve them from decay if current trends persist and accelerate:

> *For various reasons, it is very far from my intention to express any opinion concerning the value of human civilization. I have endeavoured to guard myself against the enthusiastic partiality which believes our civilization to be the most precious thing that we possess or could acquire, and thinks it must inevitably lead us to undreamt-of heights of perfection. I can at any rate listen without taking umbrage to those critics who aver that when one surveys the aims of civilization and the means it employs, one is bound to conclude that the whole thing is not worth the effort and that in the end it can only produce a state of things which no individual will be able to bear. My impartiality is all the easier to me since I know very little about these things and am sure only of one thing, that the judgements of value made by mankind are immediately determined by their desires for happiness; in other words, that those judgements are attempts to prop up their illusions with arguments. I could understand it very well if anyone were to point to the inevitable nature of the process of cultural development and say, for instance, that the tendency to institute restrictions upon sexual life or to carry humanitarian ideals into effect at the cost of natural selection is a developmental trend which is impossible to avert or divert, and to which it is best for us to submit as though they were natural necessities. I know, too, the objection that can be raised against this: that tendencies such as these, which are*

*believed to have insuperable power behind them, have often in
the history of men been thrown aside and replaced by others. My
courage fails me, therefore, at the thought of rising up as a
prophet before my fellow-man, and I bow to their reproach that I
have no consolation to offer them; for at bottom this is what they
all demand—the frenzied revolutionary as passionately as the
most pious believer.*

*The fateful question of the human species seems to me to be
whether and to what extent the cultural process developed in it will
succeed in mastering the derangements of communal life caused by
the human instinct of aggression and self-destruction. In this connection, perhaps the phase through which we are at this moment
passing deserves special interest. Men have brought their powers of
subduing the forces of nature to such a pitch that by using them
they could now very easily exterminate one another to the last
man. They know this—hence arises a great part of their current
unrest, their dejection, their mood of apprehension. And now it
may be expected that the other of the two 'heavenly forces', eternal
Eros, will put forth his strength so as to maintain himself along-
side of his equally immortal adversary.*

Does not Freud, despite his ironic disclaimers, still afford us
some consolation? He concludes, with no apparent irony, by championing love against death, while acknowledging the immortality
of both antagonists. Proust, tragic-comedian of sexual jealousy
and its discontents, will serve as complement to this last stand of
civilization.

MARCEL PROUST

Sexual jealousy is the most novelistic of circumstances, just as incest, according to Shelley, is the most poetical. Proust is the novelist of our era, even as Freud is our moralist. Both are speculative thinkers, who divide between them the eminence of being the prime wisdom writers of the age.

Proust died in 1922, the year of Freud's grim and splendid essay "Certain Neurotic Mechanisms in Jealousy, Paranoia, and Homosexuality." Both of them great ironists, tragic celebrants of the comic spirit, Proust and Freud are not much in agreement on jealousy, paranoia, and homosexuality, though both start with the realization that all of us are bisexual in nature.

Freud charmingly begins his essay by remarking that jealousy, like grief, is normal, and comes in three stages: *competitive* (or normal), *projected,* and *delusional.* The competitive or garden variety is compounded of grief, due to the loss of the loved object, and of the reactivation of the narcissistic scar, the tragic first loss, by the infant, of the parent of the other sex to the parent of the same sex. As normal, competitive jealousy is really normal Hell, Freud genially throws into the compound such delights as enmity against the successful rival, some self-blaming, self-criticism, and a generous portion of bisexuality.

Projected jealousy attributes to the erotic partner one's own actual unfaithfulness or repressed impulses, and is cheerfully regarded by Freud as being relatively innocuous, since its almost

delusional character is highly amenable to analytic exposure of unconscious fantasies. But delusional jealousy proper is more serious; it also takes its origin in repressed impulses toward infidelity, but the object of those impulses is one's own sex, and this, for Freud, moves one across the border into paranoia.

What the three stages of jealousy have in common is a bisexual component, since even projected jealousy trades in repressed impulses, and these include homosexual desires. Proust, our other authority on jealousy, preferred to call homosexuality "inversion," and in a brilliant mythological fantasia traced the sons of Sodom and the daughters of Gomorrah to the surviving exiles from the biblical Cities of the Plain that Yahweh destroyed. Inversion and jealousy, so intimately related in Freud, become in Proust a dialectical pairing, with the aesthetic sensibility linked to both as a third term in a complex series.

On the topos of jealousy, Proust is fecund and generous; no writer has devoted himself so lovingly and brilliantly to expounding and illustrating the emotion, except of course Shakespeare in *Othello* and Hawthorne in *The Scarlet Letter*. Proust's jealous lovers—Swann, Saint-Loup, above all Marcel himself—suffer so intensely that we sometimes need to make an effort not to empathize too closely. It is difficult to determine just what Proust's stance toward their suffering is, partly because Proust's ironies are both pervasive and cunning. Comedy hovers nearby, but even tragicomedy seems an inadequate term for the compulsive sorrows of Proust's protagonists. Swann, after complimenting himself that he has not, by his jealousy, proved to Odette that he loves her too much, falls into the mouth of Hell:

He never spoke to her of this misadventure, and ceased even to think of it himself. But now and then his thoughts in their wandering course would come upon this memory where it lay unobserved, would startle it into life, thrust it forward into his consciousness, and leave him aching with a sharp, deep-rooted pain. As though it were a bodily pain, Swann's mind was powerless to alleviate it; but at least, in the case of bodily pain, since it is independent of the mind, the mind can dwell upon it, can note that it has diminished, that it has momentarily ceased. But in this case the mind, merely by recalling the pain, created it afresh. To determine not to think of it was to think of it still, to suffer from it still. And when, in conversation with his friends, he forgot about it, suddenly a word casually uttered would make him change countenance like a wounded man when a clumsy hand has touched his aching limb. When he came away from Odette he was happy, he felt calm, he recalled her smiles, of gentle mockery when speaking of this or that other person, of tenderness for himself; he recalled the gravity of her head which she seemed to have lifted from its axis to let it droop and fall, as though in spite of herself, upon his lips, as she had done on the first evening in the carriage, the languishing looks she had given him as she lay in his arms, nestling her head against her shoulder as though shrinking from the cold.

But then at once his jealousy, as though it were the shadow of his love, presented him with the complement, with the converse of that new smile with which she had greeted him that very evening—and which now, perversely, mocked Swann and shone with love for another—of that droop of the head, now sinking

*on to other lips, of all the marks of affection (now given to
another) that she had shown to him. And all the voluptuous
memories which he bore away from her house were, so to speak,
but so many sketches, rough plans like those which a decorator
submits to one, enabling Swann to form an idea of the various
attitudes, aflame or faint with passion, which she might adopt
for others. With the result that he came to regret every pleasure
that he tasted in her company, every new caress of which he had
been so imprudent as to point out to her the delights, every fresh
charm that he found in her, for he knew that, a moment later,
they would go to enrich the collection of instruments in his secret
torture-chamber.*

[*Translated by* TERENCE KILMARTIN]

Jealousy here is a pain experienced by Freud's bodily ego, on
the frontier between psyche and body: "To determine not to think
of it was to think of it still, to suffer from it still." I would say that,
as the shadow of love, jealousy resembles the shadow cast by the
earth up into the heavens, where by tradition it ought to end at the
sphere of Venus. Instead, it darkens there, and since the shadow is
Freud's reality principle, or our consciousness of our own mortality, Proust's dreadfully persuasive irony is that jealousy exposes not
only the arbitrariness of every erotic object choice but also marks
the passage of the loved person into a teleological overdetermination, in which the supposed inevitability of the person is simply
a mask for the inevitability of the lover's death. Proust's jealousy
thus becomes peculiarly akin to Freud's death drive, since it,
too, quests beyond the pleasure/unpleasure principle. Our secret

torture chamber is furnished anew by every recollection of the beloved's erotic prowess, since what delighted us has delighted others.

Swann experiences the terrible conversion of the jealous lover into a parody of the scholar, a conversion to an intellectual pleasure that is more a deviation than an achievement, since no thought can be emancipated from the sexual past of all thought (Freud) if the search for truth is nothing but a search for the sexual past:

> *Certainly he suffered as he watched that light, in whose golden atmosphere, behind the closed sash, stirred the unseen and detested pair, as he listened to that murmur which revealed the presence of the man who had crept in after his own departure, the perfidy of Odette, and the pleasures which she was at that moment enjoying with the stranger. And yet he was not sorry he had come; the torment which had forced him to leave his own house had become less acute now that it had become less vague, now that Odette's other life, of which he had had, at that first moment, a sudden helpless suspicion, was definitely there, in the full glare of the lamp-light, almost within his grasp, an unwitting prisoner in that room into which, when he chose, he would force his way to seize it unawares; or rather he would knock on the shutters, as he often did when he came very late, and by that signal Odette would at least learn that he knew, that he had seen the light and had heard the voices, and he himself, who a moment ago had been picturing her as laughing with the other at his illusions, now it was he who saw them, confident in their error, tricked by none other than himself, whom they believed to*

be far away but who was there, in person, there with a plan, there with the knowledge that he was going, in another minute, to knock on the shutter. And perhaps the almost pleasurable sensation he felt at that moment was something more than the assuagement of a doubt, and of a pain: was an intellectual pleasure. If, since he had fallen in love, things had recovered a little of the delightful interest that they had had for him long ago— though only in so far as they were illuminated by the thought or the memory of Odette—now it was another of the faculties of his studious youth that his jealousy revived, the passion for truth, but for a truth which, too, was interposed between himself and his mistress, receiving its light from her alone, a private and personal truth the sole object of which (an infinitely precious object, and one almost disinterested in its beauty) was Odette's life, her actions, her environment, her plans, her past. At every other period in his life, the little everyday activities of another person had always seemed meaningless to Swann; if gossip about such things was repeated to him, he would dismiss it as insignificant, and while he listened it was only the lowest, the most commonplace part of his mind that was engaged; these were the moments when he felt at his most inglorious. But in this strange phase of love the personality of another person becomes so enlarged, so deepened, that the curiosity which he now felt stirring inside him with regard to the smallest details of a woman's daily life, was the same thirst for knowledge with which he had once studied history. And all manner of actions from which hitherto he would have recoiled in shame, such as spying, to-night, outside a window, to-morrow perhaps, for all he knew, putting

adroitly provocative questions to casual witnesses, bribing ser-
vants, listening at doors, seemed to him now to be precisely on a
level with the deciphering of manuscripts, the weighing of evi-
dence, the interpretation of old monuments—so many different
methods of scientific investigation with a genuine intellectual
value and legitimately employable in the search for truth.

In fact, poor Swann is at the wrong window, and the entire passage is therefore as exquisitely comic as it is painful. What Freud
ironically called the overevaluation of the object, the enlargement
or deepening of the beloved's personality, begins to work not as
one of the enlargements of life (like Proust's own novel) but as the
deepening of a personal Hell. Swann plunges downward and outward, as he leans "in impotent, blind, dizzy anguish over the bot-
tomless abyss" and reconstructs the petty details of Odette's past
life with "as much passion as the aesthete who ransacks the extant
documents of fifteenth-century Florence in order to penetrate further into the soul of the Primavera, the fair Vanna or the Venus of
Botticelli."

The historicizing aesthete—John Ruskin, say, or Walter Pater—
becomes the archetype of the jealous lover, who searches into lost
time not for a person but for an epiphany or moment-of-moments,
a privileged fiction of duration:

When he had been paying social calls Swann would often come
home with little time to spare before dinner. At that point in the
evening, around six o'clock, when in the old days he used to feel
so wretched, he no longer asked himself what Odette might be

about, and was hardly at all concerned to hear that she had people with her or had gone out. He recalled at times that he had once, years ago, tried to read through its envelope a letter addressed by Odette to Forcheville. But this memory was not pleasing to him, and rather than plumb the depths of shame that he felt in it he preferred to indulge in a little grimace, twisting up the corners of his mouth and adding, if need be, a shake of the head which signified "What do I care about it?" True, he considered now that the hypothesis on which he had often dwelt at that time, according to which it was his jealous imagination alone that blackened what was in reality the innocent life of Odette—that this hypothesis (which after all was beneficent, since, so long as his amorous malady had lasted, it had diminished his sufferings by making them seem imaginary) was not the correct one, that it was his jealousy that had seen things in the correct light, and that if Odette had loved him more than he supposed, she had also deceived him more. Formerly, while his sufferings were still keen, he had vowed that, as soon as he had ceased to love Odette and was no longer afraid either of vexing her or of making her believe that he loved her too much, he would give himself the satisfaction of elucidating with her, simply from his love of truth and as a point of historical interest, whether or not Forcheville had been in bed with her that day when he had rung her bell and rapped on her window in vain, and she had written to Forcheville that it was an uncle of hers who had called. But this so interesting problem, which he was only waiting for his jealousy to subside before clearing up, had precisely lost all interest in Swann's eyes when he had ceased to be

jealous. Not immediately, however. Long after he had ceased to feel any jealousy with regard to Odette, the memory of that day, that afternoon spent knocking vainly at the little house in the Rue La Pérouse, had continued to torment him. It was as though his jealousy, not dissimilar in that respect from those maladies which appear to have their seat, their centre of contagion, less in certain persons than in certain places, in certain houses, had had for its object not so much Odette herself as that day, that hour in the irrevocable past when Swann had knocked at every entrance to her house in turn, as though that day, that hour alone had caught and preserved a few last fragments of the amorous personality which had once been Swann's, that there alone could he now recapture them. For a long time now it had been a matter of indifference to him whether Odette had been, or was being, unfaithful to him. And yet he had continued for some years to seek out old servants of hers, to such an extent had the painful curiosity persisted in him to know whether on that day, so long ago, at six o'clock, Odette had been in bed with Forcheville. Then that curiosity itself had disappeared, without, however, his abandoning his investigations. He went on trying to discover what no longer interested him, because his old self, though it had shrivelled to extreme decrepitude, still acted mechanically, in accordance with preoccupations so utterly abandoned that Swann could not now succeed even in picturing to himself that anguish— so compelling once that he had been unable to imagine that he would ever be delivered from it, that only the death of the woman he loved (though death, as will be shown later on in this story by a cruel corroboration, in no way diminishes the sufferings caused

by jealousy) seemed to him capable of smoothing the path of his life which then seemed impassably obstructed.

Jealousy dies with love, but only with respect to the former beloved. Horribly a life-in-death, jealousy renews itself like the moon, perpetually trying to discover what no longer interests it, even after the object of desire has been literally buried. Its true object is "that day, that hour in the irrevocable past," and even that time was less an actual time than a temporal fiction, an episode in the evanescence of one's own self. Paul de Man's perspective that Proust's deepest insight is the nonexistence of the self founds itself upon this temporal irony of unweaving, this permanent parabasis of meaning. One can remember that even this deconstructive perspective is no more or less privileged than any other Proustian trope, and so cannot give us a truth that Proust himself evades.

The bridge between Swann's jealousy and Marcel's is Saint-Loup's jealousy of Rachel, summed up by Proust in one of his magnificently long, baroque paragraphs:

Saint-Loup's letter had come as no surprise to me, even though I had had no news of him since, at the time of my grandmother's illness, he had accused me of perfidy and treachery. I had grasped at once what must have happened. Rachel, who liked to provoke his jealousy (she also had other causes for resentment against me), had persuaded her lover that I had made sly attempts to have relations with her in his absence. It is probable that he continued to believe in the truth of this allegation, but he had ceased to be in love with her, which meant that its truth or falsehood

had become a matter of complete indifference to him, and our friendship alone remained. When, on meeting him again, I tried to talk to him about his accusations, he merely gave me a benign and affectionate smile which seemed to be a sort of apology, and then changed the subject. All this was not to say that he did not, a little later, see Rachel occasionally when he was in Paris. Those who have played a big part in one's life very rarely disappear from it suddenly for good. They return to it at odd moments (so much so that people suspect a renewal of old love) before leaving it for ever. Saint-Loup's breach with Rachel had very soon become less painful to him, thanks to the soothing pleasure that was given him by her incessant demands for money. Jealousy, which prolongs the course of love, is not capable of containing many more ingredients than the other products of the imagination. If one takes with one, when one starts on a journey, three or four images which incidentally one is sure to lose on the way (such as the lilies and anemones heaped on the Ponte Vecchio, or the Persian church shrouded in mist), one's trunk is already pretty full. When one leaves a mistress, one would be just as glad, until one had begun to forget her, that she should not become the property of three or four potential protectors whom one pictures in one's mind's eye, of whom, that is to say, one is jealous: all those whom one does not so picture count for nothing. Now frequent demands for money from a cast-off mistress no more give one a complete idea of her life than charts showing a high temperature would of her illness. But the latter would at any rate be an indication that she was ill, and the former furnish a presumption, vague enough it is true, that the forsaken one or

forsaker (whichever she be) cannot have found anything very remarkable in the way of rich protectors. And so each demand is welcomed with the joy which a lull produces in the jealous one's sufferings, and answered with the immediate dispatch of money, for naturally one does not like to think of her being in want of anything except lovers (one of the three lovers one has in one's mind's eye), until time has enabled one to regain one's composure and to learn one's successor's name without wilting. Sometimes Rachel came in so late at night that she could ask her former lover's permission to lie down beside him until the morning. This was a great comfort to Robert, for it reminded him how intimately, after all, they had lived together, simply to see that even if he took the greater part of the bed for himself it did not in the least interfere with her sleep. He realised that she was more comfortable, lying close to his familiar body, than she would have been elsewhere, that she felt herself by his side—even in an hotel—to be in a bedroom known of old in which one has one's habits, in which one sleeps better. He felt that his shoulders, his limbs, all of him, were for her, even when he was unduly restless from insomnia or thinking of the things he had to do, so entirely usual that they could not disturb her and that the perception of them added still further to her sense of repose.

The heart of this comes in the grandly ironic sentence: "Jealousy, which prolongs the course of love, is not capable of containing many more ingredients than the other products of the imagination." That is hardly a compliment to the capaciousness of the imagination, which scarcely can hold on for long to even three

or four images. Saint-Loup, almost on the farthest shore of jealousy, has the obscure comfort of having become, for Rachel, one of those images not quite faded away, when "he felt that his shoulders, his limbs, all of him, were for her," even when he has ceased to be there, or anywhere, for her, or she for him. Outliving love, jealousy has become love's last stand, the final basis for a continuity between two former lovers.

Saint-Loup's bittersweet evanescence as a lover contrasts both with Swann's massive historicism and with the novel's triumphant representation of jealousy, Marcel's monumental search after lost time in the long aftermath of Albertine's death. Another grand link between magnificent jealousies is provided by Swann's observations to Marcel, aesthetic reflections somewhat removed from the pain of earlier realities:

> It occurred to me that Swann must be getting tired of waiting for me. Moreover I did not wish to be too late in returning home because of Albertine, and, taking leave of Mme de Surgis and M. de Charlus, I went in search of my invalid in the card-room. I asked him whether what he had said to the Prince in their conversation in the garden was really what M. de Bréauté (whom I did not name) had reported to us, about a little play by Bergotte. He burst out laughing: "There's not a word of truth in it, not one, it's a complete fabrication and would have been an utterly stupid thing to say. It's really incredible, this spontaneous generation of falsehood. I won't ask who it was that told you, but it would be really interesting, in a field as limited as this, to work back from one person to another and find out how the story

arose. Anyhow, what concern can it be of other people, what the Prince said to me? People are very inquisitive. I've never been inquisitive, except when I was in love, and when I was jealous. And a lot I ever learned! Are you jealous?" I told Swann that I had never experienced jealousy, that I did not even know what it was. "Well, you can count yourself lucky. A little jealousy is not too unpleasant, for two reasons. In the first place, it enables people who are not inquisitive to take an interest in the lives of others, or of one other at any rate. And then it makes one feel the pleasure of possession, of getting into a carriage with a woman, of not allowing her to go about by herself. But that's only in the very first stages of the disease, or when the cure is almost complete. In between, it's the most agonising torment. However, I must confess that I haven't had much experience even of the two pleasures I've mentioned—the first because of my own nature, which is incapable of sustained reflexion; the second because of circumstances, because of the woman, I should say the women, of whom I've been jealous. But that makes no difference. Even when one is no longer attached to things, it's still something to have been attached to them; because it was always for reasons which other people didn't grasp. The memory of those feelings is something that's to be found only in ourselves, we must go back into ourselves to look at it. You mustn't laugh at this idealistic jargon, but what I mean to say is that I've been very fond of life and very fond of art. Well, now that I'm a little too weary to live with other people, those old feelings, so personal and individual, that I had in the past, seem to me—it's the mania of all collectors—very precious. I open my heart to myself like a sort of

showcase, and examine one by one all those love affairs of which
the rest of the world can have known nothing. And of this col-
lection, to which I'm now even more attached than to my others,
I say to myself, rather as Mazarin said of his books, but in fact
without the least distress, that it will be very tiresome to have to
leave it all. But, to come back to my conversation with the Prince,
I shall tell one person only, and that person is going to be you."

We are in the elegy season, ironically balanced between the
death of jealousy in Swann and its birth in poor Marcel, who literally does not know that the descent into Avernus beckons. When
the vigor of an affirmation has more power than its truth, clearly
we are living in a fiction, the metaphor or transference that we call
love, and might call jealousy. Into that metaphor, Marcel moves
like a sleepwalker, with his obsessions central to *The Captive* and
insanely pervasive in *The Fugitive*. A great passage in *The Captive*,
which seems a diatribe against jealousy, instead is a passionately
ironic celebration of jealousy's aesthetic victory over our merely
temporal happiness:

However, I was still at the first stage of enlightenment with
regard to Léa. I was not even aware whether Albertine knew her.
No matter, it came to the same thing. I must at all costs prevent
her from renewing this acquaintance or making the acquain-
tance of this stranger at the Trocadéro. I say that I did not know
whether she knew Léa or not; yet I must in fact have learned this
at Balbec, from Albertine herself. For amnesia obliterated from
my mind as well as from Albertine's a great many of the state-

ments that she had made to me. Memory, instead of being a duplicate, always present before one's eyes, of the various events of one's life, is rather a void from which at odd moments a chance resemblance enables one to resuscitate dead recollections; but even then there are innumerable little details which have not fallen into that potential reservoir of memory, and which will remain forever unverifiable. One pays no attention to anything that one does not connect with the real life of the woman one loves; one forgets immediately what she has said to one about such and such an incident or such and such people one does not know, and her expression while she was saying it. And so when, in due course, one's jealousy is aroused by these same people, and seeks to ascertain whether or not it is mistaken, whether it is indeed they who are responsible for one's mistress's impatience to go out, and her annoyance when one has prevented her from doing so by returning earlier than usual, one's jealousy, ransacking the past in search of a clue, can find nothing; always retrospective, it is like a historian who has to write the history of a period for which he has no documents; always belated, it dashes like an enraged bull to the spot where it will not find the dazzling, arrogant creature who is tormenting it and whom the crowd admire for his splendour and cunning, jealousy thrashes around in the void, uncertain as we are in those dreams in which we are distressed because we cannot find in his empty house a person whom we have known well in life, but who here perhaps is another person and has merely borrowed the features of our friend, uncertain as we are even more after we awake when we seek to identify this or that detail of our dream. What was one's

mistress's expression when she told one that? Did she not look happy, was she not actually whistling, a thing that she never does unless she has some amorous thought in her mind and finds one's presence importunate and irritating? Did she not tell one something that is contradicted by what she now affirms, that she knows or does not know such and such a person? One does not know, and one will never know; one searches desperately among the unsubstantial fragments of a dream, and all the time one's life with one's mistress goes on, a life that is oblivious of what may well be of importance to one, and attentive to what is perhaps of none, a life hagridden by people who have no real connexion with one, full of lapses of memory, gaps, vain anxieties, a life as illusory as a dream.

Thrashing about in the void of a dream in which a good friend perhaps is another person, jealousy becomes Spenser's Malbecco: who "quite / Forgot he was a man, and Jealousy is hight." Yet making life "as illusory as a dream," hagridden by lapses and gaps, is Marcel's accomplishment, and Proust's art. One does not write an other-than-ironic diatribe against one's own art. Proust warily, but with the sureness of a great beast descending on its helpless prey, approaches the heart of his vision or jealousy, his sense that the emotion is akin to what Freud named as the defense of isolation, in which all context is burned away, and a dangerous present replaces all past and all future.

Sexual jealousy in Proust is accompanied by a singular obsessiveness in regard to questions of space and of time. The jealous lover, who, as Proust says, conducts researches comparable to

those of the scholar, seeks in his inquiries every detail he can find as to the location and duration of each betrayal and infidelity. Why? Proust has a marvelous passage in the *Fugitive* volume of *In Search of Lost Time*:

> It is one of the faculties of jealousy to reveal to us the extent to which the reality of external facts and the sentiments of the heart are an unknown element which lends itself to endless suppositions. We imagine that we know exactly what things are and what people think, for the simple reason that we do not care about them. But as soon as we have a desire to know, as the jealous man has, then it becomes a dizzy kaleidoscope in which we can no longer distinguish anything. Had Albertine been unfaithful to me? With whom? In what house? On what day? On the day when she had said this or that to me, when I remembered that I had in the course of it said this or that? I could not tell. Nor did I know what her feelings were for me, whether they were inspired by self-interest or by affection. And all of a sudden I remembered some trivial incident, for instance that Albertine had wished to go to Saint-Martin-le-Vêtu, saying that the name interested her, and perhaps simply because she had made the acquaintance of some peasant girl who lived there. But it was useless that Aimé should have informed me of what she had learned from the woman at the baths, since Albertine must remain eternally unaware that she had informed me, the need to know having always been exceeded, in my love for Albertine, by the need to show her that I knew; for this broke down the partition of different illusions that stood between us, without having

ever had the result of making her love me more, far from it. And now, since she was dead, the second of these needs had been amalgamated with the effect of the first: the need to picture to myself the conversation in which I would have informed her of what I had learned, as vividly as the conversation in which I would have asked her to tell me what I did not know; that is to say, to see her by my side, to hear her answering me kindly, to see her cheeks become plump again, her eyes shed their malice and assume an air of melancholy; that is to say, to love her still and to forget the fury of my jealousy in the despair of my loneliness. The painful mystery of this impossibility of ever making known to her what I had learned and of establishing our relations upon the truth of what I had only just discovered (and would not have been able, perhaps, to discover but for her death) substituted its sadness for the more painful mystery of other conduct. What? To have so desperately desired that Albertine—who no longer existed—should know that I had heard the story of the baths! This again was one of the consequences of our inability, when we have to consider the fact of death, to picture to ourselves anything but life. Albertine no longer existed; but to me she was the person who had concealed from me that she had assignations with women at Balbec, who imagined that she had succeeded in keeping me in ignorance of them. When we try to consider what will happen to us after our own death, is it not still our living self which we mistakenly project at that moment? And is it much more absurd, when all is said, to regret that a woman who no longer exists is unaware that we have learned what she was doing six years ago than to desire that of ourselves, who will be

dead, the public shall still speak with approval a century hence?
If there is more real foundation in the latter than in the former
case, the regrets of my retrospective jealousy proceeded none the
less from the same optical error as in other men the desire for
posthumous fame. And yet, if this impression of the solemn
finality of my separation from Albertine had momentarily sup-
planted my idea of her misdeeds, it only succeeded in aggravat-
ing them by bestowing upon them an irremediable character. I
saw myself astray in life as on an endless beach where I was
alone and where, in whatever direction I might turn, I would
never meet her.

"The regrets of my retrospective jealousy proceeded none the
less from the same optical error as in other men the desire for
posthumous fame"—is that not as much Proust's negative credo as
it is Marcel's? Those "other men" include the indubitable precursors,
Flaubert and Baudelaire, and Proust himself as well. Here, the aesthetic agon for immortality is an optical error, yet this is one of those
errors about life that are necessary for life, as Nietzsche remarked,
and is also one of those errors about art that is art. Proust has
swerved away from Flaubert into a radical confession of error; the
novel is creative envy, love is jealousy, jealousy is the terrible fear that
there will not be enough space for oneself (including literary space),
and that there never can be enough time for oneself, because death
is the reality of one's life. A friend once remarked to me, at the very
height of her own jealousy, that jealousy was nothing but a vision of
two bodies on a bed, neither of which was one's own, where the
hurt resided in the realization that one body ought to have been

one's own. Bitter as the remark may have been, it usefully reduces the trope of jealousy to literal fears: where was one's body, where will it be, when will it not be? Our ego is always a bodily ego, Freud insisted, and jealousy joins the bodily ego and the drives of love and death as another frontier concept. Proust, like Freud, goes back after all to the prophet Jeremiah, that uncomfortable sage who proclaimed a new inwardness for his mother's people. Jeremiah said that the law is written upon our inward parts. For Proust also, this law is justice, but the god of law is a jealous god, though he is certainly not the god of jealousy.

Freud, in "The Passing of the Oedipus Complex," writing two years after Proust's death, set forth a powerful speculation as to the difference between the sexes, a speculation that Proust neither evades nor supports, and yet illuminates, by working out of the world that Freud knows only in the pure good of theory. Freud is properly tentative, but also adroitly forceful:

> Here our material—for some reason we do not understand—becomes far more shadowy and incomplete. The female sex develops an Oedipus-complex, too, a super-ego and a latency period. May one ascribe to it also a phallic organization and a castration complex? The answer is in the affirmative, but it cannot be the same as in the boy. The feministic demand for equal rights between the sexes does not carry far here; the morphological difference must express itself in differences in the development of the mind. "Anatomy is Destiny," to vary a saying of Napoleon's. The little girl's clitoris behaves at first just like a penis, but by comparing herself with a boy play-fellow the child perceives that

she has "come off short," and takes this fact as ill-treatment and as a reason for feeling inferior. For a time she still consoles herself with the expectation that later, when she grows up, she will acquire just as big an appendage as a boy. Here the woman's "masculine complex" branches off. The female child does not understand her actual loss as a sex characteristic, but explains it by assuming that at some earlier date she had possessed a member which was just as big and which had later been lost by castration. She does not seem to extend this conclusion about herself to other grown women, but in complete accordance with the phallic phase she ascribes to them large and complete, that is, male, genitalia. The result is an essential difference between her and the boy, namely, that she accepts castration as an established fact, an operation already performed, whereas the boy dreads the possibility of its being performed.

The castration-dread being thus excluded in her case, there falls away a powerful motive towards forming the super-ego and breaking up the infantile genital organization. These changes seem to be due in the girl far more than in the boy to the results of educative influences, of external intimidation threatening the loss of love. The Oedipus-complex in the girl is far simpler, less equivocal, than that of the little possessor of a penis; in my experience it seldom goes beyond the wish to take the mother's place, the feminine attitude towards the father. Acceptance of the loss of a penis is not endured without some attempt at compensation. The girl passes over—by way of a symbolic analogy, one may say—from the penis to a child; her Oedipus-complex culminates in the desire, which is long cherished, to be given a child by her

father as a present, to bear him a child. One has the impression that the Oedipus-complex is later gradually abandoned because this wish is never fulfilled. The two desires, to possess a penis and to bear a child, remain powerfully charged with libido in the unconscious and help to prepare the woman's nature for its subsequent sex role. The comparative weakness of the sadistic component of the sexual instinct, which may probably be related to the penis-deficiency, facilitates the transformation of directly sexual trends into those inhibited in aim, feelings of tenderness. It must be confessed, however, that on the whole our insight into these processes of development in the girl is unsatisfying, shadowy and incomplete.

[*Translated by* JOHN STRACHEY]

Anatomy is destiny in Proust also, but this is anatomy taken up into the mind, as it were. The exiles of Sodom and Gomorrah, more jealous even than other mortals, become monsters of time, yet heroes and heroines of time also. The Oedipus complex never quite passes, in Freud's sense of passing, either in Proust or in his major figures. Freud's castration complex, ultimately the dread of dying, is a metaphor for the same shadowed desire that Proust represents by the complex metaphor of jealousy. The jealous lover fears that he has been castrated, that his place in life has been taken, that true time is over for him. His only recourse is to search for lost time, in the hopeless hope that the aesthetic recovery of illusion and of experience alike will deceive him in a higher mode than he fears to have been deceived in already.

PART III

CHRISTIAN

WISDOM

CHAPTER 8

THE GOSPEL OF

THOMAS

The popularity of the Gospel of Thomas among Americans is another indication that, as I have argued elsewhere, there is indeed "the American Religion": creedless, Orphic, enthusiastic, proto-gnostic, post-Christian. Unlike the canonical gospels, that of Judas Thomas the Twin spares us the Crucifixion, makes the Resurrection unnecessary, and does not present us with a God named Jesus. No dogmas could be founded upon this sequence (if it is a sequence) of apothegms. If you turn to the Gospel of Thomas, you encounter a Jesus who is unsponsored and free. No one could be burned or even scorned in the name of this Jesus, and no one has been hurt in any way, except perhaps for those bigots, high church or low, who may have glanced at so permanently surprising a work.

I take it that the first saying is not by Jesus but by his twin, who states the interpretive challenge and its prize: more life into a time

without boundaries. That was and is the blessing: "The kingdom is inside you and it is outside you." Scholars are wary when it comes to naming these hidden sayings as gnostic, but I will not hesitate in making this brief commentary into a gnostic sermon that takes the Gospel of Thomas for its text. What makes us free is the *gnōsis*, and the hidden sayings set down by Thomas form a part of *gnōsis* available to every Christian, Jew, Humanist, skeptic, whoever you are. The trouble of finding, and being found, is simply the trouble that clears ignorance away, to be replaced by the gnostic knowing in which we are known even as we know ourselves. The alternative is precisely what Emerson and Wallace Stevens meant by "poverty": imaginative lack or need. Knowledge only is the remedy, and such knowledge must be knowledge of the self. The Jesus of the Gospel of Thomas calls us to knowledge and not to belief, for faith need not lead to wisdom; and this Jesus is a wisdom teacher, gnomic and wandering, rather than a proclaimer of finalities. You cannot be a minister of this gospel, nor found a church upon it. The Jesus who urges his followers to be passersby is a remarkably Whitmanian Jesus, and there is little in the Gospel of Thomas that would not have been accepted by Emerson, Thoreau, and Whitman.

Seeing what is before you is the whole art of vision for Thomas's Jesus. Many of the hidden sayings are so purely antithetical that they can be interpreted only by our seeing what they severely decline to affirm. No scholar ever will define precisely what gnosticism was or is, but its negations are palpable. Nothing mediates the self for the Jesus of the Gospel of Thomas. Everything we seek is already in our presence, and not outside ourself.

What is most remarkable in these sayings is the repeated insistence that everything is already open to you. You need but knock and enter. What is best and oldest in you will respond fully to what you allow yourself to see. The deepest teaching of this gnostic Jesus is never stated but always implied, implied in nearly every saying: there is light in you, and that light is not part of the created world. It is not Adamic. I know of only two convictions essential to the *gnōsis*: Creation and Fall were one and the same event; and what is best in us was never created, so cannot fall. The American Religion, *gnōsis* of our Evening Land, adds a third element if our freedom is to be complete. That ultimate spark of the pre-created light must be alone, or at least alone with Jesus. The living Jesus of the Gospel of Thomas speaks to all the followers, but in the crucial thirteenth saying he speaks to Thomas alone, and those secret three sayings are never revealed to us. Here we must surmise, since those three solitary sayings are the hidden heart of the Gospel of Thomas.

Thomas has earned knowledge of the sayings (or words) by denying any similitude for Jesus. His twin is not like a just messenger or prophet, nor is he like a wise philosopher, or teacher of Greek wisdom. The sayings then would turn upon the nature of Jesus: what he is. He is so much of the light as to be the light, but not the light of heaven, or of the heaven above heaven. The identification must be with the stranger or alien God, not the God of Moses and of Adam, but the man-god of the abyss, prior to creation. Yet that is only one truth out of three, though quite enough to be stoned for, and then avenged by divine fire. The second saying must be the call of that stranger God to Thomas, and the third

must be the response of Thomas, which is his realization that he already is in the place of rest, alone with his twin.

Scholars increasingly assert that certain sayings in the Gospel of Thomas are closer to the hypothetical "Q" document than are parallel passages in the synoptic gospels. They generally ascribe the gnostic overtones of the Gospel of Thomas to a redactor, perhaps a Syrian ascetic of the second century of the Common Era. I would advance a different hypothesis, though with little expectation that scholars would welcome it. Of the veritable text of the sayings of a historical Jesus, we have nothing. Presumably he spoke to his followers and other wayfarers in Aramaic, and except for a few phrases scattered through the Gospel, none of his Aramaic sayings has survived. I have wondered for some time how this could be, and wondered even more that Christian scholars have never joined in my wonder. If you believed in the divinity of Jesus, would you not wish to have preserved the actual Aramaic sentences he spoke, since they were for you the words of God? But what was preserved were Greek translations of his sayings, rather than the Aramaic sayings themselves. Were they lost, still to be found in a cave somewhere in Israel? Were they never written down in the first place, so that the Greek texts were based only upon memory? For some years now, I have asked these questions whenever I have met a New Testament scholar, and I have met only blankness. Yet surely this puzzle matters. Aramaic and Greek are very different languages, and the nuances of spirituality and of wisdom do not translate readily from one into the other. Any sayings of Jesus, open or hidden, need to be regarded in this context, which ought to teach us a certain suspicion of even the most nor-

mative judgments as to authenticity, whether those judgments rise from faith or from supposedly positive scholarship.

My skepticism is preamble to my hypothesis that the gnostic sayings that crowd the Gospel of Thomas indeed may come from Q, or from some *ur*-Q, which would mean that there were proto-gnostic elements in the teachings of Jesus. The Gospel of Mark, in my reading, is far closer to the J writer, or Yahwist, than are the other versions of the Gospel; and while I hardly find any gnostic shadings in Mark or the Yahwist, I do find uncanny moments not reconcilable with official Christianity and Judaism. Moshe Idel, the great revisionist scholar of Kabbalah, persuades me that what seem gnostic elements in Kabbalah actually stem from an archaic Jewish religion, anything but normative, of which what we call gnosticism may be an echo or a parody. Christian gnosticism also may be a belated version of some of the teachings of Jesus. All of gnosticism, according to the late Ioan Couliano, is a kind of cre-ative misinterpretation or strong misreading or misprision of both Plato and the Bible. Sometimes, as I contemplate organized, insti-tutional Christianity, historical and contemporary, it seems to me a very weak misreading of the teachings of Jesus. The Gospel of Thomas speaks to me, and to many others, Gentile and Jewish, in ways that Matthew, Luke, and John certainly do not.

This excursus returns me to my professedly gnostic sermon upon the text of the Gospel of Thomas. How do the secret sayings of Jesus help to make us free? What knowledge do they give us of who we were, of what we have become, of where we were, of wherein we have been thrown, of whereto we are hastening, of what we are being freed, of what birth really is, of what rebirth is?

A wayfaring Jesus, as presented in Burton Mack's *A Myth of Innocence*, is accepted by many as the Jesus of the Gospel of Thomas,
an acceptance in which I am happy to share. Mack rightly emphasizes that every text we have of Jesus is late; I would go a touch further and call them anxiously "belated." Indeed, I return to my
earlier question about our lack of the Aramaic text of what Jesus
said: Is it not an extraordinary scandal that *all* the crucial texts of
Christianity are so surprisingly belated? The Gospel of Mark is
at least forty years later than the passion that supposedly it
records, and the hypothetical Q depends on collating materials
from Matthew and Luke, perhaps seventy years after the event.
Mack's honest and sensible conclusion is to postulate a Jesus
whose career does not center on crucifixion and resurrection but
on the wanderings of a kind of sage. Such a sage, in my own reading of the Gospel of Thomas, may well have found his way back to
an earlier version of the Jewish religion than any we now recognize. And that earliness, as Idel has shown, anticipated much of
what we now call gnosticism.

What begins to make us free is the *gnōsis* of who we were,
when we were "in the light." When we were in the light, then we
stood at the beginning, immovable, fully human, and so also
divine. To know who we were is to be known as we now wish to
be known. We came into being before coming into being; we
already were, and so never were created. And yet what we have
become altogether belies the origin that was already an end. The
Jesus of the Gospel of Thomas refrains from saying precisely how
dark we have become, but subtly he indicates perpetually what we
now are. We dwell in poverty, and we *are* that poverty, for our

imaginative need has become greater than our imaginations can fulfill.

The emphasis of this Jesus is upon a pervasive opacity that prevents us from seeing anything that really matters. Ignorance is the blocking agent that thwarts the ever-early Jesus, and his implied interpretation of our ignorance is: belatedness. The hidden refrain of these secret or dark sayings is that we are blinded by an overwhelming sense that we have come after the event, indeed, after ourselves. What the gnostic Jesus warns against is retroactive meaningfulness, repetitive and incessant aftering. He has not come to praise famous men, and our fathers who were before us. Of men, he commends only John the Baptist and his own brother, James the Just. The normative nostalgia for the virtues of the fathers is totally absent. Present all around us and yet evading us are the intimations of the light, unseen except by Jesus.

An admonition against retroactive meaningfulness is neither Platonic nor normatively Jewish, and perhaps hints again at an archaic Jewish spirituality, of which apparent gnosticism may be the shadow. The gnostic hatred of time is implicit in the Gospel of Thomas. Is it only a vengeful misprision both of Plato and the Hebrew Bible, or does it again hint at an archaic immediacy that Jesus, as wandering teacher, seeks to revive? Moshe Idel finds in some of the most ancient extrabiblical texts the image we associate now with Hermeticism and Kabbalah, the primordial Human, whom the angels resented and envied. To pass from that Anthropos to Adam is to fall into time, by a fall that is only the creation of Adam and his world. Certainly the Jesus of the Gospel of Thomas has no fondness for Adam, who "came from great power and great

wealth, but he was not worthy of you," where "you" is Jesus, but a Jesus who stands for all of us.

Where were we, then, before we were Adam? In a place before creation, but not a world elsewhere. The kingdom, which we do not see, nevertheless is spread out upon the earth. Normative Judaism, from its inception, spoke of hallowing the commonplace, but the Jesus of the Gospel of Thomas beholds nothing that is commonplace. Since the kingdom is inside us and outside us, what is required is that we bring the axis of vision and the axis of things together again. The stones themselves will then serve us, transparent to our awakened vision. Though the Gospel of Thomas avoids using the gnostic terms for the fullness, the Pleroma, and the cosmological emptiness, the Kenoma, their equivalents hover in the discourse of the wandering teacher of open vision. The living Jesus, never the man who was crucified or the god who was resurrected, is himself the fullness of where once we were. And that surely is one of the effects of the Gospel of Thomas, which is to undo the Jesus of the New Testament and return us to an earlier Jesus. Burton Mack's central argument seems to me unassailable: The Jesus of the churches is founded on the literary character Jesus, as composed by Mark. I find this parallel to my argument, in *The Book of J*, that the Western worship of God—Judaic, Christian, Islamic—is the worship not only of a literary character, but of the wrong literary character, the God of Ezra the Redactor rather than the uncanny Yahweh of the J writer. If the Jesus of the Gospel of Thomas is also to be regarded as a literary character, then at least he too will be the right literary character, like the Davidic-Solomonic Yahweh.

Wherein, according to Thomas's Jesus, have we been thrown? Into the body, the world, and our temporal span in this world, or in the sum: Have we been thrown into everything that is not ourselves? I would not interpret this as a call to ascetic renunciation, since other sayings in the Gospel of Thomas reject fasting, almsgiving, and all particular diets. And though the Jesus of Thomas is hardly a libertine Gnostic, his call to end both maleness and femaleness does not read to me as an evasion of all sexuality. We are not told what will make the two into one, and we should interpret this conversion into one composite gender as something beyond the absorption of the female into the male. Everything here turns upon the image of the entrance of the bridegroom into the wedding chamber, which can be accomplished only by those who are solitaries, elitist individuals who in some sense have transcended gender distinctions. But this solitude need not be an ascetic condition, and it repeats or rejoins the figure of the pre-Adamic Anthropos, the human before the fall-into-creation. That figure, whether in ancient Jewish speculation (as Idel shows), or in Gnosticism, or in Kabbalah, is hardly removed from sexual experience.

Whereto are we hastening? Few of the hidden sayings of Jesus suggest that the destination of most of us is a solitary entrance into the wedding chamber. Whatever gnosticism was, or is, it must clearly be an elitist phenomenon, an affair of intellectuals, or of mystical intellectuals. The Gospel of Thomas addresses itself only to a subtle elite, those capable of knowing, who then through knowing can come to see what Jesus insists is plainly visible before them, indeed all around them. This Jesus has not come to take away the sins of the world, or to atone for all humankind. As one

who passes by, he urges his seekers to learn to be passersby, to cease hastening to the temporal death of business and busyness that the world miscalls life. It is the busy world of death-in-life that constitutes the whatness from which we are being freed by the Jesus of the Gospel of Thomas. There is no haste in this Jesus, no apocalyptic intensity. He does not teach the end time, but rather a transvaluation of time, in the here of our moment.

What really is birth? The peculiar emphasis of the question, in this context, is authentically gnostic, and reverberates throughout the hidden sayings of Jesus. Here the transcendental bitterness of logion 79 is wholly appropriate:

> *A woman in the crowd said to him, "Fortunate are the womb that bore you and the breasts that fed you."*
>
> *He said to [her], "Fortunate are those who have heard the word of the father and have truly kept it. For there will be days when you will say, 'Fortunate are the womb that has not conceived and the breasts that have not given milk.'"*

This relates to the enigmatic saying 101, where the "true" mother evidently is distinguished from the natural or actual mother, and to the strikingly antithetical 105:

> *Jesus said, "Whoever knows the father and the mother will be called the child of a whore."*

The crux there is "knows," since only the original self or spark should be known, instead of one's natural descent. Like many

other wisdom teachers, this Jesus practices a rhetoric of shock in order to break down preconceived associations. His onslaught on one's own mother and father implicitly justifies its violence by questioning not so much motherhood or fatherhood as birth itself. Even the natural birth of Jesus still participates in the creation-fall, still resists rebirth in the spirit and in a father, whose fatherhood is only a metaphor for a dwelling together.

I have been founding this sermon-as-commentary on a famous Valentinian gnostic formula, and the Gospel of Thomas has no specific sayings that are Valentinian as such. But the Valentinian chant has features so broad that by it we can chart most other varieties of gnostic religion. Its culminating and crucial question asks what rebirth really is, and many of the hidden sayings of Jesus turn ultimately upon answering that question. Rebirth involves joining Thomas as a sharer in the solitude of Jesus, or being a passerby with Jesus. In the United States, this hardly requires commentary, since it is the situation of the Baptist walking alone with Jesus, whether he or she be black Baptist or moderate Southern Baptist or independent. The American Jesus, from the nineteenth century through now, is far closer to the wanderer of the Gospel of Thomas than to the crucified Jesus of the New Testament. The "living Jesus" of Thomas has been resurrected without the need of having first been sacrificed, which is the paradox also of the American Jesus.

My gnostic sermon has concluded; the coda is a postsermon reflection on the allied strangenesses of gnosticism, and of Christianity in any of its varieties, permutations even more bewildering than

those of what Hans Jonas taught us to call the gnostic religion. Between Jesus and any Christianity, at least a generation of silence intervenes. There is a grand, almost tragic absurdity in attempting to translate any text back into Aramaic. Nietzsche, himself a master of aphorism, insisted that an exclusive writing or teaching by aphorism was a decadent mode. Kafka, this century's master of aphorism, turned to it as the most desperately appropriate of literary modes. Long a kind of Jewish gnostic, I remember still my unhappy aesthetic shock at first reading translations of the Nag Hammadi texts. The fragments quoted by the heresiologists, particularly the magnificent fragments of Valentinus, far surpassed any of the newly discovered texts, with the single exception of the Valentinian Gospel of Truth. It is the sorrow of ancient Gnosticism that, except for Valentinus, it produced no author worthy of its imaginative energies. Jesus, whoever he was and whatever he was, appears in Q and in the Gospel of Thomas as a great verbal artist in the oral tradition. That was Oscar Wilde's vision of Jesus, and G. Wilson Knight's, following Wilde, and I prefer Wilde and Wilson Knight on Jesus to almost all of the New Testament scholars, who are not exactly out to ruin the sacred truths. Sacred truths have a way of turning out to be either bad literary criticism or else coercion, whether open or concealed.

But the Jesus of the Gospel of Thomas is not interested in coercion, nor can anyone coerce in his name. The innocence of Gnosticism is its freedom from violence and fraud, from which historical Christianity cannot be disentangled. No one is going to establish a gnostic church in America, by which I mean a professedly gnostic church, to which tax exemption would never be

granted anyway. Of course we have gnostic churches in plenty: the Mormons, the Southern Baptists, the Assemblies of God, Christian Science, and most other indigenous American denominations and sects. These varieties of the American Religion, as I call it, are all involuntary parodies of the *gnōsis* of the Gospel of Thomas. But ancient Gnosticism is neither to be praised nor blamed for its modern analogues. What is surely peculiar is the modern habit of employing "gnosis" or "gnosticism" as a conservative or institutionalized Christian term of abuse. An elitist religion, gnosticism almost always has been a severely intellectual phenomenon, and the Jesus of the Gospel of Thomas is certainly the most intellectualized figure among all the versions of Jesus through the ages. The appeal of this Jesus is not to the mind alone, and yet his rhetoric demands a considerable effort of cognition if it is to be unpacked:

Fortunate is the lion that the human will eat, so that the lion becomes human. And foul is the human that the lion will eat, and the lion will become human.

Perhaps there is a recondite reference here to the Gnostic figure of the demiurgical false creator, sometimes depicted as a lion, but the imaginative strength of this apothegm does not depend on an esoteric mythology. Whether or not you judge the Gospel of Thomas to be gnostic in its orientation, you are confronted here by what I would suggest is an ancient humanism, one that is difficult to reconcile either with late Judaism or early Christianity. This hard saying of Jesus opposes two ways of becoming human, one blessed and the other foul. If we devour the lion in us, we are

blessed, and if the lion feasts on the knowing part of us, then we are lost. For the kingly lion in us knows nothing except its projection outward of its own being as lord of creation, but what is most human in us is no part of creation. And there is the center of the aphorisms that make up the Gospel of Thomas, a center that goes back to the origin, to the fullness of the abyss that preceded creation. There too, as I interpret it, is the last negation of the Gospel of Thomas, which we wrong by interpreting merely as an exhortation to asceticism:

> Simon Peter said to them, "Mary should leave us, for females are not worthy of life."
> Jesus said, "Look, I shall guide her to make her male, so that she too may become a living spirit resembling you males. For every female who makes herself male will enter heaven's kingdom."

This violently figurative language can be weakly misread as the ascetic's revulsion from nature or the female, a misreading particularly troublesome at our time, in our place, as it were. But "life" or "living" here means what it does in "the living Jesus" of the prologue to the Gospel of Thomas. That "living" Jesus certainly is not male in the literal but in a metaphorical sense, the metaphor belonging to the Gnostic sense of the original abyss, at once our forefather and our foremother. Whatever surges beneath the surface of the Gospel of Thomas, it is not a Syrian Christian wisdom teaching of the second century. The ascetic accepts creation, but always upon the basis of having fallen from it, and

always with the hope of being restored to it. That is hardly the aspiration of Jesus in the Gospel of Thomas. Like William Blake, like Jakob Böhme, this Jesus is looking for the face he had before the world was made. That marvelous trope I appropriate from W. B. Yeats, at his most Blakean. If such is your quest, then the Gospel of Thomas calls out to you.

CHAPTER 9

SAINT AUGUSTINE

AND READING

Though some scholars have discovered a Christian wisdom in Cervantes or in Shakespeare, I remain unpersuaded. Looking back over this book, I am made aware that a normative Christian wisdom is unrepresented in a panoply that begins with a quest for wisdom in the ancient Hebrews and Greeks, and then in Cervantes and Shakespeare. My second part, examining ideas that became events in Montaigne, Bacon, Johnson, Goethe, Emerson, Nietzsche, Freud, and Proust, gives only one consistent Christian moralist, in Dr. Johnson. By going on after the Gospel of Thomas to Saint Augustine, who seems to me the most challenging of Catholic intellectuals, I have some hope of contriving balance. The twenty-first century may be dominated by religious war between some elements in Islam and an emerging alliance of Hindus, Jews, and Christians. Augustine has Paul as precursor, and Dante, Calvin, perhaps Luther, as inheritors. War is the most terrible of unwis-

doms, and religious war a terrifying manifestation of ideas transmuted into events. What the commentaries on the Koran are to Islam, *The City of God* is to Christianity. Whether the United States in its role as the new Roman Empire will enforce a Roman peace, or fall eventually as Rome fell, its potential history and defense is prefigured in Augustine's *City of God*. Since my subject is confined to wisdom and literature, I will confine myself here to only a few instances of Augustine's Christian wisdom.

2
—

Freud speaks of "frontier concepts"; Augustine is a frontier conceptualizer, poised between the ancient works of Greek thought and of biblical religion, and the Catholic synthesis of the High Middle Ages. A good recent study by John M. Rist, *Augustine* (1994), has the useful subtitle *Ancient Thought Baptized*. In that particular sense, Augustine is the creator of Christian wisdom. In our own time, historical bridges are in disrepair or already are collapsed. The Augustinian bridge between the ancients and Dante will go on standing, if only because historical coherence would vanish without it.

Augustine and Freud are totally antithetical to each other, except in one trait: they are the most tendentious writers I have ever read. Each has a palpable design on the reader, and knows precisely where he desires to take you. As rhetoricians devoted to absolute persuasion, they are unique. But once we set aside rhetoric and design, they cannot coexist. The "unconscious sense

of guilt" in *Civilization and Its Discontents* shares nothing with Augustine's guilt of Original Sin. I resist *Civilization and Its Discontents,* while fundamentally assenting to much of what Freud says. I agree with absolutely nothing in *The City of God,* but then the book is not addressed to a Jew and a gnostic.

Ernst Robert Curtius, from whom my belief in the necessity of a literary canon is derived, traced his fascination with medieval culture to E. K. Rand's *Founders of the Middle Ages* (1928). Rand's heroes were Saint Ambrose, Saint Jerome, Boethius, and the linked pair of Saint Augustine and Dante, a linking that was developed further by Charles Singleton and John Freccero. The connection between saint and poet is authentic, though Singleton and sometimes even Freccero make me nervous when they regard Dante as versified Augustine rather than versified Dante, as it were. Rand emphasizes Augustine's sustained love for Vergil, a passion carried so far as to associate Vergil's version of an earthly Rome at perpetual peace with Augustine's own version of the City of God.

The philosopher Hannah Arendt, in her most useful book, *Between Past and Future* (1961, enlarged 1968), shrewdly notes that for Augustine "even the life of the saints is a life together with other men." Political life therefore goes on even among the sinless. In her youth, Arendt wrote her doctoral dissertation, *Love and Saint Augustine,* which appeared posthumously in English in 1996. Departing from her teacher (and lover) Heidegger, she argued that Augustinian love depends on the faculty of memory, and not upon the expectation of death.

Augustine remains the most profound theorist of memory ever to appear, at least before those pragmatic geniuses of mem-

ory, Shakespeare and Proust, to whom perhaps we should add Freud.

Christian wisdom in Augustine anticipates Shakespeare by what looks like an invention of the inner self. Plato's Socrates inaugurates inwardness, but in nothing like the radical abyss of the perpetually growing inner self of Hamlet, whom Emerson called a Platonist. If thought and love alike depend on memory, as they do in Augustine, then memory, in reviewing itself, will assume new thoughts, like an interpretation of the self. But is that interrogation itself an invention and finding, a form of wisdom, or is it something slighter?

A recent book by Phillip Cary, *Augustine's Invention of the Inner Self* (2000), sees Augustine as a radically new kind of Christian Platonist, one who makes Christ identical with wisdom—that is, the wisdom of God. The clearest guide I know to Augustine is his definitive biographer, Peter Brown, author of *Augustine of Hippo* (1967), who illuminates his great subject by showing us that Christ in Augustine's childhood was profoundly different from what he has been since:

> *Above all, the Christianity of the fourth century would have been presented to such a boy as a form of 'True Wisdom'. The Christ of the popular imagination was not a suffering Saviour. There are no crucifixes in the fourth century. He was, rather, 'the Great Word of God, the Wisdom of God'. On the sarcophagi of the age, He is always shown as a Teacher, teaching His Wisdom to a*

coterie of budding philosophers. For a cultivated man, the essence of Christianity consisted in just this. Christ, as the 'Wisdom of God', had established a monopoly in Wisdom: the clear Christian revelation had trumped and replaced the conflicting opinions of the pagan philosophers; 'Here, here is that for which all philosophers have sought throughout their life, but never once been able to track down, to embrace, to hold firm . . . He who would be a wise man, a complete man, let him hear the voice of God.'

So prevalent was this view that it helped the Manichees convert the young Augustine to their dualistic heresy, in which an elect group of ascetics, female and male, offered a Christianity purified of the Hebrew Bible, and of most of the Catholics' concessions to everyday realities. North Africa, a harsh environment, was a perfect context for the Manichaeists, who regarded the natural world and all people but the elect as hopelessly evil.

Augustine was born in Algeria in 354 C.E., the son of a pagan Roman father and of the formidable Catholic Monica, who eventually achieved sainthood, like her gifted son. She patiently outwaited her husband's infidelities and her son's heresies, and inevitably they became Latin Christians.

As for the invention of the inner self, Augustine achieved so much authentic wisdom (however harsh) that it seems misleading, to me, to turn him into Martin Luther, let alone William Shakespeare, both of whom are likelier candidates as inventors of the inner self. Essentially literary, a great lover and teacher of Vergil's poetry, Augustine became the center of African Roman culture

and of the Catholic religion. Even Aquinas has not surpassed Augustine as the fundamental Catholic thinker, an ascendancy that has now lasted sixteen centuries.

Aside from his vast contributions to theology, Augustine invented reading as we have known it for sixteen centuries. I am not unique in my elegiac sadness at watching reading die, in the era that celebrates Stephen King and J. K. Rowling rather than Charles Dickens and Lewis Carroll. Augustine was essentially the first theorist and defender of reading, though as an ethical interpreter he would have repudiated a stance like my own, which seeks a secular wisdom fused with a purely aesthetic experience at once freely hedonistic and cognitively strong. The essential supplement to Peter Brown's classic biography is Brian Stock's *Augustine the Reader* (1996), where the author of the *Confessions* and *The City of God* is clearly demonstrated to be the inventor not of the burgeoning inner self but of the conviction that only God is the ideal reader. To read well (which for Augustine means absorbing the wisdom of Christ) is the authentic imitation of God and the angels.

It is from Augustine that we learn to read, since he first established the relationship between reading and memory, though for him the purpose of reading was our conversion to Christ. Nevertheless, I read poetry aloud and seek to possess it by memory because of Augustine, and like Hamlet I set the will above the Word, in conscious defiance of Augustine. Shakespeare, in my judgment, invented the inner self, but only because Augustine had made it possible, by creating autobiographical memory, in which one's own life becomes the text. We think because we learn to remember our reading the best that can be read—for Augustine

the Bible and Vergil, Cicero and the Neoplatonists, to which we have added for ourselves Plato, Dante, Cervantes, and Shakespeare, with Joyce and Proust in the century just past. But always we remain the progeny of Augustine, who first told us that the book alone could nourish thought, memory, and their intricate interplay in the life of the mind. Reading alone will not save us or make us wise, but without it we will lapse into the death-in-life of the dumbing down in which America now leads the world, as in all other matters.

3

What is the specifically Christian wisdom of Augustine? He returns to Saint Paul's preaching of the crucified Jesus as "the power of God and the Wisdom of God," but for Augustine the power and the wisdom were one. Brian Stock, analyzing Augustine's final comments on the Trinity, concludes his own book by finding a type of skepticism in Augustine, not concerning the wisdom of God's power but concerning the reader:

> *The use of theory teaches that the problems of reading and interpretation cannot be solved through the imposition of a conceptual scheme; they can be addressed only by means of a system of deferrals in which the authority for the text is ultimately removed from the reader's control. Augustine believes that reading is essential for "spiritual" development in the individual, but he is pessimistic about the degree of "enlightenment" that reading*

itself confers. As a consequence, his notion of illumination is an expression of hope as well as an acknowledgement of the hopelessness of human interpretive efforts. Even if he had made no other contribution to the field, this relational view of reading, writing, and self-expression would assure him a lasting place in the history of human understanding.

But is *that* all the Christian wisdom at the end of Augustine's quest? Is Freud to offer us more pragmatic wisdom in *Civilization and Its Discontents* than Augustine does? Do Koheleth and Samuel Johnson, with their own grim kind of reality testing, teach us more usefully than Augustine does? Goethe, pagan and prideful, at least states a kind of wisdom we can carry away with us by joining him in renunciation of much of our desire. Cervantes and Shakespeare, by giving us exemplary persons—Quixote, Sancho, Falstaff, Hamlet—give us also the difficult wisdom these figures incarnate. Montaigne invaluably tells us not to study dying: we will know well enough how to do it when the time comes. Augustine, surely *the* Christian sage, if there is a single one, has to tell us more than that we must read, but cannot hope for enlightenment.

Belief and wisdom are one sphere; wisdom and literature can be quite another. Nothing else in Augustine fuses the spheres, for me, as does his outcry in section 154 of Erich Przywara's *An Augustine Synthesis* (1958):

These days have no true being; they are gone almost before they arrive; and when they come they cannot continue; they press upon one another, they follow the one the other, and cannot check

themselves in their course. Of the past nothing is called back
again; what is yet to be expected is something which will pass
away again; it is not yet possessed, whilst as yet it is not arrived;
it cannot be kept when once it is arrived. The Psalmist therefore
asks, 'what is the number of my days' (Ps. xxxviii, 5), what is,
not what is not; and (for this confounds me by a still greater and
more perplexing difficulty) both is and is not. For we can neither
say that that is, which does not continue, nor that it is not when
it is come and is passing. It is that absolute IS, that true IS, that
IS in the strict sense of the word, that I long for, that IS which is
in the Jerusalem which is the bride of my Lord, where there shall
be no death, where there will be no failing, where the day shall
not pass away but shall endure, a day which no yesterday pre-
cedes nor a morrow ousts. This number of my days, which is, I
say, make Thou known to me.

Proust, meditating in this mode, places his faith in art. Augustine appeals to God, whose bride is Jerusalem, the City of God.
Augustine's wisdom refuses to go in search of lost time. The
reader need not choose between Proust and Augustine. If one
brought Saint Paul into the contest, one would have to choose:
"The last enemy to be destroyed is death." Augustine remains a
lifelong reader of Vergil, and yearns for the farther shore, which he
calls Jerusalem.

CODA:

NEMESIS AND WISDOM

William James observed that wisdom was learning what to overlook. Prince Hamlet is the most intelligent of literary characters, but by James's pragmatic test the doom-eager Shakespearean charismatic is anything but wise. Hamlet can overlook nothing, and so sets the pattern for all who can illuminate wisdom yet cannot themselves embody it. The genius, or daemon, of Hamlet insists on making him aware of everything at once. Thinking much too well, Hamlet perishes of the truth. Whoever you are, your daemon will become your nemesis and make you your own worst enemy, incapable of learning what to overlook.

My former student Davide Stimilli, an authority on the daemonic, remarks that Nemesis, Daughter of the Night, was a venerable goddess in the Greek pantheon. She is our mortality, our ill fortune, our self-punishment, our universal inability to forgive

ourselves everything. All our unwisdom is centered in her. Freud, in *Civilization and Its Discontents*, equates her with our unconscious sense of guilt. She floats in empty air, waiting to pounce upon us. Of the wisdom writers discussed in this book, Goethe is our best guide to defend against Nemesis, because he tells us to rely on our personal daemon, or genius, to ward her off. Emerson, our American Goethe, counsels self-reliance, yet yielded later to the deity he called Fate, a homelier version of Nemesis. Though Emerson organized his Party of Hope, he acknowledged it would win few elections in the lengthening shadows of our Evening Land, home base of the New World Order. The national Nemesis of the United States may prove to be our globalization of the Wilsonian illusion that other countries can be made safe for democracy.

Still, my question in this book is wholly in my Jobean title: *Where Shall Wisdom Be Found?* The fear of Yahweh appears to be the American as it was the Hebraic answer, but does that not make God into merely a male Nemesis? Christianity, from Saint Paul through Saint Augustine, counters Nemesis or the Torah ("teaching") of Yahweh with the hope incarnated in Jesus of Nazareth, King of the Jews, legitimate seed of David's valor and Solomon's wisdom. Whether the genius, or daemon, of America is truly at one with the American Jesus was a prophetic doubt of Reinhold Niebuhr, whose spirit seems absent now from our public life.

A Jobean wisdom is scarcely American; our national epics are *Moby-Dick,* which defies Job's God, and Whitman's *Leaves of Grass,* an inextricable mingling of hope and torment. Neither work is Christian. Is the wisdom of the Greeks and Hebrews, or of the

great moral essayists, still as available to us as is the dark comedy of Cervantes or the sublimity of Shakespearean tragedy? This book has summoned these up, in conjunction with the enigmas of a Jesus varied enough to encompass the Gospel of Thomas, Saint Augustine, and Kierkegaard's indirect communication of the difficulty of *becoming* a Christian in a supposedly Christian society that actually worships Nemesis despite arguing for hope. As Davide Stimilli suggests, Nemesis is not a moral power: she is the goddess of retribution, Homeric and Freudian, and not Christian or Platonic. Goethe and Emerson, themselves not Christian, try to teach us that there is a god in us who can, for a time anyway, hold out against Nemesis. Pragmatically, that became William James's benign insight that wisdom had to become a capacity to overlook what cannot be surmounted. Is that our only answer now to the query of where shall wisdom be found? At least it does constitute a difference that helps get us through the hard or unlucky days.

I personally hope that wisdom literature, as surveyed in this book, can offer us something more than that. Western monotheism—Judaic, Christian, Islamic—is perhaps not so much opposed as it is complemented by the reliance of Goethe, Emerson, and Freud on individual genius, or daemonic Eros. Secular wisdom tradition and monotheistic hope may not finally be reconcilable, at least not wholly, but the greatest of writers ancient and modern—Homer, Dante, Cervantes, Shakespeare—contrive balances (however precarious) that allow prudential wisdom and some intimations of hope to coexist. We read and reflect because

we hunger and thirst after wisdom. Truth, according to the poet William Butler Yeats, could not be known but could be embodied. Of wisdom, I personally would affirm the reverse: We cannot embody it, yet we can be taught how to know wisdom, whether or not it can be identified with the Truth that might make us free.